303671

STATIC LOAN

C llege
b

WITHDRAWN

Psychology for Musicians

Psychology for Musicians

Understanding and Acquiring the Skills

Andreas C. Lehmann
John A. Sloboda
Robert H. Woody

OXFORD

UNIVERSITY PRESS

2007

OXFORD
UNIVERSITY PRESS

Oxford University Press, Inc., publishes works that further
Oxford University's objective of excellence
in research, scholarship, and education.

Oxford   New York
Auckland   Cape Town   Dar es Salaam   Hong Kong   Karachi
Kuala Lumpur   Madrid   Melbourne   Mexico City   Nairobi
New Delhi   Shanghai   Taipei   Toronto

With offices in
Argentina   Austria   Brazil   Chile   Czech Republic   France   Greece
Guatemala   Hungary   Italy   Japan   Poland   Portugal   Singapore
South Korea   Switzerland   Thailand   Turkey   Ukraine   Vietnam

Published by Oxford University Press, Inc.
198 Madison Avenue, New York, New York 10016

www.oup.com

Oxford is a registered trademark of Oxford University Press

Library of Congress Cataloging-in-Publication Data
Lehmann, Andreas C., 1964–
Psychology for musicians: understanding and acquiring the skills /
Andreas C. Lehmann, John A. Sloboda, Robert H. Woody.
p.   cm.
Includes bibliographical references
ISBN-13 978-0-19-514610-3
ISBN 0-19-514610-7
1. Musicians—Psychology.   2. Music—Psychological aspects.
I. Sloboda, John A.   II. Woody, Robert H.   III. Title.
ML3838.L464   2006
781'.11—dc22   2006007991

1 3 5 7 9 8 6 4 2
Printed in the United States of America
on acid-free paper

Preface

The idea for this book came a few years back, when we were discussing the different classes we were teaching for musicians, psychologists, and educators. Each of us had discovered how difficult it was to find materials that matched the interests and previous knowledge of our students. All our students had experience as music listeners, and the great majority of them played a musical instrument or sang, albeit at different levels of proficiency. Yet the questions they posed regarding the psychology of music were quite similar. This book aims to answer precisely those questions.

The topics covered here contain relevant information for musicians who perform or teach, for students of psychology who want to know more about music and the mind, and for musically inclined persons who seek personal growth and enrichment. Although we steer clear of giving recipes for musicians on how to do things (which is, after all, the responsibility of methods teachers and practitioners), we try to provide a basis for informed decisions on why and how things might or might not work. When talking to students or people in the street, we have come across strongly held beliefs or myths about music. Some of them have no sound scientific basis and, in fact, might be counterproductive. For example, it is not true that absolute (or perfect) pitch is an indicator of innate musical talent, that music is exclusively processed in the right brain hemisphere, that listening to a lot of Mozart will make you smarter in general, or that there is just one way of learning to perform from memory. These and other firmly held beliefs will be addressed in the appropriate chapters.

In order to stay close to music making and listening, we had to leave out a wealth of fascinating information that lies on the boundaries of our main focus. We only touch on such topics as musical acoustics and the early stages of cognitive processing (psychoacoustics), music and computer technology (music and artificial intelligence), music theory, music therapy, music medicine, and the cognitive neurosciences of music. Specialized publications exist in these emergent fields. We have included some of their findings, but for more detailed information we refer the interested reader to representative sources in those areas.

There are many excellent publications available in the field of music psychology, ranging from more general coverage (e.g., Deutsch, 1999; Hodges, 1996) to specialized topics (e.g., Peretz & Zatorre, 2003, on cognitive neuroscience; Juslin & Sloboda, 2001, on emotion; Butler, 1992, and McAdams & Bigand, 1993, on perception; Parncutt & McPherson, 2001, Williamon, 2004, and Davidson, 2004, on performance; Hargreaves & North, 1997, on social psychology; Deliège & Sloboda, 1996, Colwell, 1992, and Colwell & Richardson, 2002, on developmental psychology and music education). However, none of those edited books attempts a panoramic view of music making and listening based on cognitive theory in conjunction with the cultural context in which the music occurs. Perhaps the closest publication is John Sloboda's (1985b) monograph *The Musical Mind,* to which this book could be considered a sequel.

While being professional academics, each of us has a distinct specialization and musical competency. As an interdisciplinary team, we draw from our individual fields of expertise: psychology and administration in higher education (JAS), general and music education (RHW), and musicology and psychology (ACL). We are all avid music lovers who enjoy listening to and making music in different musical settings and "cultures." Since our earlier and formative years as performance majors or music educators, we have moved our focus to researching and writing about musical topics from psychological, sociological, musicological, and educational standpoints. Together we decided on the overall plan of the book, as well as the content of the individual chapters. Although only one of us was responsible for each chapter, all of us had a hand in every chapter. Hence, this publication is a true three-author book.

This book can be used in different ways. Initially written with the classroom situation in mind, its 12 chapters allow for use during an average semester. Following an introduction in which we present some basic ideas and concepts (chapter 1), the remaining 11 chapters divide into three sections: Musical Learning, Musical Skills, and Musical Roles.

- The first part, on musical learning, contains chapters on musical development, motivation, and practice. Chapter 2 covers the controversial debate surrounding talent and the environment in fostering musical development, chapter 3 addresses motivational issues in music, and chapter 4 discusses practice as the key activity in skill building.
- The second part, on musical skills, enumerates the skills that are part of music making, such as expressivity and interpretation (chapter 5), reading and remembering (chapter 6), improvising and composing (chapter 7), and managing performance anxiety (chapter 8).

- In the last part, on musical roles, we elaborate on the different roles that musical actors can assume as performers (chapter 9), teachers (chapter 10), listeners (chapter 11), and music users/consumers (chapter 12).

All chapters are structured similarly and start with a main text, which includes a brief chapter overview. The number of references used in each chapter has been intentionally limited. Interested readers can find many more by using appropriate search terms in relevant databases or by consulting the references mentioned under "Further Reading" as starting points. From our teaching experience, we have gathered a number of tried-and-tested self study exercises or demonstrations that readers can do to experience (and write about) a central concept of the chapter. Also, knowing that our readers are likely to be most familiar with the Western art music tradition, we have tried to broaden the perspective by creating a box called the "Cross-cultural Perspective" (except in chapter 12). The idea is to show how cultural practices differ across time and space. Due to limits of space we have chosen one important and methodologically typical key study per chapter, which is reported in some detail. Finally, we added a few study questions as starting points for discussions or term papers.

Many of our students lack scientific knowledge and are not comfortable with technical terminology and formal scientific writing. Therefore, we have—like many other colleagues—developed ways of putting scientific findings across in ways that musicians are likely to understand and find relevant. This book is written in such a manner that everybody interested in music should understand.

This book would not have reached its current form without the help of a number of people. We thank Anders Ericsson for having inspired all of us, Aaron Williamon, Wolfgang Auhagen, Lucy Green, two anonymous reviewers, and various others for their helpful comments on chapter drafts. We are thankful to the School of Music at the University of Nebraska–Lincoln, for hosting us on their campus for a productive week during the fall of 2003. We also acknowledge the people at Oxford University Press, especially Linda Donnelly, for their patience and help with this project. Most of all, we would like to thank Maria S. Lehmann for her editorial supervision and help throughout.

Contents

Psychology for Musicians

Part I

Musical Learning

1

Science and Musical Skills

Psychology should offer some points of reference for musicians in their activities as teachers or performers or in their everyday lives at home where they practice, rehearse, or play for their own entertainment. Before delving into topics such as musical development, practice, performance anxiety, and various other aspects of the psychology of music, we must clarify basic concepts and ideas behind our approach to these topics. We assume that music making and listening involve a host of different skills and subskills that are strongly linked to the environment in which they are used, thus connecting every musical activity to a unique cultural time and place. For example, singing in a rock band only became possible in the twentieth century in the Western hemisphere, playing the sitar still mainly happens in India, and the pygmies of the Ituri rain forest do not require a music critic.

Although the skills required by the preceding examples might look quite disparate, what unites them from a psychological standpoint is that their smooth functioning is made possible by internal mechanisms that are largely developed in the course of training. The vocalist, the sitar player, and the music critic have acquired internal mental representations of music that allow them to memorize, perform, compare, and talk about music that they have experienced. These introductory examples imply that musicians manipulate information more or less skillfully in response to certain demands. In this book, we ask how musicians perform those tasks, why some may be better at it than others, and how they have developed their faculties.

In this chapter we will highlight the following points:

1. There are different ways of learning about and discussing important issues in music psychology and music education. We propound the scientific approach to complement other, more traditional approaches.

2. Musical skills are highly culture-specific; they vary across time and space; and they share important characteristics with skills in other areas of human behavior, such as games, science, and sports.
3. Music making and listening skills require the development of mental representations and supporting cognitive adaptations, a process we know as musical learning. It has been the subject of much study by researchers and educators.

Key Questions about Music Making and Listening

Humans come in contact with music by producing, re-creating, or simply listening to it. However, the intensity with which we engage in the different activities varies considerably. Everybody is first and foremost a listener, but not everybody creates or re-creates music. In the classical music tradition of today, creating and re-creating music are even two separate professional specializations, whereas in other musical genres, such as rock or jazz music, the performers are often also the composers. It is worthwhile to consider for a moment the different musical activities and the key psychological questions they imply.

As *listeners* we are at the mercy of the acoustical stimuli surrounding us because our ears cannot be closed (see chapter 11). Although music is sometimes experienced as a noxious stimulus, it generally evokes positive feelings, and sometimes we go away from a concert completely moved. The music may have deeply touched us and resonates even after the event (see chapter 5). How can the music or the performance have this effect on us? How can even soft and slow music be stimulating? Does it have the same effect on everyone else? Why do some find this performance breathtaking, whereas others may be disappointed? Does everybody hear the same things in a piece of music?

Performers might have a different set of questions relating to the skills involved and the performing situation. They have to learn the music either from notation or by ear, practice and refine the performance, and even memorize (see chapters 4 and 6). Furthermore, at the time of performance they have to cope with nervousness while interacting possibly with other musicians and definitely with the audience (see chapter 8). All these performance-related activities are not equally well developed in each performer, and musicians have to come to terms with their personal strengths and weaknesses. One performer might memorize a piece almost automatically, whereas another musician may struggle. Classical musicians sometimes wonder how jazz performers can make up music on the fly. How much and what type of practice and training does it take to become fluent with an instrument? Why do some performances go better than others, and why does one audience react differently from another?

Improvisers and *composers* are considered among the most creative musicians (see chapter 7). Many classical musicians feel that they are inadequately prepared for these activities, but most other people (especially children) find it normal to invent music (see chapter 2). How do you become a composer or an improviser in the first place? How do composers and improvisers achieve their constant generation of new musical ideas? Is improvised music always completely different or are there common parts to repeated performances? How do improvising musicians communicate with each other on stage (see chapter 9)?

Finally, *teachers* may not always be credited explicitly, but they are definitely important in the development of musical skills. Through teaching we ensure the historical continuity in music, be it by singing and transmitting folk songs to the next generation or by formally instructing a musician in advanced techniques on an instrument (see chapter 9). We might wonder why some teachers produce highly successful students whereas others do not. How do teachers motivate themselves to teach and students to practice (see chapters 3 and 4)? Does talent matter (see chapter 2)? What is the right sequence of teaching materials, and should this sequence be the same for every student? Can adults still learn to play an instrument?

Psychology for musicians cannot provide definitive answers to all these questions, but it can provide tentative answers based on our current knowledge. There are three different approaches to answering relevant questions, which we outline here.

Possible Approaches to Answering Questions about Music

In every aspect in our lives we are confronted with questions. We can either refuse to answer them (e.g., because we have no interest in knowing how a nuclear power plant works), or we can search for explanations. In the latter case there are different approaches we can use, such as the intuitive approach, the reflective approach, and finally the scientific approach. Each approach has its particular strengths and weaknesses, and no single one will be sufficient to get anyone through life in every situation. Our preferred view, however, is the scientific approach, because it informs the practitioner and even the lay person in powerful ways.

The Commonsense and Intuitive Approaches

Questions and problems in our lives occur in relation to technology, health, culture, administration, and many other areas. Most often we are lay persons in a certain field, also called a *domain*, and we respond by following our intuitions, feelings, and habits. Sometimes we have quite strong feelings on these matters, and our responses come naturally without further thinking. For example, most people talk to children more melodically and simply than they would to other adults. It is possible that some of our intuitive behaviors are biologically programmed and truly adaptive and useful. Other things, on the contrary—such as the strong cravings for alcohol or drugs that some people experience—are known to be biologically and psychologically damaging. Some behavior is simply false transfer of existing knowledge—for example, when our first reaction to put out a fire in a frying pan would be to pour water on it. Although we feel strongly inclined to do a particular thing, this does not mean that it is the right or healthy thing to do. However, the great advantage of following our intuitions is that, given the many decisions that we face every day, they provide rough and ready responses to recurring problems.

Another way of responding to problems is to appeal to "common sense," usually a set of shared beliefs and practices that are passed down in communities and families. Health issues of babies and children are often governed by such practices. For instance, one often hears the advice not to go swimming after eating. Although this advice ranks among the myths in medical science, there is a grain of truth to it (just search the Internet for a lively discussion of this topic). After a meal, the flow of blood to the stomach and intestines increases to absorb nutrients. Hence heavy exercise after eating creates a competition for blood flow between the digestive organs and other muscles, which could result in muscular cramps and stitches. Most parents do not explain this connection between swimming and eating but simply reiterate what they have been told by their own parents. Despite its usefulness, common sense can enshrine practices that have no clear benefit or that can even be harmful. Although folk wisdom provides simple tried and tested advice and is backed by some reasoning, it is not the motor that drives major advances in many areas.

There are also musical intuitions and folk wisdom. For example, some people consider themselves not musical enough to learn, understand, or perform music in the classical music tradition; some parents think that the trumpet is not an appropriate instrument for girls and the flute is not for boys; some view absolute pitch as an innate disposition. Whether or not such folk wisdom is true can only be answered by a music expert.

Consulting the Informed Practitioner or Professional

In a world in which knowledge is rapidly expanding, it becomes less and less possible for any one individual to be well informed in all areas. Most societies respond to this problem by encouraging individuals to become specialized professionals. But today even professionals have to struggle to keep up with their fields, leading to a further narrowing of specialization. This is as true for musicians as it is for medical doctors or researchers. Musicians do not learn all instruments but only a selected few, and many classically trained musicians even exclude composition and improvisation from their practice. Thus music professionals are experts in their respective fields only.

Individuals wishing to become professionals obtain qualifications (e.g., degrees), and communities of such professionals monitor each other as a means to ensure quality. Some areas do not have formal training and certification agencies, but they have different selection mechanisms (e.g., competitions, apparent success). Doctors, engineers, and teachers usually receive degrees that allow them to practice, whereas athletes, artists, and poets gain a reputation within their respective fields. Music teaching is interesting because some teachers start out as teachers, whereas others start out as performing artists and become teachers without formal qualifications.

Practitioners draw on what they have learned during their formative years and the experience accumulated as they work in their fields. Although it is well established that mere experience does not necessarily increase performance on routine tasks, most experts do become better over time in dealing with rare and complicated problems, especially if they deliberately try to improve (Ericsson, 2004; Ericsson & Lehmann, 1997). Thus practitioners' advice, whether given in person or in writing, is a prime source of information in many domains—including music. However, even experts can disagree or make doubtful decisions. For example, why can two different doctors come to different diagnoses? Or how is it possible that two professional voice teachers disagree in their assessments during a student audition for entry into a conservatory?

Sometimes even professionals have to use an unsound knowledge base because the relevant knowledge needed at a given time might not exist. For example, it is difficult to predict a musician's success based on selected performances during an audition, and the jurors' assessments may rest on different perceptions. Sometimes a prospective student may have had insufficient training despite favorable assessments. Although one could dismiss a disappointed student's skepticism toward the jurors' decision as arrogance, it is true that there is little or no scientific basis for the theories and practices espoused by many practitioners whose expertise does not replicate well under controlled conditions. But in most cases the professionals themselves are not to blame: They simply do not have access to the information that would allow a useful assessment or prediction.

Historical changes in knowledge and practices provide good examples for fluctuations in assessment. For example, a physician 80 to 100 years ago probably could not deal successfully with smallpox or pneumonia, whereas today these are easily curable. Today we are struggling with various cancers and HIV instead. Sometimes there are irrational resistances to change among practitioners. For example, for many years most children in the United States have been vaccinated against chicken pox. Only now are German doctors considering the widespread use of this vaccine, which was deemed unnecessary—or even dangerous—before. As knowledge and theories become available, they are bound to trickle down to the practitioner, who can then use them, often without clear reference to where this knowledge came from. In turn, it simply becomes common knowledge in the field (for better or worse).

We often follow the advice of an expert based not so much on the quality of the advice (we often have no way of assessing this) but on extraneous factors, such as the apparent trustworthiness or persuasiveness of the individuals concerned or their reputations, which depend on other people whom we respect. Sometimes our willingness to follow advice is based on whether or not we like the person who is advising us! Such a situation occurs when a music student plays a piece of music she doesn't like just to please the teacher.

The musical expert or reflective practitioner is conspicuously present in the writings of philosophers, aestheticians, critics, performers, composers, and teachers. Indeed, most sources used in musicology and performance practice consist of such writings. They are informative and reflect the experiences of one individual with a specific background, which may or may not apply to other people, times, and places. Personal opinions are elevated to hard-and-fast truth by the writers. The benefits we can derive from them for performing, teaching, and listening today depend on the authors and our ability to read and apply their writings to our own situations.

Some words of caution are in order. Accounts of personal experience (e.g., autobiographies) are often written for specific purposes that may distort the message by emphasizing or deemphasizing certain facts. For example, why would a performer confess weaknesses or lack of motivation to practice as a student? This would be bad for his or her image.

At other times, the report of a performance comes so long after the event happened that natural distortions of memory are likely. For example, as an old man Carl Czerny, who had been a student of Ludwig van Beethoven as a child, reminisces about Beethoven's execution of his own piano sonatas. How accurate can his description possibly be? Despite these shortcomings of historical and contemporary phenomenological accounts, many of them have changed the musical world and allowed stimulating, unique insights.

The writings of famous teachers who act more as researchers, such as Francesco Geminiani, Leopold Mozart, C. P. E. Bach, J. J. Quantz, or their modern counterparts, are somewhat different, leading us to more systematic ways of seeking answers. As Auer (1921/1980, p. vii) states in the preface to his famous book:

> I have simply and frankly endeavoured to explain the art of violin playing as well-nigh sixty years of experience as an interpreting artist and teacher have revealed it to me. My advice, my conclusions are all the outcome of my experience. They have all been verified by years of experiment and observation.

Instrumental music education has a long and successful tradition of imparting extremely high levels of human performance by refining and handing down skills from generation to generation. Teachers' advice comes in the form of easy-to-understand rules and basic principles to follow. They may not work for everybody, but they usually worked for the person who is giving the advice—and they might work for us. Teachers see many students throughout their lives and can hone and test their personal theories. However, great teachers are often flexible and therefore may deviate from their own prescriptions for the sake of accommodating the individual needs of a student.

The Scientific Approach to Answering Questions about Music

The most recent approach developed in the history of civilization up to now is the scientific approach, and it is this one that we want to convey as a useful addition to the traditional ones. Science as a fully fledged and distinct branch of intellectual activity did not establish its full credentials until the nineteenth century. In many areas of our lives, scientific evidence provides the cornerstone against which all knowledge can be assessed. For example, new protective clothing for firefighters, new and exciting beverage tastes, and drugs to fight cancer are all developed with scientific methods. Our forefathers believed that many natural phenomena were caused by supernatural beings. Rituals, such as Mardi Gras or Carnival, were held to scare ghosts away or request their assistance. Science has demystified many of those natural phenomena, giving us powerful explanations and even the ability to predict or foresee certain events (e.g., severe weather).

As in other areas of life, music making, listening, and teaching are accessible via scientific methods, and a lot of research has been done on music over the past 150 years. The scientific approach is useful and can often provide an alternative and maybe better basis for solving certain problems than the other approaches. Just as we enjoy experiences such as Mardi Gras or a thunderstorm despite our knowledge of their origins, the expert music listener can consciously follow the harmonic progression in a piece, identify the performer, or single out every instrument from a complex sound—and still feel the joy of listening. We believe that knowledge and understanding do not preclude amazement, surprise, and admiration (see chapter 12).

At least three important features—namely, *objectivity*, *generalizability*, and *explanation* or *prediction*—distinguish science from other approaches of knowledge production. Although much philosophical discussion revolves around those principles, they are generally accepted as the basis of scientific work. We now explain the three features in more detail, because they affect music research.

Although true objectivity may be desirable, it is impossible, for various reasons. Therefore, scientists try to seek information that depends as little as possible on the individual person making the observation or gathering the data. This principle is violated in the case of Auer's historical observations and his supposed objectivity because we do not know whether someone else would have made the same observations and come to the same conclusions. Everybody seeks objectivity sometimes: Many students, for example, record themselves in the practice room or on stage and listen to themselves afterward, thus distancing themselves from the event, excitement, and personal involvement. This

Cross-Cultural Perspective: Entering the Culture of Science

In everyday life we seldom think about music as a topic of scientific research. Yet we notice our thoughts and feelings about a piece of music, and maybe even verbalize them in a diary or in conversations with friends and teachers. Researching music is going one step further by deriving theories and hypotheses from our observations and intuitions and putting them to a test. This process has certain requirements (see the text for further details):

We need people who cooperate with us, who fill out survey forms or answer questions, or who perform or listen to music in a laboratory situation. Although we thereby isolate them from the natural context in which music making and listening occurs, we assume that most of the concepts we are after will be stable even under these changed conditions (e.g., that the listener might still like rap music and the guitarist can still perform a certain song). But researchers may also go out into the field to observe, interview, or record people "in their natural habitat."

It is absolutely necessary to obtain consent from those people we seek to investigate, and we are not allowed to deceive them (unless we tell them afterward, as in the television show *Candid Camera*). Ethical considerations are extremely important, even when the research cannot harm the individual and is noninvasive. Similarly, we have to accept that people may choose not to answer or participate (American Psychological Association, 2002).

Research requires certain skills. Finding and applying the appropriate research methodology is the only way to obtain meaningful results, and many books have been written on the topic. To finally enter into a discourse with the scientific community, one needs to learn how to acquire and analyze data (Huron, 1999), and adequately write up the research (American Psychological Association, 2001).

We would encourage the reader to join our quest for a better understanding of our human relationship with music. Just as discovering more about a composer and the piece we are currently rehearsing can add to our enjoyment of this music, finding out about the people-music-interaction can enhance our appreciation for the skills involved in listening to and making music.

example also demonstrates that science and technological development often go hand in hand (e.g., microscopes, recording equipment, measuring devices). However, many scientific observations can be made with little or no complex equipment, especially in psychology. Interviews and surveys can achieve a high degree of objectivity by sophisticated new qualitative research methods. At the very least, the researcher can unveil possible sources of bias for the reader, hence making the research process transparent (see the box on cross-cultural aspects).

Psychologists seek commonalities in human thought and behavior. This is often achieved by counting, which is the reason this method is also called the *nomothetic* approach. Science is keen on establishing facts that are true not only at one place and time but that are also true in general. This makes science distinctly different from disciplines such as music and history, which describe the unique facts about a particular event, place or time (*ideographic* method). It also sets science apart from most of our everyday activities. Generality can be established only by making a sufficiently large number of similar observations in an appropriate range of different situations. Whereas scientific progress can sometimes be slow and expensive and is by its very nature always lagging behind the problem, the practitioner can generate solutions and answers very quickly. This is the reason that research should try to tackle truly important questions (e.g., How much practice time is necessary and useful?) and not those to which the answers are trivial (e.g., Do students slow down when the music gets difficult?). Although science can make generalized statements, specific answers for individual problems are beyond the reach of science. A typical example would be dosages for most medications: The instruction leaflet lists different dosages for different ages, mostly disregarding height, weight, gender, or other individual features. Because making recommendations for each individual would require individual testing, scientists are sometimes reluctant to draw firm conclusions from their research. This is where the practitioner is needed.

Prediction and explanation is one goal of psychology. Scientists ask the "why" question in seeking to understand and explain the facts they observe. Ultimately, they would like to be able to predict future behavior or performance. They do this through propounding and testing theories. A theory is often a conjecture about an underlying mechanism that, if it operates as envisaged, would necessarily produce the results observed. For example, one of the most significant advances in medicine was brought about by the work of Louis Pasteur (1822–1895) and others who tried to understand why so many people died after surgery or childbirth. They conjectured that infections could be accounted for if they were carried by invisible entities transported through the air into open wounds. This theory was successfully validated by protecting wounds and washing hands, but they still did not have a means to finally explain the phenomenon. Of course, after the invention of the microscope, their theory could be confirmed and the bacteria observed. Similarly today, some promoters of alternative medicines claim to have evidence for the effectiveness of their cures, yet they offer no scientifically valid explanation, and their current evidence is also often questionable. It remains to be seen if their claims will be confirmed or debunked.

Modern psychology started to study music in the second half of the nineteenth century by investigating phenomena of acoustics and basic perception (consonance, resonance, auditory perception, etc.). More complex behaviors were studied in the twentieth century with the advent of wax cylinders and phonographs to record and play back music in laboratory settings. (The same equipment also aided ethnomusicology.) More applied research into the mechanics of performance and practice was undertaken in the 1920s (e.g., vibrato, musical aptitude, practice, piano performance) using newly emerging technology. In the 1930s, research methods from marketing and radio research (questionnaires, survey, observation, etc.) were adopted to investigate musical preferences, emotional experiences, and performance anxiety. Since the end of World War II, research in the psychology of music has continued to encompass every possible topic touching on the human (or machine) relationship with music, and the interest has increased during recent years.

Research in music psychology has been useful in designing concert halls and musical instruments, in managing radio and TV stations, in finding and optimizing applications of music in industry or therapy, in fostering our understanding of how children learn music, and in informing performers and teachers about better methods for learning, practicing, and performing. Many things we know today have been found by researchers or reflective practitioners in the past and have slowly made their way into our "common sense."

Science can synthesize a music performance that is hardly distinguishable from that of a human being, thereby demonstrating that we understand the performer's use of expressive devices (see chapter 5). Science can also roughly predict the success of a performer based on training data. But science will never "produce" or attempt to produce a first-rate performer, composer, or teacher or a perfect listener. Science can inform, explain, and suggest, but every individual is unpredictable, has a free will, and is subject to chance.

Music Making and Listening as Skills

In this book we consider music listening and music making to be learned behaviors or skills. Our goal is to understand the mechanisms involved in these activities and to explain possible individual differences among people with regard to these skills. For example, it would be nice to know what makes students practice effectively or what effective learners do. This can be useful in explaining why some people achieve more than others. As we know from other areas of the social sciences (e.g., sociology, anthropology), understanding human thought and behavior requires consideration of the cultural context in which it occurs.

Depending on where and when we grow up or live, we develop differently: Our physiology and psychology are influenced by our surroundings. One of the striking pieces of evidence with regard to physiology is the development in body height. Over the past hundred years, the average height of the population has increased by several inches, and this effect has been different for the United States and Europe: Americans used to be taller, but Europeans caught up after World War II. Researchers attribute the difference in height to the availability of health care and food (Komlos & Baur, 2004). Psychology is also affected by geographical location and historical times. For example, we know that people in different parts of the world have different cultural practices and mentalities. In fact, even though we tend to think that all cultures ought to have the same maladies, clinical psychologists are confronted with different symptoms and cures in different cultures (cf. Scupin, 1999).

Musicians often do not consider their performances to be a skill, such as riding a bike, typing, or speaking a foreign language, but rather an art that defies the laws of mundane skills to a certain degree. However, as researchers continue to discover, all skills share certain features, and so do experts in the different domains of human endeavor. This is confirmed by the writings of Auer and many other musicians, who imply that art becomes possible only through the mastery of a skill. How else would an improviser display his or her splendid imagination other than by executing it with extreme *artistic* and *technical finesse*? It is not our purpose to engage in a philosophical discourse on art, but rather to show how skills contribute to it.

The Distribution of Musical Skills in Society

When we claim that someone is a skilled musician, we actually mean that this person displays a certain level of performance, although the level of mastery may vary from one individual to another. It is therefore useful to talk about the distribution of musical skills in society (see figure 1.1). Fewer people reach the higher levels of performance. The variation in level of performance also coincides with changes in a person's past training history, resulting musical identity, and professional role in society. For simplicity's sake we assume four levels.

The first and lowest level of proficiency, which we jokingly call the "Happy Birthday" level, is that manifested by the average population without specific training. At this level people are capable of performing basic musical tasks, such as singing a limited repertoire of familiar songs (e.g., "Happy Birthday to You," the national anthem, congregational singing), tapping along to a beat, or listening to music of their culture and understanding its basic messages. Central to this category is that the musical skill is imparted through acculturation passively or through the intermediary of whatever public education is available to everybody.

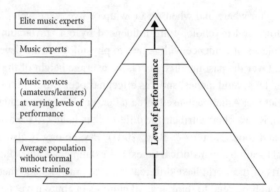

Figure 1.1. Pyramid model of distribution of musical skills in society. Fewer individuals attain higher levels of music performance. Individual differences within levels are considerable.

The second level is that of the novice or amateur and includes the beginning string student, as well as the semiprofessional rock guitarist or the decade-long member of a church choir. They all have some type of formal or informal training, but they do not earn their livings with music. It is difficult to set a clear dividing line between this level and the next, the expert level, because many amateurs perform at expert levels. Therefore, the division cannot be primarily imposed with regard to the attained level of performance but also with regard to a person's chosen group of reference (e.g., "I am an amateur pianist, not a professional").

The third level encompasses the experts. They have sought and received extensive training with the goal of making music their professional careers as teachers, performers, composers, and so forth. Classical musicians typically have gone through formal training and examinations, whereas other types of musicians have successfully completed noninstitutional means to professionalization. We could even include university music students in this level, as they are clearly on the way to professionalism.

In addition to performing, we should consider listening a skill. In the course of learning an instrument, or even through intensive listening, we become more discriminating (see chapter 11). The simple fact that music from a different musical culture often does not touch us emotionally or is difficult to understand supports the notion of music listening as a skill. Some people make a living as listening experts (e.g., music critics, recording engineers, sound designers). It is from this third level of expertise that the fourth one emerges, the elite experts.

The elite experts are those professionals who are recognized by other experts in the field as being superior. In music, the elite experts are the big-time international performers we know from recordings or the performers and composers included in the encyclopedias (e.g., Clara Schumann, Ravi Shankar, the

Beatles, Dizzy Gillespie, David Bowie). They make an impact in their domains, either by perfecting the art (as Mozart perfected music of the classical style), by setting new standards (as pianist Franz Liszt did in achieving a hitherto unknown virtuosity), or by clearly inventing a new domain (as Dizzy Gillespie did in "inventing" bebop).

Even among people of similar acculturation or training, that is, within one slice of our pyramid, we would expect individual differences in performance (e.g., some 14-year-old brass-band members play better than others). Statistics tell us that those differences should be distributed in a systematic fashion following the well-known bell curve. Roughly two-thirds of a given population fall in the middle portion of the normal distribution, and one-third is divided between its remaining left and right tail ends. Of this third, about 2% of the population will be found in the far right and far left ends of the curve. One example is IQ scores (population average is 100). Two-thirds of all people fall between 85 and 115; this is 100 plus or minus 15 (which is 1 standard deviation from the mean). Another third would fall evenly under 85 and over 115, of which roughly 2% each would fall under 70 and over 130. We have no index in music that resembles the IQ, but if we had, the upper 2% would include people with unusually high musical skills or aptitudes (see chapter 2), whereas the lowest 2% would contain individuals with learning difficulties in music (see chapter 11).

Musical Skills and Culture

Having claimed that skills vary within society, we can now show how skills vary across time and place (see also chapter 12). Anthropologists and ethnologists have provided rich descriptions of musical behaviors that differ from our Western experiences. Compare, for example, the average level of performance of a South African and a German adult. The African adult might know many songs (some even polyphonic), can perform rather complicated rhythms vocally and in dance, and has no qualms about participating in a public musical event (see the cross-cultural box in chapter 2). In contrast, the average German adult will have learned to play simple tunes on the recorder in primary school, will know very few songs, will likely hand clap on beats 1 and 3 regardless of the music, and will be scared to death to perform in public. In Hungary, where the Kodály method is extensively practiced in public schools, the average proficiency of amateur choirs is rather high, as it is in some Eastern European and Scandinavian countries that have a strong choir tradition.

Also, the emergence and level of performance of a skill are influenced by the surroundings and vary over time. In sports we see quite clearly how levels of performance have changed. In 100-meter freestyle swimming, for example, the 60-second record was broken by Johnny Weissmuller (who later played Tarzan) in 1924, causing considerable media attention. Forty years later, the first woman, Dawn Fraser, undercut this very threshold. Today, 80 years later,

60 seconds is a reasonable high-school or college amateur time (see figure 1.2). Similarly, researchers have shown that the proficiency of young instrumentalists has soared over the past century as demands have changed and competition has grown for some instruments (Lehmann & Ericsson, 1998a). For example, a technique that has recently gained importance in classical wind instrument playing—circular breathing—seemed difficult at first. Only high-level soloists, such as Heinz Holliger (oboe) or Wynton Marsalis (trumpet), used it. Today it is mastered by many young instrumentalists. Moreover, there are pieces for nearly every instrument that were deemed unplayable at the time of their composition, such as Beethoven's *Hammerklavier* Sonata, but that are today part of the standard repertoire. The increase in skill is particularly tangible when new instruments emerge (e.g., electric guitar). Thus skills can increase or decrease over time depending on the demand for this skill in society.

Skills are embedded in specific cultural contexts. Without trying to summarize the extensive discussion of music and culture that has taken place in cultural studies (see, e.g., Bohlman, 2002; Cook, 1998; Frith, 1996; Rogoff, 2003), and at the risk of sounding simplistic, we can talk of different musical cultures, dominant and nondominant ones, or we can introduce the problematic distinction between high and popular culture, a topic extensively covered by cultural sociologists. A skill that is a valued and useful behavior in a particular context may be totally useless in another (see also chapter 12). For example, a hip-hop music disk jockey requires a totally different set of skills from that of a Western classical musician, and a traditional Indian musician requires yet another set. By studying and talking about skills, researchers and scholars take part in a larger societal discourse about their value and cultural contextualization.

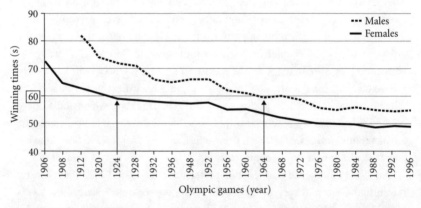

Figure 1.2. Historical development of swimming times for the 100-meter freestyle. The lines indicate gold medal times of men and women. By permission of Oxford University Press.

Personal characteristics of the person exhibiting a skill are also important. Literature in anthropology and ethnomusicology tells us that in some cultures women were not allowed to play certain instruments, at least not to perform in public. For example, didgeridoo music, which today is a cliché for Australian music, was actually the music of a few select tribes and exclusively played by males for sacred rituals.

This book mostly deals with research on traditional Western art music rather than popular music and non-Western music, because types of music outside the Western classical art-music tradition have unfortunately not received much attention from researchers in psychology. Although current research efforts are already starting to fill this gap, nonclassical music has been studied by researchers in other disciplines. However, as we explained earlier, the discovered similarities between mental skills in different domains make it more than likely that results found in one musical domain also apply to others.

Mental Representations as the Essence of a Skill

Musicians and music teachers in any musical culture would agree that music making is not primarily a physical but a mental skill, in which the hands, fingers, breathing apparatus, and so forth, merely follow directions from higher levels. Skilled music listening is a solely mental activity. We therefore propose that the common mechanisms that mediate the execution of skills are internal mental representations and auxiliary processes that act on those representations (see chapters 4 through 8).

What exactly is a mental representation? The concept of mental representation is ubiquitous in psychology and refers to the internal reconstruction of the outside world. Here is a simple everyday life example: We are standing at one end of a furnished room and want to get to the door at the opposite end of the room. For this, we have to circumvent the obstacles in our way. Now, if we were to attempt this in a darkened room or with eyes closed, we would have to re-create the approximate location of the objects in the room in our heads and attempt to compute our own location while moving about. The internal image we generate, unlike a color photograph, is a more reduced, simplified version of the external image. For example, the ceiling is likely not represented, nor is the exact pattern of the chair's fabric. Not only do we have to represent the outside world, but we also have to manipulate the information in useful ways in order to image, problem solve, anticipate, teach, remember, learn, practice, and create. That such representations are built and manipulated in music making and listening is uncontroversial from the psychologist's (Weisberg, 1992) as well as the musician's perspective. The famous piano teacher Neuhaus (1967) calls it the "artistic image," the music educator Gordon (1987) speaks of "audiation," and some people use "inner hearing" or similar terms.

Self Study: Mental Representation in Listening

Try to play or sing a very short melody (5–10 notes) and ask another student to recall it by singing or on his or her instrument, like a call-and-response exercise. This is generally no problem. Your partner should be able to keep the information in working memory and reproduce it from there. Now try the same thing with increasingly longer and complex melodies. Mistakes now start to emerge as the melody can no longer be recalled exactly but has to be reconstructed using a mental representation of it. This reconstructive process involves reading and inference and crystallizes around salient features such as rhythms, harmony, contour, or other musical structures (cf. Sloboda & Parker, 1985). More familiar and structured melodies are easier to recall than less structured ones. To get an idea of how extensively this process can be trained, listen to Gregorio Allegri's *Miserere,* which Wolfgang Amadeus Mozart allegedly transcribed in Rome (assisted by his father) at the age of 14 after hearing it only a few times (see also chapter 6).

Here is a simple musical demonstration of an internal representation: Try to find which word of the song "Happy Birthday" receives the highest note or pitch. You have likely hummed the song to yourself until you reached that last *bir-* shortly before the name of the celebrant; just to make sure the answer is correct, you might have continued until the end. In this way, you attempt to represent the song and scan it for the highest note, which is not difficult to do. Young children may not be able to do this.

Neuropsychologists have found that hearing and imaging music activate the same brain areas (Halpern, 2003). Thus, when representing the external world internally, we partly draw on those mechanisms that are involved in its perception. However, musical representations need not be solely of an auditory nature. We can think in terms of music theory, emotions, images, and kinesthetic and other aspects (see also chapter 6).

Internal representations naturally become more complex when we make music. We have to represent not only what we are going to play or sing but also how it will be executed on the instrument and what is currently being played. This last process is necessary for musicians in order to monitor and improve their performance. We can describe these representations using a triangular model (see figure 1.3), incorporating the representation of the current performance, the goal representation, and the motor representation (Lehmann & Ericsson, 1997a; 1997b; Woody, 2003). The performers might ask themselves, How do I currently sound? How do I want to sound? How does this feel on the instrument? Each of these representations can theoretically be assessed and

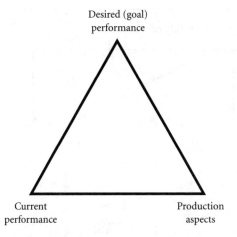

Figure 1.3. Triangular model of the three necessary mental representations for music making. From "Research on Expert Performance and Deliberate Practice: Implications for the Education of Amateur Musicians and Music Students," by A. C. Lehmann and K. A. Ericsson, 1997, *Psychomusicology, 16*, p. 51. Copyright © 1998 by *Psychomusicology*. Reprinted with permission.

trained independently. Our model is consistent with general psychological theories. Failure to construct and use representations can lead to problems, as the following typical example demonstrates. The teacher asks the student to do something (e.g., to play a crescendo); the student gives a rendition without a crescendo but insists that he or she played what the teacher wanted. This incident demonstrates how the student can short-circuit his or her representations by mistaking intentions for output.

It is important to emphasize mental representations because they underlie the whole range of musical skills, starting with remembering music to reproducing and creating it. A convincing scientific proof for this bold claim can be gleaned from the studies by McPherson and collaborators (see McPherson & Gabrielsson, 2002, for an overview). In a 3-year longitudinal study with more than 100 instrumental students, they assessed performance on several musical subskills, including playing by ear, sight-reading, playing rehearsed music, and improvisation. The researchers also interviewed students about their musical development and music training. Figure 1.4 shows their results in a schematic way. The thicker lines indicate stronger influences of one variable on another; thinner arrows represent weaker ones. Note that all relationships between musical subskills were positive, which means that students who played well by ear also tended to sight-read and improvise better, and so forth. What could be the common denominator that led to these positive associations? We are tempted to say that this is the person's ability to encode and manipulate musically relevant information, in essence, to construct and manipulate mental representations.

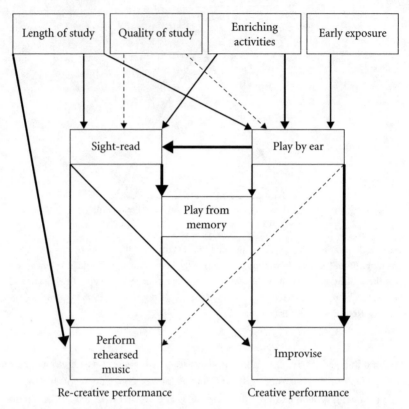

Figure 1.4. McPherson's empirically based model of the interrelation of musical skills with training/environmental factors. From *The Science and Psychology of Music Performance,* edited by R. Parncutt & G. McPherson, 2002, p. 108. Copyright © 2002 by Oxford University Press, Inc. Used by permission of Oxford University Press.

Palmer and Meyer (2000) uncovered this hidden ability in two experiments in which they studied whether meaningful (conceptual) and motor learning facilitate learning a new task. Such so-called positive transfer is generally regarded as a sign of successful learning. Sixteen adult pianists participated in the first experiment, and 16 piano-playing children took part in the second one. In both experiments the participants first learned a melodic line consisting of 12 notes during a training phase, and then they were asked to perform another melody. They played either the same or a slightly altered melody with the same or a different hand (which required different fingering). The training trials, as well as the transfer trials, were performed on an electric piano, and the researchers could thus analyze every single keystroke. The hypothesis was that the more similar the transfer melody was to the original melody, the greater the transfer would be. Positive transfer was even predicted for a change in hand with unchanged melody. The idea was that playing difficulties would slow down the performance, whereas the benefits from previous training would facilitate performance. Therefore, the measure of most interest was the time it took the participants to play the transfer trial, and the experimenters predicted that more positive transfer would result in performance durations that were relatively close to those of the final training trials. The adult pianists' results fulfilled the predictions. They did quite well regardless of the hand, as long as the melody was the same. The children, however, did best when both hand (motor) and melody (conceptual) aspects were unchanged. Here, imposed changes in motor performance increased duration of performance. Interestingly, the more experienced group of pianists (5–7 years) showed better transfer than the less experienced group (3–4 years). Note that children in both groups were comparable in age (average 11.2 and 11.9 years). The authors concluded that:

> As skill increases, mental representations for performance become dissociated from the movements required to produce a musical sequence; advanced performers' mental plans are based on abstract, conceptual pitch relations. . . . In contrast to the results for skilled adults, the results for novice children showed transfer of learning that reflected the movements as much as the abstract pitch relationships. (p. 67)

This clearly shows that learning to play the piano does not primarily consist in learning to press keys but in gaining a conceptual understanding for music that is relatively independent of the more technical matters.

In this chapter we have argued for the scientific approach in answering important questions in music regarding creating, re-creating, and listening to music. This particular and fairly recent way of thinking offers a powerful source of insights for understanding music making and learning and could assist reflective practitioners in their everyday lives as performers, teachers, or listeners. At the core of the scientific approach is the view of music as a skill. Consequently, we can adopt the notion that mental representations, namely the individual's ability to reconstruct the outside world in order to act effectively on that information, is at the heart of becoming an expert. This theory is compatible with writings of expert teachers in music. As further chapters demonstrate, these cognitive mechanisms are acquired in the course of long-term training, which is the reason that we emphasize the importance of optimal teaching and learning (e.g., chapters 2, 3, 4, and 10).

Study Questions

1. Which groups of people (see figure 1.1) possess the varying levels of musical proficiency in our society with regard to different musical genres (e.g., jazz, rock, and classical music)?
2. In what way does the issue of mental representations feature in the writ-

ings of famous music pedagogues and musicians? Find examples and rephrase them in more scientific terms.

3. Discuss what implications the findings of Palmer and Meyer (2000) may have for the music teacher with regard to teaching beginners and more advanced students.

Further Reading

Ericsson, K. A. (Ed.). (1994). *The Road to Excellence.* Core articles in the area of expertise research that introduce a skill approach; especially chapters 1 and 4.

Proctor, W., & Dutta, A. (1995). *Skill Acquisition and Human Performance.* An excellent introduction to the general psychology of skills without specific emphasis on music.

Chaffin, R., & Lemieux, A. F. (2004). *General perspectives on achieving musical excellence.* Music performance is placed in a broader psychological context.

2

Development

There are many important questions on which almost every musician is expected to have an opinion. How do musical skills emerge in the normal child? Can we know anything about musical capacity before and shortly after birth? Is there a normal path of musical development that most children follow? How do we account for differences in musical ability between children? Is absolute pitch a sign of special musical ability? What kinds of activity and environment will best assist children in their musical development? Is there an optimum age for beginning formal musical instruction? Musicians who teach (as most musicians do) will shape their teaching and their advice to parents according to the views they hold on these questions. These are also questions on which people tend to hold quite strong views, not all of which are supported by scientific evidence. This chapter may help dispel some prevalent myths, drawing from current scientific knowledge (see also Runfola & Swanwick, 2002, and Gembris, 2002, for reviews).

A commonly held view is that musical ability is a somewhat rare "talent" within the population. According to this view, only a few talented individuals can become musicians; thus a key task for the music profession is the detection or early identification of talent so that it may be properly encouraged and nurtured.

Our assessment of the scientific evidence makes us question the value of thinking about talent in this way. The evidence we review here suggests that:

1. All normal human babies display an astonishing array of musically related skills and aptitudes, lying just beneath their apparently "helpless" appearances.
2. These skills show a typical developmental progression through childhood that is to a certain extent independent of training and education.

3. Parents and caregivers can provide environments that significantly accelerate the rate of acquisition of musical skills.
4. It is very difficult to predict later musical outcomes on the basis of "tests of aptitude" or "early signs of talent." Many professional musicians displayed no distinctive early signs.
5. Supposedly "special" abilities, such as absolute pitch, are less influential in musical development than more mundane factors, such as parental support and involvement and sustained practice. Little firm evidence exists that high-achieving musicians are genetically different from lower-achieving ones.

If the evidence we present supports these conclusions, what are the implications? One implication is that music education should be seen as a birthright for all children (just as math or literacy education is), not as a resource to be allocated to the "talented" few. Another implication is that we should expect most children to be capable of attaining high levels of musical accomplishment if they are properly motivated, taught, and encouraged. However, scientific research does not imply that all children could become Mozart, Beethoven, and the like. The attainment of genius is a complex combination of biological, cognitive, motivational, cultural, and historical factors (Eysenck, 1995; Simonton, 1999), and an explanation of genius is at the far limits of what science is capable of. We believe that there is nothing inherent to prevent most human beings (with some exceptions outlined later) from achieving a level of musical proficiency that would be comparable to those displayed by professional performers. Whether they achieve this potential is a matter of motivation, opportunity, and resource, rather than biological capacities or limitations.

The Preverbal Infant

The understanding of musical development has been revolutionized by the development of experimental methods for testing the knowledge of very young babies, who are unable to talk or follow instructions. For instance, researchers are able to measure subtle changes in body movement (head or eye turns, rate of sucking) or internal processes (heart rate) that demonstrate a baby's awareness of change. There are now many demonstrations that infant music perception is far more sophisticated than overt behavior would suggest. Only carefully constructed experiments can elicit the full extent of these perceptual abilities, which would normally go unnoticed even by the most observant parent.

Innovative techniques have been able to establish that musical sensitivity and learning exists prior to birth. For example, newborn babies respond with greater attention to music tracks that were repeatedly played by their mothers before birth than to novel melodies (Hepper, 1991). This means that babies have already picked up and stored quite specific information about the music around them prior to birth. This becomes possible because the auditory system appears to be fully developed by the end of the fourth month of pregnancy (Lecanuet, 1996).

Turning to the months following birth, researchers have shown that 5-month-old babies are already more sensitive to melodic pattern or contour than to pitch as such (see Trehub & Trainor, 1993, for a review). When a melodic pattern to which the babies had become familiarized was transposed up or down by 3 semitones, there was relatively little response. However, when the pattern itself was changed, this provoked strong reaction. Already at 5 months, babies attach relatively little importance to the absolute pitch at which they hear a melody. What is more important to them is the invariant set of contours and intervals that distinguish one melody from another. In this respect, babies display musical "intelligence" that older children or even adults show.

Babies also appear to be sensitive to certain aspects of musical structure. Jusczyk and Krumhansl (1993) showed that babies prefer tonal melodies in which pauses are introduced at the end of phrases rather than the same melodies with pauses occurring at other points. Trainor and Trehub (1993) trained 9-month-old babies to respond to an intensity change in a series of repeating melodic fragments. When the intensity increased, babies were rewarded if they turned their heads at least 45 degrees to the left. The reward was a brief illumination of four lights and a set of mechanical toys. Previous research had shown that the opportunity to look at interesting moving objects is rewarding for babies of this age. Figure 2.1 shows an example of a typical experimental environment for testing infant perception.

The test phase used a repeating five-note pattern. The background pattern could be either (1) a major triad (e.g., C E G E C) or (2) an augmented triad (e.g., C E G# E C). Each repetition of this pattern began on a different pitch, which meant that only relative pitch information was available to the baby. A "change trial" occurred when the third note of the pattern was lowered by a semitone; thus (1) would become C E F# E C and (2) would become C E G E C. The experiment was carried out using both babies and adults (adults signaled a change trial by raising their hands). The proportion of trials in which participants correctly detected a change was recorded. Figure 2.2 shows the percentage scores for adults and infants, given separately for the major triads and the augmented triads. This shows that adults and infants performed very similarly. Both groups performed well on the major triads but much more poorly on the augmented triads.

The authors concluded that there is some special feature of a major triad that allows babies (and adults) to process and store it more efficiently. A major fifth is more consonant (having a simpler frequency ratio) than an augmented fifth. It

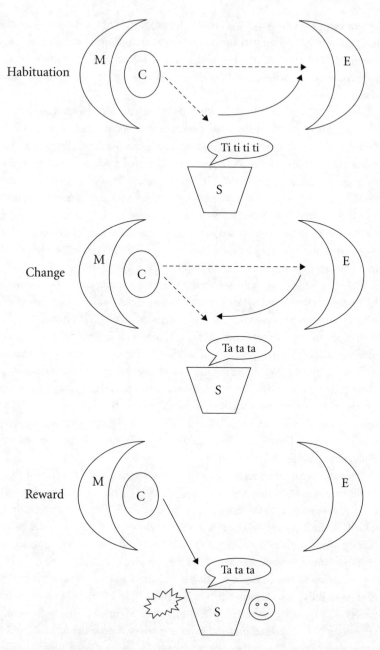

Figure 2.1. Schematic diagram of a typical experimental environment for testing infants' perceptual capacities. The child (C) sits on its mother's (M) lap and hears a stimulus from a loudspeaker (S). The experimenter (E) watches the child. Once the child loses
interest in the new stimulus and habituates (top panel), the stimulus changes (middle
panel). Renewed interest in the changed stimulus is rewarded by lights or a toy (lower
panel), and a new trial begins.

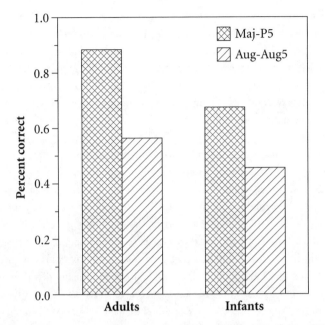

Figure 2.2. Percent correct performance for infants and adults in Trainor and Trehub's (1993) experiment. The bars show performance for the major chord and for the augmented chord. From "What Mediates Infants' and Adults' Superior Processing of the Major over the Augmented Triad?" by L. J. Trainor & S. E. Trehub, 1993, *Music Perception, 11,* p. 190, Figure 1. Copyright © 1993 by the Regents of the University of California. Reproduced with permission.

also occurs more often in music. Nine-month-old babies have a surprisingly adult capacity to make use of these special features. These and similar studies show that in many respects human babies are "pretuned" to music, able to extract key information necessary for perception and memory of the complex melodic and rhythmic sequences that make up music.

Babies are not simply passive recipients of musical information. The early use of their voices also shows their musical capacities. Long before they are able to produce recognizable words or tunes, babies experiment with their voices, playing with the elements that will later be incorporated in speech and in singing. This activity is called *babbling* and includes cooing, gliding, and the repetition of specific pitch and vowel-consonant patterns (e.g., "da-da-da"). Much of this experimentation takes place in the context of interactions between the infant and the caregiver (usually the mother). Adults interacting with babies alter their vocalizations in very specific ways. This "infant-directed speech" is more rhythmical and songlike than normal speech, uses affective archetypes, and imitates specific features of vocalizations of the infant in order to attract the infant's attention (Papousek, 1996). The imitation is two way: Infants also imitate pitches and melodic contours that they hear in adult speech (Kessen, Levine, & Wendrich, 1979). Some of these skills are apparent well before 6 months of age. Babies are much more attentive to mothers singing than to mothers speaking the same text (Trehub, 2003). When mothers sing to their babies, they use raised pitch level, decreased tempo, and a more emotive voice quality. Music is thus an essential part of babies' behavior and interaction from the very beginning of life.

All the evidence we have demonstrates that babies can do quite sophisticated things musically. This is very strong backing for the conclusion that musical capacity is a universal inherent human capacity: It is part of what it means to be human. The achievements just described are not the achievements of "superbabies"—they are what every average baby achieves. Indeed, the literature on infant capacity is notable for the absence of studies demonstrating large and systematic individual differences between babies in their musical capacities. Even studies that have specifically searched for early signs of difference between able and less able young musicians have failed to find consistent evidence that high achievers were exceptional babies, musically speaking (Howe, Davidson, Moore, & Sloboda, 1995). Of course, in any given study, babies' responses do differ, but many of these differences are more likely to be caused by differences in attentiveness and arousal than differences in underlying capacity. We know of no studies on babies in which individual differences in response have been linked to long-term differences in musical ability or achievement.

If music is a universal capacity of the human brain, it is important to ask whether anything could ever go wrong with a brain to render it incapable of dealing with music. We know from some astonishing life histories (e.g., the percussionist Evelyn Glennie) that even profound deafness does not automatically exclude high levels of musical achievement. The prime contender for a "brain-disabling" condition is congenital amusia (see Peretz & Hyde, 2003, for a review; see chapter 11). This condition (sometimes self-diagnosed as "tone deafness") afflicts about 4% of the population to a greater or lesser extent (Kalmus & Fry, 1980). People with congenital amusia have long-standing deficiencies in detecting pitch and rhythm changes in melodies, even though their speech and hearing is normal. This means that they fail on simple musical tasks (such as telling two melodies apart) on which most musically untrained adults are able to perform perfectly. Psychometric tests now exist to identify and pinpoint the nature of amusic deficiencies, but we still do not understand the precise neurological underpinnings of this condition, nor has anyone yet identified a congenitally amusic baby. It still remains possible that amusia is acquired during or after infancy rather than being a genetically determined deficiency. Whatever the final outcome of research into congenital amusia, we can already be fairly certain that at least 96% of the general population has the innate capacity to deal with music.

Normal Development: From the Onset
of Speech to School Age

Although the differences among individuals preoccupy many people in music education, the vast thrust of research on child development over this past century has emphasized how similar children are to one another in the fundamental path of development. This similarity comes about because of three important factors: (1) All humans share a common genetic heritage—all human beings are genetically more similar to each other than to any nonhuman animal; (2) all humans share a common environment—we all live on the surface of the same planet, surrounded by similar objects, plants, animals, and humans, which affect us in broadly similar ways; (3) the way in which the environment affects our bodies and brains to bring about physical and psychological change is determined jointly by our genetic makeup and the specific characteristics of our shared environments. Large developmental differences often appear to be caused by extreme abnormalities in *social* environment (e.g., children deprived of significant human contact and who are socially retarded and lack language; or children "hothoused" in abnormally stimulating early environments and who display characteristics of child prodigies).

One of the most important contributors to the scientific study of common developmental patterns was the Swiss psychologist Jean Piaget. He was the first to provide a systematic account of children's intellectual and moral development in terms of a fixed sequence of phases (or stages) through which most normal children pass in the same order at very comparable ages (Piaget, 1958). His research strategy was to devise a set of tasks presented to the children as games or puzzles, which most children would invariably get wrong or answer randomly at one age but which the same children would almost invariably get right a few months later.

One such task involves laying out two rows of identical small objects, such as coins or sweets (see figure 2.3). Row A has more objects in it than row B. However, row B is spaced out so that its ends are farther apart. The question asked of the children is, Which row has more?

Children under the age of about 7 find this difficult. They either answer inconsistently or, overwhelmed by the visual cue of length, they choose B. Over the age of 7, most children instantly give the correct answer, because they count each row and rely on the outcome of the counting operation, regardless of all other cues. Although psychologists have argued intensely over what precise

A. * * * * * * * *
B. * * * * * * *

Figure 2.3. Schematic representation of a typical Piagetian comparison task.

cognitive changes underlie this shift in performance, the fact of the shift is un-doubted. This type of shift, at around this age, has been observed with children from a wide range of cultures and social backgrounds. Piaget proposed that at age 7 children enter a stage of "concrete operations," in which they tend to apply rules and logical reasoning to the tasks that confront them. Note that children were able to count—correctly—for some time before they decided to prioritize counting over all other means of arriving at the answer to this problem. Their success at the task was not due to suddenly mastering the skill of counting; rather, it signaled a broader cognitive reordering in which they consistently grasped *why* counting was the most appropriate strategy (from among a range of strategies available) for problems such as this. Piaget had little or nothing to say about music, but researchers who follow him have been eager to discover whether and how musical development might be similarly constrained by common phases of development across a wide range of cultures and situations.

A very considerable body of data now exists to suggest that musical development does indeed display a common sequence of stages and typical ages at which specific abilities are displayed. These stages have been demonstrated for perceptual skills (Dowling, 1999), singing (Davidson, McKernon, & Gardner, 1981), notation (Bamberger, 1991; Davidson & Scripp, 1988), and emotional and aesthetic judgment (Gardner, 1973; Kratus, 1993).

One of the most comprehensive stage models available is the "spiral" model (Swanwick & Tillman, 1986, cited in Runfola & Swanwick, 2002; see figure 2.4). This model was developed to account for observed changes in children's performed compositions in classroom contexts (see also chapter 7). Data were gathered from children between the ages of 3 and 15 and, on the basis of this, four main levels of operation were proposed (with two sequential modes nested within each level, reflecting, respectively, the child's internal motivation and more external cultural features of music):

Level 1, materials level: up to age 4. In the first "sensory" mode, children explore the pleasantness of sound through spontaneous vocalizations and soundings of instruments and other objects. Experimentation focuses particularly on loudness and timbre. In the subsequent "manipulative" mode, children acquire greater ability in handling musical instruments, showing awareness of instrument-specific techniques. Their music making may reflect a regular pulse and other simple conventions of music, such as repeated rhythmic and melodic patterns.

Level 2, expression level: ages 5 to 9. This begins with the "personal expressiveness" mode, during which children convey emotions and stories through spontaneous music, particularly through singing. Expressiveness concentrates on changes in tempo and dynamics. In the "vernacular" mode that follows, children show a greater conformity to established musical conventions. Their music making is marked by the presence of melodic and rhythmic patterns, regular meter, and standard phrase lengths.

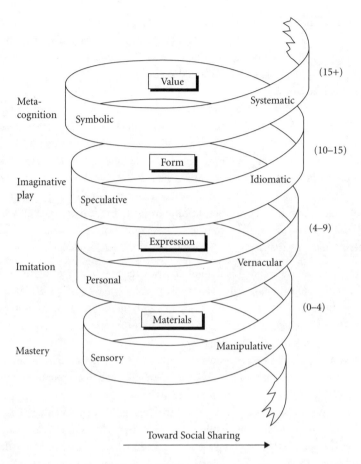

Figure 2.4. Swanwick and Tillman's (1986) spiral of musical development. From "The Sequence of Musical Development," by K. Swanwick and J. Tillman, 1986, *British Journal of Music Education*, 3(3), p. 306. Reprinted with the permission of Cambridge University Press.

Level 3, form level: ages 10 to 15. In the first "speculative" mode, young musicians show growing interest in deviating from the musical conventions discovered in the previous mode. They experiment with ways of varying patterns and adding contrast to their music, often at the expense of larger structural cohesion. In the subsequent "idiomatic" mode, they are better able to integrate their imaginative ideas into recognizable styles. Musical authenticity becomes very important, as does technical, expressive, and structural control. There is greater emphasis on imitating existing musical styles, often popular ones.

Level 4, value level: ages 15 and up. This level may never be attained by some people. In the "symbolic" mode, musicians become aware of its language-like affective function. Larger compositional qualities, such as groups of timbres or harmonic progressions, are given greater attention. In the final "systematic" mode, advanced musicians begin to approach music in innovative or sophisticated ways. This may mean employing novel compositional systems or studying and discussing music from various intellectual perspectives (e.g., philosophical, psychological).

The initial observations that led to this particular model were culturally specific. They took place in state-funded schools in the United Kingdom as part of a teaching program that encouraged and supported children in developing and presenting their own compositions. Some of the classificatory methods used have been criticized for being insufficiently scientifically rigorous (Lamont, 1995). Nonetheless, Swanwick (1991) has provided evidence for similar patterns of development in different countries. In sum, from all the available data, of which this model systematizes only a small part, it is possible to see a number of broad patterns emerging that seem to characterize normal musical development:

1. Receptive (perceptual and aural) skills precede productive (performance and compositional) skills. Children are able to make discriminations and distinctions in what they hear significantly before they are able to produce those features reliably. In this, music is exactly similar to most other symbolic skills (such as language).
2. Spontaneity precedes control in productive skills. Children begin with free, somewhat undisciplined experimentation and then naturally move to more ordered and controlled use of elements.
3. Concrete operations precede abstract ones. Early conceptualizations are holistic. Only later can children acquire the capacity to break down musical objects into their component parts and transform and recombine them (going from global to local features). For example, the ability to imagine musical objects appears relatively late in the developmental sequence.
4. Key developmental changes occur through acculturation (see chapter 1). This is the normal exposure gained by all children within a culture, excluding specific specialist training. There is considerable evidence that children who have had specific musical training (e.g., lessons on a specific instrument) do no better on a range of general perceptual and production tasks than do children without specialist training. Their superiority is found mainly in those specific tasks that the training has addressed.
5. Higher levels of achievement and the later stages of development require more support than acculturation can supply and are typically not reached at a consistent age—or at all—by significant numbers of people (see chapter 1).

What is the right age to introduce children to musical activities and have them start learning a musical instrument? This is one of the questions most often asked of professional musicians; there is no simple answer. No age is too young for some form of musical engagement that will lead to productive learning.

However, the engagement must be appropriate to the capacity and developmental stage of the child. A clear example of this relates to the teaching of musical notation (a relatively abstract skill). The evidence is quite strong that children cannot profit from formal instruction in notation until they have had considerable experience in handling musical sounds "by ear" (McPherson & Gabrielsson, 2002).

Processes of acculturation have an informal quality. The essential feature of informal learning is that the individual is free to participate or not and to take the activity at his or her own pace. Formal assessments are absent (even though feedback may be available to the participant). As such, learning through acculturation very often has a quality of play (Hargreaves, 1986). Successful early instruction builds on that informal gamelike structure rather than overturning it (e.g., parent-child song games, call and response, etc.).

The developmental literature makes quite clear that most children do not have the capacity to focus systematically on instrument-specific techniques until around the age of 4. Before that age, instruments can be used rather to illustrate general characteristics of sound-producing objects and to facilitate human interaction with those objects. Musical games involving singing, dancing, and movement, however, can be successfully introduced almost as soon as the child shows some capacity for attentive and controlled response. All early instruction requires high levels of skillful adult support and interaction to sustain a productive yet gamelike environment. Children below the age of 6 are generally not capable of solitary or self-directed study on an instrument. This is the reason that socially rich systems such as the Suzuki method appear to be necessary for very early instrumental activities. Such systems involve a great deal of group learning and the strong cooperation of parents in all aspects of the program.

Lessons that focus on structured performance targets and the deliberate improvement of control and accuracy are probably not going to mesh with the normal child's capacities until the second half of Swanwick and Tillman's (1986) expression level (vernacular mode), when the child becomes naturally able to focus on conformity to external standards and structures. Typically this occurs between the ages of 6 and 8. This is the usual age at which research has shown that professional musicians begin formal instrumental lessons (see Sloboda, Davidson, Howe, & Moore, 1996). However, even here there are considerable degrees of latitude. At one extreme are instruments such as the violin and piano, much of whose classical repertoire requires unusual degrees of manual dexterity and bodily coordination. For these instruments the highest levels of achievement require early starting ages, mostly before age 8. At the other extreme are instruments that, through their size, their repertoire, or their less demanding physical characteristics, can be successfully taken up at relatively late ages. These include the larger instruments, such as double-bass, tuba, and a range of wind and brass instruments (Linzenkirchner & Eger-Harsch, 1995).

Ability and Aptitude

Well before the age of 10, many children will come to differ from each other quite widely in what they can do musically. This happens despite the underlying similarities that have been outlined in the preceding sections. One child may be able to sight-read hymn chords on the keyboard. Another may be able to improvise effectively on the flute. A third may be able to do neither of these. These differences represent different abilities (or competencies) possessed by these children.

Musicians, their families, and those who educate them have been rightly concerned with understanding how these differences in ability come about and what implications they have for education and training (see also chapters 7, 9, and 10). One possible explanation is that different competencies arise from different preexisting aptitudes. For instance, someone who plays the violin might have special aptitude for fine finger movements and pitch discriminations, whereas someone who excels in improvisation might have special aptitude for aural memory. This explanation appears to find support from brain research. For instance, the area of the brain that receives sensory input from the fingers is larger in professional violinists than it is in nonviolinists (Elbert, Pantev, Weinbruch, Rockstroh, & Taub, 1995). However, this finding by itself does not prove that the larger brain causes the higher level of violin skill. It is also possible that practicing the violin causes these brain areas to expand. The weight of evidence from brain research actually favors the second explanation. There are many studies showing how brain areas can be radically altered by experience, either positively or negatively (Altenmüller & Gruhn, 2002; see also chapter 4).

Rather than trying to look inside the brain, some researchers have tried to discover whether there are any behavioral signs that would predict specific later competencies. The most frequently used method is the assessment of basic musical skills through age-normed tests of musical ability. These are sometimes called *aptitude tests* because they supposedly do not rely on training on specific instruments or concepts. They tend to test perception, rather than performance, and the most common type of test involves listening to two short musical sequences and judging whether they are the same as or different from each other, for example, with regard to pitch and rhythm. Different degrees of ability can be assessed by making smaller or larger changes in the dimension being tested. Examples of such tests include the Seashore Measures of Musical Talent (Seashore, Lewis, and Saetvit, 1960) and Gordon's Primary Measures of Music Audiation (PMMA; Gordon, 1979).

We know from the developmental literature that perceptual competence precedes performance competence, so we would expect children to show abilities on such perceptual tests before they demonstrate significant performance skills. It also follows that children whose perceptual skills exceed the norms for their age are more likely to acquire performance skills earlier than their peers. Conversely, children who lag behind age norms may experience difficulties in acquiring those same skills. As a result, performance on these types of tests has been shown to be moderately predictive of musical achievement at later stages of development in some research studies (e.g., Gordon, 1967). However, equally many studies have failed to find a clear relationship between early scores on aptitude tests and later musical performance (e.g., O'Neill, 1997), and for this reason many educators are extremely cautious about using aptitude tests to make major and irreversible decisions about music training (for a balanced view, see Kemp & Mills, 2002; see also chapter 3).

One reason that some people are eager to overinterpret the results of musical aptitude testing is that they believe such tests measure innate musical talent, with talent defined as a genetically predetermined advantage for the specific skill in question (in this case, music). In fact, aptitude tests measure only achievement of the sort that can be accomplished outside formal music instruction. There is remarkably scant evidence to suggest that innate talent can provide an explanation for significant further differentiation among children (apart from identifying amusics), particularly at the upper end of achievement.

The best case that has been made for genetic underpinnings of musical superiority is provided by a very small number of unusual "savants" who excel in very specific skills, often at an early age and in the absence of deliberate formal instruction. Such highly developed achievement, accomplished without the usual support, persuades many that there must be an innate ability at work. Often, these savants have significant intellectual and emotional deficits (such as autism) and seem to have retained one small pocket of excellence that, because of the lack of normal social constraints, has been obsessively developed to an extraordinarily high level (Miller, 1989; Winner, 1996). For example, one such savant, N.P., was able to perform a harmonically complex Grieg piano piece from memory with few mistakes only 12 minutes after having heard it for the first time in his life (Sloboda, Hermelin, & O'Connor, 1985). This skill had been perfected over a 15-year period during which obsessive memorizing of music had been the primary daily activity, to the exclusion of most other activities.

In general, however, children who radically exceed developmental norms for music turn out to have had highly unusual and richly supportive early environments. For instance, in an exhaustive analysis of famous piano prodigies from the seventeenth through the twentieth centuries, Lehmann (1996) could find no instance in which the child had not received extraordinarily enriched early training opportunities (often provided by a highly expert parent and/or a long-term live-in tutor providing tuition and possibly supervised practice every day).

The science of human genetics has made many advances, and we know that many differences among people (in physical characteristics, certain medical conditions, and propensity to illness) are indeed genetically influenced. However, it is extraordinarily difficult to establish genetic contributions to behavioral and psychological differences, mainly because such differences can so easily be transmitted by social and environmental, as well as genetic, routes.

Separating out the contributions of genetics and the environment is not straight-forward, and no fully satisfactory method has been devised. One method involves the study of twins (identical and, raised together and apart). Identical twins have identical genetic makeup, even if they are reared apart. Thus it is argued that if these twins are more psychologically similar to one another than are fraternal twins, this demonstrates the clear influence of genetics in bringing about their similarity. But it has also been argued that the environments of identical twins reared apart may be more similar than the environments of fraternal twins (Ceci, 1990). If that is the case, environmental explanations cannot be ruled out. In any case, the number of identical twins reared apart who are available to researchers is extraordinarily small, and it is just not possible to conduct every desirable research study on this beleaguered minority. Very few identical twins have been highly able musicians. There are almost no published twin studies on musical ability, and those that are published (e.g., Coon & Carey, 1989) have often used dubious measures of ability; that is, ability estimates were made on the basis of informal biographical data with no objective psychometric measures applied.

A different reason for being cautious about overinterpreting the results of tests of ability is the finding that test performance can be hugely dependent on motivational and emotional factors that have nothing to do with the actual level of ability. Test performance can depend on the familiarity of the testing environment, the behavior of the tester, the level of anxiety of the person being tested, and more subtle motivational factors, such as susceptibility to failure. In one study (O'Neill & Sloboda, 1997), test results were manipulated to give children the experience of either succeeding or failing the same test. The less confident children showed a significant decline in performance on a subsequent musical test, even though their earlier test performance was identical to that of more confident children. The implications are obvious. Musically able children who suffer doubts and anxieties about their musical ability will underperform in test situations, thus providing a self-fulfilling prophecy of declining expectations, confidence, and performance. Such performances tell us little about underlying capacity. Many wise educators would prefer to adopt a positive strategy by which they assume that the underlying ability is present and that it is their job to uncover and encourage it.

One specific skill that has commonly been assumed to be a sign of innate musical aptitude or talent is absolute (or perfect) pitch (AP), a skill that in its full form is reported to be found only among 1 in every 10,000 individuals. Full AP is the ability to identify instantly the nearest pitch-category name to any sounded note (e.g., C, G#, B♭). Often possessors of AP have the reverse skill—they can sing or play any named pitch without recourse to trial and error. However, in an authoritative review on the topic, Ward (1999) concludes that there is a lack of convincing scientific evidence to support the suggestion that AP is inherited. AP generally appears in people who began intensive musical training in childhood. The earlier the training begins, the more likely a person is to possess AP (Sergeant, 1969). Recent evidence also suggests that key aspects of AP are not as rare as the full syndrome. For instance, babies as young as 8 months of age can learn to recognize tonal stimuli on the basis of their absolute pitch (Saffran, 2003). Most untrained adults can sing familiar popular tunes in or close to the key in which they are habitually broadcast, even though they cannot name the notes they are singing (Levitin, 1994). Finally, AP does not appear to be correlated with other musical skills, nor is it predictive of musical success. Many, if not most, professional musicians do not possess AP, and some consider it a disadvantage (Parncutt & Levitin, 2000). As more than one possessor of AP has complained, "I don't hear melodies, I hear pitch names passing by."

Relationship between Early Experience and Adult Achievement

In classical performance, training is confined to a limited period. Professional musicians are supposed to be fully trained by their early 20s. This has implications for the level of achievement that is needed by puberty in order to gain entry to specialist institutional support for high-level achievement (such as a specialist music school or a conservatory). As we have seen, adult classical musicians have typically started some form of instrumental instruction by the age of 8. In chapter 4 (on practice) we show that the best predictor of level of musical achievement is the amount of formal practice accumulated over the life span. Given the amounts of daily practice possible for children of different ages, it turns out that it is hard to accumulate the required amount of practice in less than 10 years; more often than not, a longer time will be necessary. This means that for some highly competitive instruments, such as the piano, ages under 8 have become the usual starting age.

However, there are differences according to instrument (voice develops later; violin is a difficult instrument and needs the earliest start), as well as musical culture (rock music, which involves, in some cases, lower technical demands but higher demands on personal experience and expressivity, can be started considerably later than classical music). In this, as in so much about music, cultural and social factors play very important roles. It just happens to be a fact about Western culture that 16–19 is the normal age of entry to a conservatory. This is not some immutable law, and in cultures with different educational structures, doors of opportunity may not be so decisively shut at such an early age.

On the other hand, there is nothing inherently unnatural about early musical learning and development. Cross-cultural data suggest almost the opposite. In

Cross-Cultural Perspective: Children's "Normal" Musical Achievements

In some non-Western cultures, musical achievements are much more widespread than in our own. Messenger (1958, p. 21) provides the following account of his study of the Anang Ibibo tribe of Nigeria:

> We were constantly amazed at the musical abilities displayed by these people, especially by the children who, before the age of five, can sing hundreds of songs, both individually and in choral groups and, in addition, are able to play several percussion instruments and have learned dozens of intricate dance movements calling for incredible muscular control. We searched in vain for the "non-musical" person, finding it difficult to make enquiries about tone-deafness and its assumed effects because the Anang language possessed no comparable concept. They will not admit, as we tried so hard to get them to, that there are those who lack the requisite abilities. This same attitude applies to the other aesthetic areas. Some dancers, singers, and weavers, are considered more skilled than most, but everyone can dance and sing well.

Lucy Green (personal communication, June 19, 2004) provides an example of how African and Western cultural values may affect even very small babies. Whenever a baby of 6–12 months takes hold of a long thin object (such as a spoon), his or her natural impulse is to start banging it semirhythmically on a nearby surface, such as a table. The typical response of a Western adult is to firmly remove the spoon. The typical response in an African family would be for other family members to take up spoons and join in, embellishing the baby's efforts with more sophisticated cross-rhythms. By doing so, they both recognize the baby's inherent musicality and provide a context in which rhythmic development can take place.

many traditional societies, children acquire a wide repertoire of songs and dances at an early age, often at a level of complexity and skill that exceeds Western norms (Blacking, 1973). The level of achievement seems to be directly related to the level of opportunity freely available within the society to learn and participate in these songs and dances, which are shared by most people "in the street," rather than "behind closed doors" of the music school. It is possible to observe a similar effect across generations within Western societies. Most of us have parents or grandparents who can remember times when practical music making was much more central to everyday life. Every house had a piano, violin, or other instrument, and people gathered round it to sing (in the days before radio and TV). Everyone went to church and participated in hymn singing. Folk music was part of everyday life, and people would come together in community halls and taverns for participatory singing, dancing, and playing, unaided by recorded or printed music. Some parts of Western society have still retained strong folk music traditions. For instance, within the British Isles, folk music traditions are relatively strong in Ireland, Scotland, and Wales but relatively weak in England.

It seems likely that children who have opportunities to participate in musical activities in their everyday lives develop musical skills and abilities faster than those whose main experience is one of passive consumption. Because the first and most prevalent aspect of everyday life is the home, the level of musical activity in the home, and particularly that instigated by the parents, is likely to be a major influence on musical development. One of the few reliable early predictors of later musical achievement is the age at which a child first started to sing recognizable songs (Howe et al., 1995). To learn such songs requires that they be sung by someone else in the child's earshot. Musical songs and games initiated by parents with their babies and toddlers, although natural in many cultures, are so threatened in media-dominated cultures that special efforts are often needed to show parents what to do. Thus what is simply "routine" for parents and children in the Venda tribe of Central Africa must be laboriously reintroduced to Western urban parents and their children through "early enrichment programs" (such as the KinderMusik program popular in the United States and elsewhere). The evidence is strong that early enrichment leads to acceleration of skill acquisition. Although most of the research has concentrated on language and other skills necessary for school success (e.g., Fowler, 1990), there is clear evidence that early parental musical involvement and stimulation is a strong correlate of later musical achievement (Davidson, Howe, Moore, & Sloboda, 1996).

The research we have reviewed supports a clear and coherent account of the development of musical skills. Virtually all children are born with the full neural capacities to engage with music. These capacities are stimulated and developed by musical activities in the home environment, though in the normal Western home the level of such activities is not such as to allow the acquisition of significant performance skills (see chapter 1). Rather, children are able to enjoy music by listening, dancing, and singing along. Specific instrumental performance skills tend to develop in the context of the more formal educational inputs offered by teachers. Children have the capacity to engage in formal and self-directed classical learning from about the age of 6, and it is generally not until 3 or 4 years of such learning has taken place that parents and teachers are able to make reliable judgments about potential for long-term engagement in classical performance (Sosniak, 1985). Sustained practice over 10 or more years is the normal prerequisite for attainment of the highest levels of classical performance achievement (see chapter 9).

However, even among those children who appear to be developing good levels of performance skills, we cannot assume that all will become adult performers.

Self Study: Key Events in Your Childhood Musical Biography

Write brief answers to the following questions. In each case, rate each answer on a 4-point scale, with 1=*not at all sure this is accurate or complete;* 2=*somewhat confident in my answer;* 3=*broadly confident in my answer;* 4=*completely confident in my answer.*

1. What age were you when you first sang a complete and accurate verse of a song (e.g., a nursery rhyme or a pop song)?
2. What kind of musical activities did your parents engage in—without you and with you—before you were 5 years old?
3. At what age did you have your first formal lesson on an instrument?
4. Do you have absolute pitch? If so, can you remember at what age you first noticed that you had it?
5. Have you ever performed your own compositions? If so, when did this start, and how did it develop? Do you have recordings available?
6. At what age were you told, or did you feel yourself, that you had a special aptitude or ability for music? How did this affect you?

It can be instructive to ask your parents the same questions and compare their answers with yours. Why might their memories differ from yours? Spend some time thinking about or discussing the extent to which your experiences fit the research outlined in the chapter. What might account for different levels of certainty or confidence in your answers—age or some other factor?

Particularly in the preadolescent and adolescent years, motivational issues become increasingly important in determining whether young people persist with or abandon musical activities (see chapter 3). Without a strong will to persist with daily practice (see chapter 4), childhood achievements can often come to nothing in later life. The musical dropout is a major phenomenon of the Western educational system—and a significant headache for the music education profession. And, as always, chance is a factor that affects future success.

Study Questions

1. What human musical capacities arise naturally in human beings without the help of specialist training?

2. Review arguments and evidence for and against the idea that outstanding musical achievement is due to innate talent.

3. What research-based advice would you provide to parents and teachers who want to help the musical development of children under the age of 8?

Further Reading

Deliège, I., & Sloboda, J. A. (Eds.) (1996). *Musical Beginnings*. A compilation of commissioned chapters focusing on early development of musical behavior.

Deutsch, D. (Ed.). (1999). *The Psychology of Music* (2nd ed.). Chapter 15 discusses the development of music perception and cognition; chapter 16 concerns musical ability.

Gembris, H. (2002). The development of musical abilities. In R. Colwell & C. Richardson (Eds.), *The New Handbook of Research on Music Teaching and Learning* (pp. 487–508). This is a review of life-span musical development.

For two contrasting views on the nature-nurture controversy about the origins of musical talent:

Howe (1990). *The Origins of Exceptional Abilities.*

Winner, E. (1996). *Gifted Children: Myths and Realities.*

3

Motivation

The following could be a true but not unique story:

> Laura had everything going for her. From the age of 6 she had weekly violin lessons with outstanding teachers. Her parents spared no expense on her. She started winning competitions at a young age, and at 12 she won a coveted place in a preparatory program at a prestigious conservatory. Yet after graduating from high school, she abandoned the study of music altogether, sold her violin, and enrolled as a science major in college.

To provide a clear account of what allowed Laura to achieve so much with music—and then change life direction so abruptly—we turn to the psychology of motivation. This is a critical consideration for those trying to improve their own musicianship or for teachers and parents of young musicians. As an aspiring performer, it is one thing to know what you need to do to improve your skills, but it is quite another thing to actually do it. Similarly, it is easy for a teacher to write down a list of exercises to be practiced but much more difficult to get students to carry them out. Often musicians and teachers talk about motivation as a feeling or inner desire. But to study motivation, we have to look to its manifestations as behaviors, such as a young child saying he wants to learn to play the trumpet, a teenager continuing her music studies in school when others have dropped out, or a collegiate musician employing special strategies to maximize his practice time (Maehr, Pintrich, & Linnenbrink, 2002).

Multiple sources of motivation exist in the lives of musicians. One simple way of understanding these many sources is to categorize them as intrinsic versus extrinsic. Intrinsic motivation comes from the activity itself and the enjoyment experienced from engaging in it. In general, people make music because of the enjoyment and fulfillment they get from doing it. However, because acquiring musical skill takes much time and effort, developing musicians also rely on extrinsic motivation, or secondary nonmusical rewards that come with musical participation. This is seen when young musicians respond to the support and encouragement of people close to them, including parents, teachers, and peers. At any one time in their development, musicians may be drawing on several intrinsic and extrinsic sources simultaneously. Some performance experiences include both intrinsic and extrinsic elements. The pleasure of group music making is intrinsically rewarding, and additional extrinsic motivation is gained through the applause of an audience. It is sometimes difficult to distinguish between extrinsic and intrinsic motivation (see the later section on beliefs and values).

Although a great many people are attracted to music as children (either intrinsically or extrinsically, as in the case of parental coercion) and set out to learn an instrument, relatively few of them achieve a satisfying level of proficiency. Building a skill of any kind necessarily involves effort. In music, the effort can include a lot of concentrated time repeating musical exercises that are not intrinsically enjoyable. Many musicians in the classical tradition—even highly successful ones—admit that they do not like to practice (Hallam, 1997). But must practice be unpleasant? Popular musicians often talk of their individual and group practicing in a much more positive light. A better understanding of motivation may cause musicians to alter practice routines to make them more personally rewarding and to find ways to sustain the needed effort in the unavoidably unpleasant activities.

Based on the research that has examined motivation and music achievement, this chapter explains the following principles:

1. Music is intrinsically motivating. Early pleasurable experiences with music draw children into pursuing greater involvement, including formal training. Maintaining an intrinsic love of music can ultimately determine how long musicians will continue in the field and how rewarding it will be for them.
2. The support of parents and teachers can be the difference between a young student's benefiting from music training and dropping out altogether (see chapter 2). Motivating a child musician to do the practice necessary for skill development requires the supervision of parents and the encouragement of respected teachers.
3. Social standing among their musical peers prompts many teenagers and young adults to strengthen their commitment to music. The social structure of the "conservatory culture" exerts a strong influence on the motivation of music students.
4. The persistence that musicians show in learning activities is largely determined by their beliefs about music and about themselves. Students'

self-perceptions of ability and their expectancies for success (or failure) are strong indicators of achievement.

5. Motivation is also related to the extent to which musicians embrace challenges. Those with a mastery orientation are willing to expend the effort needed to achieve and tend to set specific goals for themselves, which makes practice activities more efficient, productive, and rewarding.

Intrinsic Motivation for Music

Human beings have a "love affair" with music. Virtually everyone claims to like music, at least some kind of music, and most people would say they *love* music. Generally speaking, making and liking music are intrinsically motivating activities. People are naturally attracted to them because the activities themselves are rewarding experiences. Research with infants suggests that attraction to music is not acquired (although tastes for certain styles of music certainly are) but is something inherently human.

Childhood Experiences

Although a person may not begin to study music until school age, the motivation for that later involvement has likely been built very early in life. Young children's home environments can differ greatly in opportunities for musical discovery and experimentation. People who go on to become musicians characterize their early childhood musical experiences as playful, fun-filled, and exciting (Bloom, 1985; Sloboda, 1990). They report music being a normal part of their home environments, often through parents or siblings (Howe & Sloboda, 1991). Toddlers' first music-making experiences involve playful singing and experimenting with musical instruments (Sloboda & Howe, 1991). Musicians' earliest memories often describe more active participation (singing, playing), as compared with more passive experiences (listening, watching) for nonmusicians. For instance, conductor and composer Michael Tilson Thomas once described his childhood:

> I couldn't pass the piano, so my parents tell me, without touching it. They always knew when I was coming and going . . . because every time I would go back and forth between the living room and another part of the house I would have to go by the piano and have to play it. (Jacobson, 1974, p. 262)

Although the inclusion of music in a child's everyday play activities can build lasting positive associations, it may be more exceptional musical events that capture one's musical interests for life. Many musicians remember having highly emotionally satisfying "peak experiences," characterized by feelings of wonder, awe, or surrender (Sloboda, 1990). The great classical guitarist Andrés

Segovia once recounted how, as a young child, he first became captivated by the instrument when a strolling flamenco guitar player came to his town:

> At the first flourish, more noise than music burst from the strings and, as if it had happened yesterday, I remember my fright at this explosion of sounds . . . rearing from the impact, I fell over backward. However, when he scratched out some of those variations he said were *soleares*, I felt them inside of me as if they had penetrated through every pore of my body. (Segovia, 1976, p. 3)

Sloboda's (1990) study found that children who have such powerful experiences, perhaps through attending a live performance, are more likely to continue with musical involvement than those who do not. This research also suggests that peak experiences are most likely to occur in environments in which no demand or threat is perceived by the child. In such situations, the intrinsically pleasurable nature of music can affect young people; as a result, many decide to become musicians, or at least to pursue musical training, at a young age.

Enjoyment and Exploration during Learning

A basic fascination with music and an enjoyment-oriented discovery approach can be powerful motivators beyond childhood. Many popular and jazz musicians cite "loving music" and "having fun" as reasons for spending so much time on their music (Green, 2002). Their musical activities are so enjoyable, consuming, and rewarding that they resist calling them "practice" or "learning." Of course, their activities are not merely musical play activities such as those of children; these musicians also show strong drive to master the music that they love. For them, the process itself is rewarding.

Of course, intrinsic motivation for music is also very important to music students who undergo formal training. McPherson and Renwick (2001) found that the beginning instrumentalists who made the most progress in their first year of music lessons tended to express intrinsic reasons for their involvement, such as wanting to play music for their own personal enjoyment. Playing "just for the fun of it" (as opposed to practicing) by oneself and being a part of group "jam sessions" with musical friends are likely very positive activities. In a study of factors that contribute to the development of musicians, Sloboda, Davidson, Howe, and Moore (1996) interviewed instrumental music students between the ages of 8 and 18 about their day-to-day musical activities, and they asked many of the students to keep a practice diary over the course of a year. Among their results, Sloboda and colleagues (1996) found a relationship between informal practice—such as playing favorite songs for personal enjoyment or musically "messing around" with friends—and performance achievement. The lowest achieving students did the least informal practice (see chapter 4). Although these activities are not likely to be important for refining performance skills, they probably offer a motivational boost to students' commitment to music training and involvement.

Cross-Cultural Perspective: Popular Musicians' Labor of Love

Virtually all initial music development comes as very young children playfully explore musical sounds. Whereas some young people soon turn to formal music instruction to build on these enjoyable early experiences, many others stay on a more exploratory path. In her study of popular musicians, Green (2002) identified several key learning practices that draw on intrinsic motivation for music. First, the music they work on—usually by listening to and copying recordings—is of their choosing. Their practice almost always has a real musical context, that is, they practice songs or parts of songs (e.g., guitar solos or shorter "licks"), as opposed to technical exercises and études. Also, much of their skill development takes place in informal group learning sessions with peers. In such get-togethers, musicians collaborate to reproduce popular songs, create new compositions, or "jam" (improvise) for fun. In addition to the social rewards of this group music making, the performing itself can be tremendously gratifying. These kinds of learning activities that popular musicians engage in are in many ways a contrast to the solitary, technique-intensive practice of assigned exercises and repertoire that formally trained students are often asked to do. Some music scholars assert that classical music performing ability is accomplished through discipline but that popular music skills are arrived at by osmosis. Green maintains, though, that the real difference between these realms is whether the time and effort invested are perceived as unpleasant or pleasant. Popular musicians describe their learning process as voluntary, enjoyable, and what they love to do.

Research suggests that freedom and choice are conditions that maintain and enhance intrinsic motivation. The development of student musicians can benefit greatly when they are given a choice in the music they work on. The great pianist Vladimir Horowitz once confessed:

> When I was a child, I was bringing to my professor the music I liked and not the music which I had to play. My mother went to him and asked, "What are you doing? Instead of Bach, he's playing Rachmaninoff!" . . . I went to the stores and bought the new music. I took it home and I played it. (Epstein, 1987, p. 8)

Music students practice differently when they are working on pieces of music they like (Renwick & McPherson, 2002). They seem to be willing to devote more time to practicing, and while they are doing it, they are more attentive and use a greater variety of strategies to improve their performances. For some musicians, a sense of freedom and choice is attained through improvisation. Moore, Burland, and Davidson (2003) found that professional musicians reported engaging in more improvisation during their development than non-professionals. It seems that intrinsic motivation for music is reinforced in an environment that is perceived as allowing personal autonomy rather than as controlling.

The act of performing music itself can be an intensely powerful experience for musicians. Making music is fundamentally pleasurable. Experiences that tap into this can reinforce musicians' intrinsic interests. In addition to the rewards of making music alone and with peers in informal situations, public performance can be a motivating factor. The presence of a live audience may prompt a heightened sensitivity on the part of performers. Thus the aesthetic rewards gained by being a part of a high-quality performance may be even more satisfying and may inspire budding musicians to greater performance achievement. Professional musicians report participating in concerts as students more often than do nonprofessionals (Moore et al., 2003).

Extrinsic Sources of Motivation for Music

The aforementioned intrinsic sources of motivation can provide a foundation for lifelong musical involvement. They can also, however, be rendered ineffective by negative experiences with music. People who at a young age were told that they were not "musical" seldom enjoy a childhood of growing musicianship (see the section on beliefs and values later in the chapter). This fact indicates just how critical extrinsic sources of motivation are in a person's musical development. The most primary sources are parents, teachers, and peers.

Parental and Family Support

Within Western cultures, parents are a main source of motivation and support in the beginning stages of their children's music development (Bloom, 1985; Davidson, Sloboda, & Howe, 1996). A parent's verbal praise and encouragement is an important reward for young children as they demonstrate their developing musical abilities and express their interest in learning more about music. Once a child begins formal study, the support of parents is especially important. In addition to simply paying for lessons and providing transportation to and from them, parents can support their children's musical achievement by becoming involved in the lessons themselves, mainly by communicating with teachers (see figure 3.1).

The highest achieving young students tend to have parents who, additionally, sit in on lessons and supervise their children's beginning practice efforts (Sloboda &

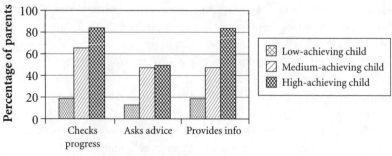

Figure 3.1. Different types of parental involvement in lessons corresponds with their children's achievement. Data from Table 2.1 in "The Role of Practice in Children's Early Musical Performance Achievement," by S. A. O'Neill, 1997. In H. Jørgensen & A. C. Lehmann (Eds.), *Does Practice Make Perfect? Current Theory and Research on Instrumental Music Practice* (pp. 53–70). Copyright © 1997 by the Norwegian State Academy of Music and the author. Adapted by permission.

Howe, 1991). Parents need not have extensive musical training or experience themselves for their supervision to be beneficial (Davidson et al., 1996; McPherson & Davidson, 2002). Their role is primarily to encourage their children to carry out the practice activities assigned by instructors. Violinist Jascha Heifetz once recalled, "Although I do not remember being made to practice, I think there were times when I would have preferred something more playful. Let us say that my father 'persuaded' me to practice; and I am glad that he did" (Axelrod, 1976, p. 138).

Parental support seems to be a basic requirement for children to continue their musical involvement. A lack of parental support is widely recognized as a deciding factor in children dropping out of music training. There is, however, a negative side of parental involvement. Parents who are too pushy (or who "hothouse" their child) run the risk of their child losing the intrinsic enjoyment of music and eventually wishing to drop out. Some parents may believe that, however negative the experience, the child will thank them later for making them take piano lessons. Research suggests, though, that among those who enjoy music success later in life, the onset of formal lessons was either initiated by or at least agreeable to the child.

Children can also be influenced by siblings who play musical instruments (Howe & Sloboda, 1991). In addition to simply making a younger child aware of music, an older sibling may serve as a musical role model. It is, of course, common for a younger child to look up to older brothers and sisters and aspire to be like them and learn to do what they can do. This phenomenon applies to music endeavors and may prompt a child to learn to play the same instrument as an idolized sibling and wish to take music lessons (even if on a different instrument). Unfortunately, this sibling dynamic can also play out in a more negative form. But even then, jealousy between siblings can also provide incentive to increase musical skills.

Teachers

Teachers, especially first teachers in an area of interest, are naturally very influential in the lives of students. Davidson, Sloboda, Moore, and Howe (1998) have shown that early instrument teachers also have a significant motivating effect on young musicians. Children who were identified as high achievers in music generally experienced their very first instrument teacher as warm, friendly, encouraging, and fun to be with. They looked forward to their lessons. Children who achieved less on their instruments or who had even given up playing altogether more often recalled their first teachers as critical, unfriendly, cold, and directive. Evidence showed that young children were incapable of appreciating the teaching or playing ability of the teacher if there was no positive personal rapport. At the younger ages (up to 10 or 11 years old), not liking the teacher led to not liking the instrument and not liking music.

Subsequent teachers are also important. Once a student has begun a committed musical involvement, the teacher is a primary source of motivation, but in a slightly different role. This person will have great influence in the young musician's developing belief system concerning the value of music involvement, and he or she can also provide encouragement to achieve. As critical as it is for an initial music teacher to be warm and friendly, subsequent teachers must have the ability to stretch their students' musical commitment in a way that is inspirational (Sloboda & Howe, 1991). At this stage, a teacher's success at becoming a role model for students becomes more linked to his or her performance skills. In fact, advanced music students will often tolerate a disliked personality if they respect the teacher's abilities as a performer. Even younger students—post-elementary-school age—can separate judgments of their teachers as persons and as professionals. This suggests that respect for a teacher as a performer and instructor can help a student overcome reservations about the teacher's personality or style.

Perhaps the primary way in which a teacher can challenge a young musician is related to practice. Teachers are responsible for teaching music students *how* to practice, and even young musicians recognize this as a characteristic of a good teacher (Sloboda & Howe, 1991). The teacher is an integral cog in a motivational cycle of practice, reward, and achievement. With better practice comes greater and more rapid skill development. For music students, improved performance skills provide important rewards—musical, social, and otherwise.

Peers

As young musicians enter adolescence, their peers become increasingly important. The extrinsic motivation provided by peers can eclipse the influence exerted
by parents and teachers; it can lead a child to either quit music instruction or continue. Social pressure can have a direct negative effect, such as when members
of a peer group claim that being in the school band is "not cool." More indirectly,
adolescent peer groups are often identified by the kind of popular music they like.
This may make a young music student come to realize that the music he or she
plays at school does not match the music of his or her peer group.

Peer relationships can also help sustain interest in music involvement. Many
teenage music students build their social peer groups with other musicians. It is
very common in high schools for musical subcultures to exist in the form of close-
knit groups of "band kids" or choir students. Social recognition within these
groups is linked to the members' musical abilities. Proficient young musicians
are often motivated to practice in order to maintain their standing among their
peers. Usually, music students enjoy the support and encouragement provided by
their peers and value joint music-making opportunities. Referring to his musical
peers, a young performer in one study explained, "At least they know what makes
me tick . . . I find it difficult to relate to people who just don't understand what
drives me to do the things I do" (Burland & Davidson, 2002, p. 127).

Immersion into a musical social structure can firm up a student's commitment to music—but it can also have some harmful effects. This is especially
true of the "conservatory culture," which can be marked by a highly judgmental
atmosphere among peers (Kingsbury, 1988). For music students who are particularly self-conscious, their practice efforts are tied to the negotiation of social
esteem. Kingsbury (1988) has likened it to a teenager who rehearses smoking
a cigarette in front of a mirror to ensure success when doing it among peers. In
college conservatories and university music programs, with the successes inevitably come some failures as well. The competitive atmosphere and the perceived social consequences for failure may drive some to maladaptive lifestyles
or result in mental health problems or in dropping out of music altogether.

Because of the prevalence of competition in music, one might believe that
it is a common source of motivation for young musicians. This is not always
the case. Competition is usually understood as a desire to outdo other people.
Therefore, competition may serve as an incentive to already competent musicians who believe they have a good chance to win or otherwise fare well. Of
course, the flip side is that less skilled music students—perhaps all except elite
performers—may be more discouraged by a competitive environment. In general,
research with music students has shown that cooperative learning situations in
which students collaborate with each other are as effective as, if not more so
than, competitive environments (Austin, 1991). Even among advanced or "gifted"
children, competition is not unanimously well received. It may motivate them to

Table 3.1 Summary of factors necessary for achieving various levels of performance success

	Initial years of playing	Later childhood years
Continuation of playing into childhood	Early Start Parental support Teachers who are friendly	
Success as a child	All of the above plus: High initial practice Teachers who are not too pushy Teacher is very friendly	Continuation of high levels of practice into fourth year of playing Teacher is not too relaxed
Success as a professional musician	All of the above plus: Mothers at home	All of the above plus: More improvisation Gradual increase in practice rather than initial big burst (avoidance of burn-out) Involvement in concerts and group activities Later teachers who are more pushy

achieve, but it can come at a greater cost in the long run. Competitive conditions can cause young people to become so focused on procuring the desired outcome in a specific competition that it diverts their time and attention away from fully developing their skills.

External sources of motivation play an important role in maintaining a student's activities in music. For instance, young musicians who engage in isolated practice but who do not also enjoy the social contact and support of musical peers may be more susceptible to "burnout" (Moore et al., 2003). However, extrinsic motivators cannot replace intrinsic motivation. That is, external support may keep children from dropping out of music, but without additional intrinsic motivation, they are not likely to improve much musically (McPherson & Renwick, 2001). Achieving the highest levels of performance success seems to require a combination of many motivational factors (see table 3.1). As young musicians develop, they begin to internalize extrinsic sources of motivation. The values of parents, teachers, and peers become part of the musicians themselves, thus becoming intrinsic. Eventually, they come to work on their music primarily because it is important to them. Their musical activities define their identity. This transition can be seen in the following autobiographical comments of concert pianist André Watts:

> I wouldn't be a pianist today if my mother hadn't made me practice . . . On days when I wasn't exactly moved to practice, my mother saw to it that I did. Sometimes she tried coaxing me to the piano by relating the careers of

famous musicians, hoping perhaps to inspire me to practice. At thirteen, however, I realized the necessity of practice. I still don't really "like" it all the time, but by now it has become second nature. (Mach, 1980, p. 182)

Beliefs and Values

In many cases, parents and teachers instill in their young musicians a belief that they are talented (Howe & Sloboda, 1991). When children are labeled as musically talented, the parents and teachers may be especially supportive, feeling a sense of obligation to nurture the gift (Bloom, 1985; see also chapters 2 and 10). Also, children who feel talented may downplay failures and work hard to unlock the potential others see in them. Beliefs and values influence what people think they can do and why they can do it.

Self-Efficacy: What You Think You Can Do

Young musicians rely on the other people in their lives in building a belief system about music. Based on the feedback they receive from parents, teachers, and peers, music students begin to solidify ideas about how good they are in certain pursuits, including music. *Self-efficacy* refers to people's beliefs about their abilities to achieve in a specific domain (Bandura, 1986). Belief in one's competencies can affect future decisions about musical activities by creating self-fulfilling prophecies.

Research in music has shown that motivation as measured by students' self-efficacy can be highly predictive of performance achievement. McCormick and McPherson (2003) studied 332 instrumentalists between the ages of 9 and 18 who were completing music performance examinations. To assess self-efficacy, the researchers had the young musicians respond to questions about how well they had mastered the music they were to play on the exam, their expected grades for the exam, and their appraisal of their general musicianship as compared with their peers. Those students who expressed the highest confidence in their abilities were also the ones who received the best performance scores.

It is important to remember that self-efficacy is inextricably linked to a musician's competence. It is not built by simply getting students to believe that they are good at music when, in fact, they are not. Self-efficacy is also understood to include the ability to "organize and execute courses of action" required to achieve competent performance (Bandura, 1986, p. 391). Thus strong self-efficacy entails not only recognizing oneself as a good musician but also judging oneself as knowledgeable about the necessary subskills and strategies responsible for performance success. This kind of motivation results in musicians having the confidence to continue in higher levels of music training and engagement, largely because they feel equipped to handle challenges they will face.

Explaining Successes and Failures

Students make decisions about continuing in music based on their beliefs about their own prospects for success in it. Generally speaking, success breeds more success; early successes in music will encourage children to pursue greater music engagement, but failures can bring discouragement. *Attribution theory*, however, maintains that students' motivation and achievement are affected not only by prior successes and failures but also by how students explain those outcomes. In other words, students ask themselves, *"Why* did I do well or do poorly in my last attempt?"* In explaining a successful performance, musicians may rely on these common causal attributions: ability/talent ("I've always been good at sight-reading"), effort ("My months of practice really paid off"), luck ("I got lucky and played well this time"), or task difficulty ("I couldn't go wrong with that easy music").

Studies of music students show that ability and effort are the most common causal attributions (Asmus, 1986). In Asmus's (1986) study of music students in grades 4 through 12, an interesting trend was revealed. As grade level rose, the number of ability attributions increased, and the number of effort attributions decreased. In other words, as students got older, they seemed to believe less and less that personal effort determined musical success, favoring talent instead as an explanation. Why would this be the case? In many formal educational settings, by the time high school age is reached, a relatively small number of high achievers will have distinguished themselves. The less accomplished music students may use attributions of talent to account for others' proficiency and success, in part to excuse themselves for not achieving more. "I could have been that good," they might think, "if only I had the talent they were born with." Austin and Vispoel (1998) reported a strong association between adolescent's musical self-concepts and their beliefs about success and failure in musical ventures. Specifically, they found that students with low self-concepts tended to attribute musical failures to a lack of ability.

Additional research suggests that certain attributions are more adaptive or productive for music learning and skill improvement than others. Rather than attributing success to talent or ability, it is perhaps more suitable for students to explain success and failure using attributes that are within their control, such as effort. Further, some attribution research has examined learners' belief in "strategy," which amounts to a subcomponent of effort. Using an expanded choice of attribution, Austin and Vispoel (1992) found that practice strategy was often chosen by elementary and junior high students to account for musical failure experiences. Further, strategy attributions were most likely to produce constructive changes in students (i.e., new motivation toward harder work and better strategies); ability attributions were least likely to result in adaptive student responses. In general, it appears that music students choose between practice (overall effort and strategies) and talent to explain music performance achievement and that they draw their motivation to pursue their own musical growth from these beliefs.

Assessing Your Prospects in Music

Research suggests that students' confidence in their musical abilities (self-efficacy) is distinct from the values they have that are related to music involvement (Eccles, Wigfield, Harold, & Blumenfeld, 1993). That is, some students may not believe that they are or will be great performers, but they persist in music involvement because the activity itself is important. In fact, children's perceptions of the importance of a particular enterprise may be more consequential than their believed prospects for success. This perception will determine their interest in participating in it and whether they decide to further their development.

Expectancy-value theory is a motivational framework developed in general educational research that has been recently applied to music (O'Neill & McPherson, 2002; Wigfield, O'Neill, & Eccles, 1999). This model incorporates the importance of personal values regarding an endeavor with expectations about what would be involved in carrying it out. This framework, which factors in both intrinsic and extrinsic sources of motivation, consists of four components. First, *attainment value* reflects the importance a person places on doing well in a musical activity. This depends on what a person believes are the consequences of successful musical involvement. The second factor is *intrinsic motivation*—in other words, the extent to which a musician expects participating in the activity itself to be pleasurable or rewarding. The third component in the model, *extrinsic utility value*, relates to whether a person sees music as being useful in achieving future goals. This is obviously a strong factor for someone hoping to make a career out of music performance, but it can also be a source of motivation for someone who sees music involvement as a "ticket" to other things (e.g., a chance to travel to interesting places with a touring ensemble, or a college scholarship to study another field). The final part of the expectancy-value framework is *perceived cost*. This reflects the amount of effort or practice, that a person believes is required to participate in a music activity.

Research in music learning supports the expectancy-value model, suggesting that these components are useful for predicting students' interests and choices related to music involvement. As we might expect, children who express a low regard for music instruction usually drop out after only a short time when given the opportunity (Wigfield et al., 1999). McPherson (2000) interviewed beginning instrumentalists ages 7 to 9 and then tracked their musical achievement over the first year of study. He found that their value statements could be subdivided according to the four components of expectancy-value theory. Most of the children expressed an intrinsic interest in learning to play an instrument, but few of them envisioned music as being an important part of their overall educational goals (extrinsic utility value). Those who expected

Self Study: Why Do You Do What You Do?

Think about your daily music making, including individual practice, group rehearsals, and any other time you spend making music. How do you classify these daily experiences? You can do so by musical style (e.g., classical music, jazz, other styles), by the skills you're working on (e.g., interpretation, sight-reading, improvisation), or by music material (e.g., scales, études, solo repertoire). However you classify the different activities of your music making, choose a few of these activities and, for each, go through the expectancy-value model of motivation in order to better understand what motivates you to do what you do. The following questions will help you identify what component of the model best explains why you do a particular music activity.

Attainment value. How important do you consider this activity? Do your beliefs about music (or other things) dictate that this activity is fundamentally valuable somehow?

Intrinsic motivation. How enjoyable or pleasing do you find this activity to be? Do you do this activity because it is personally rewarding to do so?

Extrinsic utility value. How useful is this activity in accomplishing professional or musical goals you have? Does your doing this activity serve as a means to another, more important end?

Perceived cost. How convenient or comfortable is this activity for you? Do you do this activity because it is less effortful than other activities you could (or should) be doing?

their music involvement to be a long-term engagement practiced significantly more over the course of the year and achieved higher levels of performance skill (see figure 3.2). Similarly, Hallam (1998b) found that young musicians' attitudes toward practice were a strong predictor of whether they dropped out of music lessons or continued.

Managing Challenges and Goals

For a musician by trade, it is quite common to look ahead to the next performance and prepare in light of it. In fact, research has shown that few advanced musicians report being intrinsically motivated to practice. Instead, it is the threat of an imminent performance that gets them into the practice room (Hallam, 1997). For some, the potential social consequences provide motivation (i.e., the

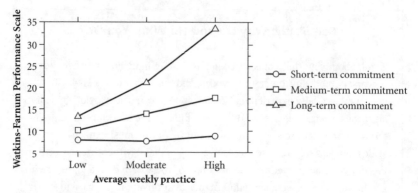

Figure 3.2. Students who express a long-term commitment to music (expectancy-value theory) practice more and achieve greater performance skill as measured by a standardized performance scale. From "Commitment and Practice: Key Ingredients for Achievement during the Early Stages of Learning a Musical Instrument," by G. E. McPherson, 2000, *Bulletin of the Council for Research in Music Education, 147*, 122–127. Copyright 2000 by the Council of Research in Music Education. Reprinted by permission.

desire to avoid looking bad in front of their peers). But also, a looming performance represents a concrete goal around which a musician can organize his or her learning activities.

A musician's attitude about challenges and goals is an important variable in motivation. Individuals who have a *mastery orientation* demonstrate persistence in learning something, even in spite of difficulties faced along the way. Bloom (1985) suggested that skilled musicians learn this work ethic as children from their parents. They tend to establish attainable goals for themselves and persist in their efforts to accomplish them. Conversely, those who show *helpless* patterns usually fail to identify reasonable goals and tend to avoid challenges altogether. These contrasting motivational patterns are the results of various underlying psychological processes and can be fairly stable in school-age children. O'Neill and Sloboda (1997) used mastery orientation to explain the performance achievement of children completing their first year of formal instrumental music training. Before the children began their music instruction, the researcher established which children possessed either mastery or helpless orientations by involving them in problem-solving exercises. At some point during these, the children were put in failure-feedback conditions in which they were told told over repeated attempts that they were answering the problems incorrectly. In response, some children's actual performance deteriorated (helpless), whereas others' performance maintained or improved (mastery oriented). After a year of receiving instrumental music lessons, the children who showed mastery motivational patterns demonstrated higher music performance achievement than those who exhibited a helpless orientation.

Musicians who are mastery oriented are motivated by goals and challenges. This type of goal orientation can be further categorized as *task involved* or *ego involved* (Maehr et al., 2002). Music students with a task-involved orientation are primarily focused on improving their performance according to self-set standards. They might, for instance, identify a performance technique that is part of a favorite type of music and reserve time in their practicing to work on it. In contrast, an ego-involved orientation leads musicians to be concerned with how their skills will be judged by others. They focus on normative performance standards and practice in order to earn recognition for themselves by outdoing the accomplishments of others. The ego-involved orientation may thrive in a competitive conservatory culture, as students labor to attain certain benchmarks in the program, such as end-of-the-term juries, auditions for select ensembles, and graded public recitals. Performance goals may then be reduced to avoiding errors and failure, instead of reflecting more artistic and self-imposed concerns. Even if some form of perfection can be attained, it may not be satisfying. Cellist Yo-Yo Ma once recounted an early performance situation:

> While sitting there at the concert, playing all the notes correctly, I started to wonder, 'Why am I here? I'm doing everything as planned. So what's at stake? Nothing. Not only is the audience bored but I myself am bored.' Perfection is not very communicative. However, when you subordinate your technique to the musical message you get really involved. Then you can take risks. It doesn't matter if you fail. (Blum, 1998, pp. 6–7)

If they adopt an ego orientation, musicians may deprive themselves of the intrinsic rewards of music making, which in the end are likely to be needed for effecting lasting musical growth and sustaining long-term involvement in the field.

Implications for Musicians and Music Teachers

Sometimes people talk about "feeling motivated"—or perhaps "being unmotivated"—to do something, as if motivation is an emotional force that comes and goes, beyond their control. As we have seen in this chapter, some sources of motivation are more related to emotions than others. Regardless, there is much that performers can do to affect their own motivation and to support the musical efforts of students they teach and other musicians around them.

There is perhaps nothing more important for performers and teachers than contributing to positive musical experiences for children. The youngest students, especially, thrive in a musical environment marked by playful engagement and exploration. As teachers guide students in their development and introduce increasing rigor in their studies, they should guard against taking all the fun out of music! Teachers are also responsible for teaching their students how to practice and build musical self-efficacy. Young aspiring musicians need help setting appropriate performance goals for themselves and being reminded about *why* they are performing. As shown by the research on task-involved and ego-involved goal orientations, a young musician's motives for performing can affect how rewarding musical experiences will be.

Musicians can also take an active role in shaping their own motivation. Performers can too often find themselves primarily responding to the expectations of others such that their own musical preferences are ignored. To remedy this, musicians may, for example, seek out informal opportunities to play a favorite musical style that is absent from their formal music involvement. Even within their usual music activities, they should look for ways to exert personal choice, perhaps in the repertoire they work on or the kind of performances they engage in (e.g., collaborative music making rather than solo performance). In most cases, it is an underlying love of music that leads us to make music an important part of our lives. We must continually work to set goals for ourselves that make our music activities appropriately challenging and rewarding for us.

Study Questions

1. What are the influences in the lives of young musicians that can threaten their intrinsic motivation for musical involvement?
2. Describe how motivation is provided by different people at different points in a musician's development.
3. According to the research, how do a musician's expectancies and goals affect his or her performance achievement?

Further Reading

Maehr, M. L., Pintrich, P. R., & Linnenbrink, E. A. (2002). Motivation and achievement. In R. Colwell & C. Richardson (Eds.), *The New Handbook of Research on Music Teaching and Learning* (pp. 348–372).
O'Neill, S. A., & McPherson, G. E. (2002). Motivation. In R. Parncutt & G. E. McPherson (Eds.), *The Science and Psychology of Music Performance: Creative Strategies for Teaching and Learning* (pp. 31–46).
The above offer comprehensive reviews of motivational theories as applied to music education.
Moore, D. G., Burland, K., & Davidson, J. W. (2003). The social context of musical success: A developmental account. *British Journal of Psychology, 94*, 529–549.
A study of the influence of parents, teachers, and peers, as well as intrinsic sources of motivation.

4

Practice

In this final chapter of the section on Musical Learning we discuss the activity that musicians engage in most: practice. "How much and how do you practice?" is not the first question we would ask famous musicians, but it is certainly one that many of us would like to know the answer to. "Have you practiced today?" is the nagging question asked by parents or peers. Music teachers too often take it for granted that their students know how to practice correctly, but the objective record from the practice room experience dispels this myth. Rather than well-organized, goal-directed work, we often hear aimless and haphazard music making. Fortunately, some teachers have their particular advice on practice for students, hoping that what worked for them personally will work for their students as well. But then they might wonder why some advice bears fruit for one student and not for another. The fact is that practice is a multifaceted behavior that has attracted a lot of attention from researchers and teachers alike. We know that practice is not only the most prevalent activity that all musicians engage in but that it is also unarguably a necessary duty. Furthermore, we know of no one who has become (even remotely) famous without it. In this chapter we show the following:

1. The scientific concept of practice is somewhat more detailed than our everyday notion of it, which does not clearly differentiate between formal and informal practice.
2. The goal of practice is not merely to learn a piece of music but to develop complex mental and physical adaptations that, in turn, enable successful long-term skill building.
3. Not surprisingly, more practice leads to better performance. This insight has some important ramifications for our understanding of skill development, namely, that there are few (if any) shortcuts to acquiring musical skills.

4. Although every musician is different, there are some common denomina-
tors of "good practice" that have emerged from the practice of experts
and that seem promising to emulate.

What Is Practice?

By first surveying the perimeter of practice from a macro perspective, we set the
stage for talking about the micro perspective, the skill-building aspect. Although
the *macro* perspective is what parents and teachers are usually confronted with
in everyday life (i.e., time spent playing an instrument, distractions, getting instruments ready to play, looking at music, stalling), researchers and teachers are
really interested in the *micro* perspective (i.e., quality time, structure, improvement, goals).

Practice as an Everyday Activity (the Macro Perspective)

In order to acquire skills in any domain of expertise, everybody has to practice.
Musicians go about it differently, yet it is puzzling how little they talk about it in
detail. When they do, musicians can be very emotional about their practice, loving or hating it at the same time (see Mach, 1980; Chaffin, Imreh, & Crawford,
2002, chapter 3, for interesting quotes). This ambivalent relationship may be
due to negative biographical experiences, such as being forced to practice or
feeling incompetent, or to positive ones, such as being rewarded or having fun
playing the instrument.

Although a fascinating indication of how a musician experiences his or her
practice, verbal information gathered from subjective biographical accounts can
be biased by several factors and therefore has to be analyzed with care. For example, some performers—similar to magicians—try to guard certain trade se-
crets and do not disclose all relevant details. The superstar image may prevent
them from talking freely about problems, worries, or failures; at other times,
musicians may be inarticulate or naive in their answers; finally, the early stages
of skill acquisition may not seem important anymore to seasoned performers or
may seem so far away in time that they cannot be clearly remembered. Gradu-
ally, however, performers and researchers alike have started opening up, allowing us a look behind the scenes (e.g., Chaffin et al., 2002; Marsalis, 1995a).

Practice has always been a major part of musicians' lives, and it even has its
own physical place, as the expression for solitary practice—"going to the
woodshed"—implies. In most industrialized countries today, young music students practice in their own rooms or in a family room under parental supervision. Conservatory students usually practice by themselves in small cubicles or
at home. One can even buy specially designed practice environments that afford
variable acoustical properties for setting up at home or in schools. Practice is

thus given a special status, and disturbances are limited, all of which points to the mental effort and concentration it requires.

But practice can also be a nuisance to those who have to bear its acoustical by-products. Some classical pianists use mute instruments (today electronic instruments) in order to practice whenever and wherever they desire. Young rock musicians often have to find a garage where they can practice without disturbing their environment. This was not always possible in history, and anecdotes exist about noise pollution. For example, Felix Mendelssohn claimed to be virtually tortured by a young girl who practiced 2 hours a day in the apartment next to his, making the same mistakes every day and playing Rossini arias at unbearably slow tempi; yet he conceded that he was probably bothering her even more with his own playing (Mendelssohn-Bartholdy, 1882, p. 25). During the 1800s large halls in the Paris conservatory contained many pianos being used for practice simultaneously. Even today, in many places (e.g., the Cuban music academy in Havana), music learners do not enjoy the solitude we often associate with optimal learning, instead practicing in the communal courtyard.

What are the constituting elements of practice (or "training," as people call it in sports)? In general, we refer to practice for activities that result in learning, that is, an ongoing change in behavior. However, the manifestation of practice may vary, depending on the skill level and type of music. Whereas advanced classical musicians work by themselves, children often practice in the presence of an adult; a singer or an instrumentalist will on occasion be accompanied by a coach; jazz or popular musicians may jam with others or practice with a play-along recording; and so forth. We also have the young conductor who might rehearse his or her gestures with one or two pianos in lieu of an entire orchestra. Characteristically, practice sessions try to either simulate the real performance situation as closely as possible or isolate specific aspects of it.

Although we recognize easily those types of practice that resemble performance, such as a trio performing for some friends to prepare for an upcoming performance, the isolation of specific performance aspects is not as easy to identify. Many activities appear marginal, and many people would not readily call them practice: reading a music psychology book, exercising Alexander technique, memorizing or analyzing a score away from the instrument, listening to someone else's or one's own recording, playing through a program in the practice room while wearing performance attire and stage makeup, taking lessons, gesturing in front of a mirror, lifting weights, or doing breathing exercises. Yet we want to include them here for good reasons. In the sports domain, these extra activities (e.g., learning about strategies in ball games, watching videos of opposing teams before an encounter, going to physical therapy) are commonly acknowledged and encouraged as improving performance. Surprisingly enough, one of the main training activities of chess players is to study published games, trying to predict the next best move (Charness, Krampe, & Mayr, 1996). Thus, in order to know exactly what constitutes practice in a certain domain, we have

---

Cross-Cultural Perspective: Practicing and Learning to Play the Gamelan

In his fascinating report on Balinese music instruction, Bakan (1994) describes a type of practice and teaching that is representative of many non-Western music traditions. His account relates how a leading musician and teacher instructs students (including Bakan himself) to play the drum (i.e., the *kendang lanang,* or "male drum" of a male-female drum pair) in the percussion-dominated Indonesian music called *Gamelan Baleganjur.* All other players of the gamelan set do not receive one-on-one tuition, but they learn their instruments in the context of full ensemble rehearsals. The drumming instruction consists mainly of a model-copy approach called "teaching with the mallet" (*maguru panggul*). The teacher plays up to 1-minute-long precomposed fixed passages (*pukulan*) from the larger composition at a stretch, offering a performance model to the student, who attempts to reproduce the movements immediately. Countless repetitions of this section at performance speed are needed until the pupil starts to grasp some of the movements. Virtually no explanation, analysis, segmenting, or slowing down accompanies the teacher's renditions. The teacher's only intervention may be occasional head movements to direct the student's attention to particular aspects of the performance. After some time, out of the student's "rhythmic rambling" emerge certain stock phrases, similar to licks in jazz, that the student subsequently uses as stepping stones from which to build mastery of his or her part. Once the student is able to play a certain part of the *pukulan*, the teacher starts to play the interlocking drum part of the "female" (*wadon*) *kendang* drum, in fact mimicking the future ensemble situation. Because the lesson takes place out of doors, passersby can join in. Although some musicians might get together outside the full ensemble situation, solitary (private) practice is almost unheard of and is met with puzzlement, if not ridiculed, by other musicians (Bakan, personal communication, October 1, 2004).

---

to identify all the activities that skilled individuals engage in and judge necessary for improving performance.

Practice also has a strong emotional component. The anecdotal literature abounds with firsthand experiences of the love-hate relationships professional musicians maintain with their practice experiences (e.g., Mach, 1980). Whereas some musicians downplay its vital role in the acquisition of expert skills, others emphasize its importance. The violin teacher Auer called it "mental labour" (Auer, 1921/1980, p. 14), whereas a more recent pedagogue talked of practicing as a type of "commitment to yourself to improve by developing skills from lesson to lesson" (Snitkin, 1997, p. 11). *Tackling the Monster* is the telling title of an educational video on practicing by trumpet virtuoso Wynton Marsalis (1995b). The range of opinions of famous pianists about practice can be gleaned from the recent book by Chaffin et al. (2002): "Claudio Arrau and Janina Fialkowska claim that practicing is 'fun,' while John Browning compares it to dishwashing. Others—Lazar Berman and Jorge Bolet—say they dislike it" (p. 43). Practice involves motivating oneself to do it, even if the process itself is not always enjoyable (see chapter 3), and those who do not cope successfully with this problem are likely to abandon music making in the long term.

A Scientific Look at Practice (the Micro Perspective)

Rather than viewing practice more holistically, this section concentrates on its skill-building aspect. A detailed analysis of practice has to start with the definition of practice as a:

> [s]tructured activity, often designed by teachers or coaches with the explicit goal of increasing an individual's current level of performance. In contrast to work and play, it requires the generation of specific goals for improvement and the monitoring of various aspects of performance. Furthermore, deliberate practice involves trying to exceed one's previous limits, which requires full concentration and effort. Consequently, it is only possible to engage in these activities for a limited amount of time until rest and recuperation are needed. (Ericsson & Lehmann, 1999, p. 695)

Interestingly, practice is set apart from paid work and play. Those activities are often performed at levels that can either be sustained for very long times without psychological and physiological breakdown (work), or they are inherently enjoyable (play). Both of them are unlikely to continuously increase our skills in the long run, although they certainly contribute experience. Think of someone working in a car wash: A smooth working procedure that can easily be maintained throughout the day has been learned after a week. It is unlikely that, after working in the business months and years, the employee would wash cars much faster or make them cleaner. Work's main objective is to provide a reliable and sustainable behavior, and play's main aim is to further well-being (physical, emotional, or cognitive). Play is inherently enjoyable because one is not pushed to the limit. Neither a recreational golfer nor an amateur tennis player will reach championship level, not even after many years. Both have settled for a comfortably functioning level.

Practice, on the other hand, is different from simple exposure, play, and work. Some types of practice are more enjoyable than others. To distinguish between these types we can speak of formal (deliberate) and informal practice. In deliberate practice, we have specific goals that lie somewhat outside of our current level of performance, and we try to attain those during bouts of great concentration.

Hence, simply playing through a piece for the third time does not satisfy this criterion because of the absence of a specific goal and the lack of feedback. Also, playing a whole evening in a club with a jazz ensemble cannot strictly be counted as practice, because an existing skill is merely exhibited (work). This does not rule out that some parts of the evening may qualify as practice—for example, when a player tries out a new solo under the critical eyes of the band members, who will later comment on it. Conversely, such an evening might also involve playful activities when musicians perform witty call-and-response games, which cannot clearly be considered deliberate practice. Merely spending time with a musical instrument does not necessarily count as practicing.

Deliberate practice is evident when there are explicit goals and the possibility of feedback. For example, a teacher or peer will comment on the quality of a trombone player's tone, or a member of a choir will nudge her neighbor with her elbow on detecting a blatant mistake. Feedback can be rendered even more precise—for example, when we listen to a slowed-down recording of ourselves, thereby amplifying all the tiny irregularities in our phrasing. In the absence of precise goals and feedback, we do not know what to do next or to listen for. A good example is a study on the synchronization of contrary finger movements (called "forks" by wind players) among musicians on different instruments, such as bagpipes, woodwinds, violins, pianos, and accordions (Walsh, Altenmüller, & Jabusch 2006). Some instruments are more or less forgiving with regard to the exactitude with which alternate finger movements have to be performed. The authors showed that the instrumentalists who alternated most accurately were the bagpipers, followed by the woodwind players (the most inaccurate were nonmusicians). Such differently graded goals of precision would not have emerged among the musicians investigated in the absence of immediate unpleasant auditory feedback.

Our earlier definition of practice mentioned effort and concentration. Those are needed to maintain the typically circular nature of practice: play–evaluate–play differently–evaluate and so forth (see the section on self-regulation, later in the chapter). When practicing, we have to maintain the goal, listen attentively, and integrate any available feedback into the next attempt. For example, the goal may be to attempt an alternate fingering. The resulting evaluation by the teacher suggests that although everything sounded right, one finger was lifted too high, which leads to a new goal for the next trial, that is, paying close attention to the respective finger. We all know from experience how tiring this type of practice is. In a survey study, music academy students were asked to rate effort and enjoyment of various music-related activities (e.g., giving lessons, practicing, playing for fun, music theory) and several everyday activities (e.g., household chores, shopping, work, sleep; see Ericsson et al., 1993). It appeared that, apart from taking part in real performances, lesson taking and practice were rated highest in effort among all listed activities. And although some pleasure is derived from those strenuous activities, playing for fun and listening to music are much less effortful and more enjoyable. Similarly, when looking at various practice activities, we find that practicing trouble spots and studying new repertoire are the most effortful activities, with trouble-spot practice being the least enjoyable (Lehmann, 2002). This negative correlation of effort and enjoyment underscores that we have to constantly motivate ourselves to practice. Its effortful nature also implies that it can be sustained for only limited amounts of time every day, usually around 4 to 5 hours for adults, without leading to psychological or physiological burnout in the long term.

What Does Practice Accomplish?

The Structure behind Skilled Behavior

For most people, the goal of practice is to be able to play a piece of music adequately, whatever that may mean at a given moment. But the observable behavior is just an indicator of more central things that are going on inside—or at least that should be going on! Mere performance of one piece could conceivably be accomplished without actually understanding the music. For instance, many people learn "Chopsticks" on the piano, but we would not consider them piano players. Similarly, you could learn to say a sentence in Russian without knowing what it means. When we truly know a piece of music, such as a flute sonata by G. F. Handel, we can stop at any given point, know what notes we are currently playing, where we stand in the piece, what the accompanist would play, and, most important, what the next notes are. In essence, practice not only enables us to perform a given piece of music but also helps establish generic cognitive (i.e., mental) representations that support the skills and enable the learner to assimilate, manipulate, memorize, and retrieve the music in appropriate ways (see chapter 1). More important, these representations allow mental and physical skills to transfer from one piece and difficulty level to the next. This mechanism allows us to learn subsequent pieces faster, because certain note combinations or expressive devices can be anticipated, and the conceptual understanding of the music becomes largely independent of the motor execution (see chapter 1; Palmer & Meyer, 2000). In sum, new learning pathways rely on previously acquired structures.

Of course, these mental representations are not acquired instantly but, rather, by learning several individual pieces with increasing difficulty. Amateurs who tend to play pieces of similar difficulty level cease to progress because the mental representations they use are likely to allow only similarly structured pieces to be acquired with ease. This effect is visible, for example, when a classical musician attempts to learn a popular piece with a Latin groove or a jazz singer tries to master a Schubert song. It then becomes evident how specific those acquired representations are. In short, practice not only requires the repetition of similar things but also demands increasing difficulty—a challenge to be met, a goal to aspire to (such as in the earlier bagpiper example).

Practice also leads to a narrow and reproducible range of performance. For example, expert musicians can reproduce their interpretations of a piece of music very accurately with respect to timing and dynamics (e.g. Seashore, 1938/ 1967). They are not only more accurate but also faster than amateur musicians. That some performers can demand large sums of money for their performances attests to the fact that they deliver the same high quality "product" every time— within small margins of error that are hardly noticeable to the audience. The small variability in performance, that is, deviation from the average, is therefore a hallmark of musical (or other domain) expert performance. On the contrary, novices stray around the target, displaying a much larger variability in performance. You may remember early music lessons when you had not practiced well and still were able to perform quite decently, or times when you had only moderate success despite having worked hard.

Thus the results of practicing are the supporting internal mechanisms that lead to the observable performance behavior. We now talk about a few other adaptive advantages that sustain performance, namely physiological, perceptual-motor, and cognitive adaptations (for more cognitive adaptations, see chapter 6 and 11).

Physiological Adaptations That Help the Performer

As music making is just one task domain among others in our daily lives, our bodies and minds respond to it in the same way they respond to habitual demands in other areas. For example, you can often distinguish people who enjoy food by their size, heavy smokers by their yellow fingers or teeth, craftspeople by coarse hands, and fitness buffs by their shaped-up bodies. Musicians also display such localized physical characteristics that occasionally even allow informed guesses as to what instrument they play. Calluses at the tips of fingers, especially on the left hand, are a giveaway for string instrument players, whereas stronger or sprung lips may indicate brass players. Violin and viola players often have a discolored spot on the neck (left side) where the instrument rests.

Not all physiological adaptations are as obvious; for example, in one study pianists were found to exhibit a reliably larger extent of inward rotation (pronation) of their forearms and violinists had a larger outward rotation (supination) compared with control participants. The overall degree of rotation remained constant in all three groups but was shifted toward the respective habitual usages for the instrumentalists (see Lehmann, 1997, for a review). Singers and brass players were found to have significantly larger vital and total lung capacities compared with controls. Sometimes the advantage or change appears only while the musician engages in habitual behavior. For instance, functional superiority in inhalation and expiration pressures in trumpet players were found only after several long notes had been played (Fiz et al., 1993). From research on runners, we know that metabolic processes in athletes reach their optimal levels while the athletes are performing their sports. Many physiological adaptations are helpful for the expert performer.

Although additional results could be reported, it would be even more interesting to know whether those changes coincide with amount and intensity of training. In fact, they do, and we focus now on those concerning the cortex, the characteristically wrinkled surface of the brain (see Münte, Altenmüller & Jäncke, 2002; and Pantev, Engelien, Candia, & Elbert, 2003, for reviews). For a long time scientists believed that the brain remained anatomically unchanged except for pathological or aging symptoms. The subtle adaptations in our brains have recently been uncovered by neurophysiologists using sophisticated imaging techniques (e.g., functional magnetic resonance imaging or fMRI). This technique allows researchers a noninvasive look into a person's brain while the person is doing something. One of the first studies that received widespread attention was one that looked at the position and size of the areas in the brain, that is, the cortical representation, in which localized increases in neural activity can be seen in response to the movement of certain fingers. Researchers found that the area representing the left hand in string players was enlarged compared to the right (Elbert et al., 1995). Also, the cortical representation on the surface of the cortex that is responsible for processing the information from individual digits of the left hand (the playing hand) was enlarged compared with the area representing the thumb. Most important, this cortical reorganization was more pronounced for persons who had started musical training at an earlier age. Other studies have since shown that this reorganizing effect is not restricted to playing but also appears when listening to music: Larger areas of the cortex are activated when musicians listen to tones of their own instruments as compared with instruments they do not play. Much research has been done comparing musicians with nonmusicians. Among other things, we find differences in the volume of gray matter in the motor, as well as the auditory and visuospatial, brain regions of professional musicians (keyboard players) compared with amateur musicians and nonmusicians. It is therefore reasonable to assume that training and practice induce far-reaching changes in our brains. But musicians are not unique; similar learning-induced changes, also called "neuroplasticity," can be found in many other populations (e.g., in athletes and the blind).

Some Physiological Adaptations That Are Counterproductive

Although some degree of physiological adaptation is presumably necessary for musicians to perform at the highest levels, these benign outward changes might also turn malign, as they can result in musculoskeletal problems, skin conditions, chronic pain, or neurological problems (see below). These signs of misuse or maladaptations are the focus of modern performing arts medicine (Brandfonbrener & Lederman, 2002), but they have been documented as far back as the lifetimes of Georg P. Telemann and Robert Schumann. Today, more than three-fourths (82%) of musicians from orchestras report medical problems, and 76% say that at least one of these problems has affected their playing (Fishbein & Middlestadt, 1989, as cited in Brandfonbrener & Lederman, 2002). Although hearing losses and performance anxiety are among the prevalent problems, research shows the particular problems that emerge for every instrument due to its design or the required playing techniques (see chapter 8).

When specialization and habitual demands become extreme, problems may evolve even from the previously mentioned neuroplasticity. Researchers had monkeys engage in repetitive hand actions and showed that the cortical representations of digits first enlarged (as discussed earlier) but then started to overlap with adjacent receptive fields that are usually sharply separated (Blake et al., 2003). As a result, moving one digit invoked an uncontrollable movement in an adjacent digit. Evidence is mounting that this fusion of digital representations may also occur in musicians as an unwanted result of extensive training and decades-long practice. The symptoms, called musician's cramp or focal dystonia, occur more often in males than in females and are instrument-specific (Lim & Altenmüller, 2003). Although we cannot rule out that heritability factors may make some musicians more or less prone to such maladaptations, no one can generally evade the lifelong plasticity of his or her brain—which normally is a blessing, for it allows us to learn even at advanced ages.

Perceptual and Psychomotor Adaptations

The physiological adaptations were discussed first because they are more surprising than the plausible and obvious cognitive changes that we would expect to coincide with changes in performance. But perceptual and psychomotor adaptations also occur. The word *psychomotor* is used instead of *motor performance* because in music making motor performance is mediated by mental processes, and it also triggers further mental activity. It is also possible to talk about perceptual-motor skills when motor skills are interconnected with vision (as in reading notation) or the auditory system. Next we discuss some general results regarding practice-related changes to the motor and perceptual system.

Musicians develop a finer frequency and loudness discrimination compared with nonmusicians (Houtsma, Durlach, & Horowitz, 1987); however, the improved discrimination of timbres and tones by musicians is so specific that it does not transfer even to speech sounds (Münzer, Berti, & Pechmann, 2002). Also, musicians playing instruments that require fine tuning of individual notes during performance develop a more accurate discrimination for pitch height, whereas percussionists acquire an improved perception of durations (Rauscher & Hinton, 2003).

Even conductors who start their training later in life develop the ability to preattentively monitor an unusually large auditory space (e.g., from first violin to cellos and basses) in which they can detect wrong notes or other inaccuracies (Nager et al., 2003). Furthermore, researchers found that pianists possess a heightened sensibility in tactile discrimination that is related to the amount of practice undertaken by the pianists (Ragert et al., as cited in Nager et al., 2003). Thus the senses can "sharpen," but this heightened acuity is very much limited to typical stimuli.

Motor researchers have also found that pianists are able to tap their *fingers* faster and more accurately than are control participants, but this advantage does not transfer to the *heels* (Keele, Pokorny, Corcos, & Ivry, 1985). Earlier we mentioned the higher accuracy of contrary finger movements exhibited by some wind instrumentalists (Walsh et al.,2006). A generalizable finding concerns eye movements, which are involuntary and which change considerably with training (Rayner & Pollatsek, 1989; see also chapter 6). Recording eye movements allows interesting insights into our cognitive processing (e.g., in reading), because those movements indicate where and how our brains try to obtain information from the outside world. Beginning text readers, for instance, show different eye movements than experts do, a finding that also applies to music reading (see chapter 6). Because changes in performance, as well as physiological and psychological aspects, seem to emerge as a result of practice, we now turn to the quantity and quality of practice.

Amount of Practice

When we hear a musician perform, we hardly ever think of the number of hours it has taken to prepare the pieces performed or to attain a given general level of performance. We could ask the same of other experts. How many meaningful chess configurations does a chess master know and how long does it take to learn those? Simon and Gilmartin (1973; as cited in Ericsson & Smith, 1991) estimated that between 10,000 and 100,000 meaningful configurations (chunks) were necessary and that it would take up to 30,000 hours to become an chess master! Because learning takes time, and even more so when a skill comprises a motor component, the amount of practice time is very important.

A seminal study in this area is the one by Ericsson, Krampe, and Tesch-Römer (1993), in which the authors assessed practice times of musicians and related them to attained levels of performance. In their first study, 30 violin students from the Berlin (Germany) Music Academy were compared with regard to the amount of time they had spent practicing over their life spans. The students were rated by their teachers as being among either the "best" or the "good" students (10 each, matched for age and sex), whereas the last group of 10 students consisted of aspiring music teachers. The mean age of the young violinists was 23.1 years. To ascertain whether the "best" students were comparable with current professionals in regard to practice times, 10 members of professional orchestras in Berlin were also surveyed. During an interview, participants reported on current durations of practice and on their musical biographies (e.g., first teacher, start of lesson, changes of teacher). Also, they estimated retrospectively how long and how many days per week they had practiced in a given year since the start of their training. Those estimates were later summed to a total duration of accumulated practice by multiplying daily estimates by the number of days of practice and the resulting weekly estimates by number of weeks per year and then adding all the yearly estimates. When comparing the lifetime accumulated durations among groups, the authors found that the superior experts ("best" students) had practiced more than the others (see figure 4.1 top). At age 18, when all the students entered the Academy, the best students had already practiced for roughly 7,400 hours; the next group, 5,300 hours; and the last group, 3,400.

In a second study involving amateurs and professionals, Ericsson et al. (1993) interviewed pianists regarding their practice times and asked them to perform several motor performance tasks (tapping and coordination, music performance; see also Krampe & Ericsson, 1996). In brief, the findings showed that practice times were again related to motor performance (simple tapping tasks and complex movement coordination): More practice resulted in shorter between-keystroke times (faster movements) and more consistency in expressive performance. Many more detailed results are reported in those studies, but for our present purpose it is important to remember that duration of practice is systematically related to attained level of performance.

A later study by Sloboda et al. (1996) confirmed the results of Ericsson et al.'s (1993) study for younger music students. A large sample of music students at five different levels of achievement was surveyed with a method similar to that of Ericsson et al. (1993; see Williamon & Valentine, 2000, pp. 355–357, for a good comparison of both studies). Students were divided in groups, ranging from those with the highest level of achievement (Group One in figure 4.1 bottom) to students who had abandoned playing altogether (reported as Group Five in the figure). The better students had practiced more, even in the beginning stages of learning, whereas the least industrious ones were also the ones most likely to drop out of lessons. More important, the best students needed as many hours to progress from one level to the next as did the less proficient students. Sloboda et al.'s (1996) data show that there is no "fast track" to achievement; a minimum number of hours is simply necessary to reach a certain level of proficiency. The better students in the study spent more time tinkering with their instruments, suggesting that they enjoyed playing them. Similar findings relating amount of relevant practice to performance also come from other domains outside of music (see Ericsson & Lehmann, 1997; Ericsson, 2004, for a review).

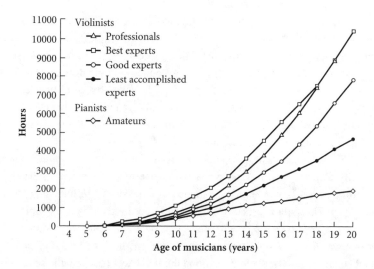

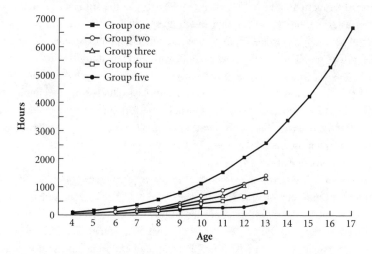

Figure 4.1. Relation between accumulated lifetime deliberate/formal practice and attainment of instrumental music performance (top panel for experts; bottom panel for novices). See text for details.

Assessing deliberate practice is usually done by interviewing the participants and obtaining retrospective estimates of practice for every year since the start of practice. Critics have suggested that these estimates may be unreliable and that time spent practicing alone may not be a good indicator of deliberate practice. Ericsson et al. (1993) included a diary study in their project to compare estimates of current practice times with week-long diary entries. It became apparent that all students had slightly overestimated their practice. Therefore, the overall pattern of results remains: Practicing more leads to better performance in the long run, but the absolute magnitude of amounts indicated by the respondents may have been slightly inflated. The precise amount of (individual) practice is not as interesting because it varies substantially among instruments—with string and keyboard players practicing most, followed by wind players, and ending with vocalists (Jørgensen, 1997). This difference is not due to the laziness of some instrumentalists (or singers) but, rather, likely reflects physiological limitations and teaching traditions.

Although practice times are quite telling in the long run, researchers have rightfully claimed that they are not as indicative of performance in the short run—for example, when learning a single piece of music (Williamon & Valentine, 2000). The authors asked pianists at different levels to practice a piece of music and to record their practice using a tape recorder. Although the amount of practice was not related to final quality of performance, the length of practice segments in the middle stage of learning the piece was (see also the section on phases of practice, later in this chapter). Possibly some students acquired the piece faster and had fewer problems with its specifics. After all, someone with little experience playing Bach may face problems that an experienced Baroque player does not. This would be consistent with another study that found that a musician's personally estimated difficulty of a piece, along with its objective amount of content—or the number of notes to play—did predict the amount of time a musician needed to learn this music for performance (Lehmann & Ericsson, 1998b). In brief, the mere duration of practice cannot be used independently from a more detailed analysis of the quality of practice when it comes to short-term practice efforts.

If practice times are more important in the long run, could one not simply increase the number of practice hours every day? This is, alas, not possible, largely because mental effort is needed to practice effectively, and human attention capacity is limited, as everybody knows. Ericsson et al. (1993) estimate that approximately 4 hours' worth of concentrated daily mental effort is possible without long-term physiological or psychological burnout. Beginners in a domain and children can probably concentrate for shorter amounts of time (also Williamon & Valentine, 2000). This fact leads to varying amounts of practice over a lifetime, starting with shorter stretches and leading up to (overly) long hours of practice prior to the start of the career (or before college exams). Up to this point musicians are still building skills.

Later the focus may shift to maintaining existing skills, which is likely to require less practice. Moreover, competing activities, such as managing one's life, career, and family or teaching obligations, force performers to practice less. To our knowledge, allegations of little or even no practice by performers must be misinterpretations of ambiguous remarks. When musicians claim not to need to practice, it may be that concertizing, or other activities which they may not view as practicing, suffice to keep their skills up.

Very much later in life, performers ought to practice more because they have to counteract the adverse effects of aging. Incidentally, research shows that musicians who keep practicing can actually delay those negative effects (Krampe & Ericsson, 1996). The finding that their musical cognitive-motor skills decay comparably less than their nonmusical cognitive skills do offers a hopeful perspective for all active musicians. Age effects can also be met with compensatory strategies, such as choosing technically less demanding pieces or playing more slowly.

What we learn from all these studies is that the amount of optimized practice is related to the attained performance. The expertise view does not rule out possible individual differences in innate aptitude; it merely focuses our view on those aspects of skill acquisition that we can influence as educators. As educators, we know that it is not the quantity of practice alone that is so important but also the quality, a subject to which we now turn.

Quality of Practice: What Is Good Practice?

We now point out why some types of practice are qualitatively superior to others. In a letter to his wife in 1898, Busoni (1983) stated 12 noteworthy rules on how to practice the piano, and many piano teachers since have made similar recommendations. Much advice is sound and grounded in lifelong experience; other advice appears haphazard. Sometimes, advice comes in the form of recipes that, when applied thoughtlessly, may have little or no effect. Take, for example, the idea of "slow practice," which is often hailed as a simple remedy for all sorts of problems. However, as the scientifically well-informed piano teacher Tobias Matthay states, slow practice without actually imagining the upcoming note in your head "is only a useless fetish" (1926, p. 12; see chapter 6). Sometimes an observable behavior may look right (e.g., someone practicing slowly), but it is accompanied by the wrong thoughts (e.g., thinking about lunch). Following an experienced practitioner's advice may be wise, but we also have to ask ourselves why something works or why it does not.

Despite our best intentions to work effectively (whatever this means at a given time), our goals often escape us; we fail to listen to our results; we simply do not know how to practice a certain trouble spot; or we are too tired to muster up the necessary attention. A number of other factors influence the effectiveness of practice, including person-related and task-related aspects. Among the person-related aspects, we can list age and maturational factors, motivation, personality traits (see chapter 9), socioeconomic background and education, current psychophysiological states (e.g., fatigue, hunger, unhappiness, mental presets), and musical self-concepts. Other aspects pertain more to the practice activity itself, such as length of practice time, distribution of practice across time (especially over longer periods of time), use of practice strategies, and supervision (see Barry & Hallam, 2002; Jørgensen, 2004, for reviews). In brief, as conditions become less favorable—for example, when we are hungry, feel that the piece is too difficult, or lack effective strategies—practice as a whole becomes a waste of time. Consequently, a student's apparent lack of progress in spite of reported adequate amounts of practice might actually be related to sub-optimal conditions during practice, that is, the microstructure of his or her prac-tice. Because practice is influenced by so many factors, it is not surprising that individuals differ greatly from each other in the ways they practice.

Phases of Practice

From observing experts and novices practicing, we can learn a lot about the mi-crostructure of practice. For example, the learning of a new piece for perfor-mance occurs in distinguishable stages (Chaffin et al., 2002, chapters 6 and 10). During the brief first stage, the musician tries to get the big picture of the piece; in the longer second stage, technical practice is undertaken to master the piece; and in the third stage, the performance itself is practiced. The fourth stage, the maintenance of a piece, occurs over very long periods of time between concerts or recordings. The stages are as follows:

1. The first stage entails reading through the piece or, more generally, getting an aural representation of the piece in its entirety. Already at this point, strategies may vary, depending on the musician's preferred work methods (e.g., sight reading, analyzing, and listening to recordings).
2. Now begins the second stage, in which the piece is worked on in sections that increase in length as practice progresses. Those sections emerge from the first stage and already align, at least among experts and better student performers, with the compositional and artistic conceptions of the piece (see also Williamon & Valentine, 2000). The interpretation is developed either intuitively (i.e., evolving during the course of learning to play the piece) or analytically (i.e., through structural analysis, comparison of in-terpretations, and listening to music; Hallam, 1995). During this elabora-tive stage of practice, the motor programs become largely automatized, resulting in a first incidental memorization of the piece. Better performers reach this stage earlier in the process than less proficient players, presum-ably because they either understand the music better or have fewer techni-cal difficulties to overcome.
3. In the third stage, the performance is polished and prepared more directly by putting all the pieces together and ironing out the seams between them. Memory, which up to now was largely motor memory, creates an internal map of the piece with close attention to the order of the parts (see chapter 6). As performance approaches, memory is repeatedly tried and tested. Musicians often play slowly and perform for an imagined or real audience

---

Self Study: Stages and Duration of Practice

Think of the most recent piece you prepared, from first encounter to public performance. What were the steps you went through to prepare it for the event? Try to estimate the frequency (times) or duration (days) you used for certain activities.

You will notice that the stages identified for example by Chaffin et al. (2002) can also be traced in your own preparation. If rehearsing performance is usually not all that important for you, you might think again. If you rely on the incidental memory until the very end, and if you could not write out part of the piece or sing a particular voice, the image you have of the music may not be entirely clear. Also, note how regular or irregular your practice is with regard to time and procedure. More regularity is generally advisable.

(e. g., a friend), refine interpretational details, bring all sections up to the correct tempo (or even slightly above it), and clean up technical problems on the way. If possible, musicians even practice under performance conditions (i.e., in concert attire and in different locations) to prevent context effects of memory (Mishra, 2002). Although this final polishing and preparation process is the longest one and might never truly end, the returns diminish as the phase turns into maintenance work.

4. Maintenance of a piece may involve slight modifications in the interpretation at later points and general upkeep of the technical and memory aspects. Performers will maintain some pieces for many decades.

Learning to Practice Correctly through Self-Regulation

Because experts and novices differ in their observable practice (e.g., Gruson, 1988), we can conclude that practice has to be learned. Beginners, especially children, have the problem of creating the necessary representations and structuring their practice accordingly. Sometimes written procedures can fulfill this function. Barry (1990) found that students who practiced according to a written procedure learned more during a specified 30-minute session than students who practiced freely (presumably less structured). Unlike in sports, in which the aspiring athlete works under the watchful eye of a coach, music students have to become their own coaches. Three different studies—one on American concert pianists (Sosniak, 1985), one on historical piano prodigies (Lehmann, 1997), and one on successful children from a specialist music school (Davidson, Sloboda,

& Howe, 1996)—found that high-achieving and successful children were supported in their practice. In addition to ensuring that practice happens for a specified amount of time, supervising teachers or parents provide practice goals and feedback. For this, the tutor does not necessarily have to be a musician—everybody can hear wrong notes, encourage lovingly, and watch the clock. Parents and children with no prior experience in learning to play an instrument, however, may have faulty expectations about what needs to be done and for how long (McPherson & Davidson, 2002). As musicians become more self-sufficient, they can regulate practice to correspond to the task difficulties and, if necessary, change practice behaviors.

Optimizing practice is mainly achieved through self-regulation. This means that a person can select appropriate strategies, plan, monitor the outcome, and revise according to the difficulties encountered (e.g., McPherson & Zimmerman, 2002, for an in-depth discussion). Nielsen (1999) videotaped two organ students and had them verbalize their thoughts as they were practicing and again while watching the taped practice. It became clear that they cycled repeatedly through the sequences of problem recognition, choice of strategy, performance, and evaluation of performance, while also considering short-term and long-term goals. Possible ways of practicing vary considerably from instrument to instrument, from piece to piece, and from player to player (see Jørgensen, 2004, and Hallam, 1998a, chapter 7, for useful advice).

That this self-regulation is partly dependent on the motivation of the student was shown in a study of children practicing by themselves (Renwick & McPherson, 2002). A child who was unmotivated because she did not like her piece displayed little to no self-regulation as she simply stumbled through the material. The same child was able to practice effectively, that is, self-regulate successfully, when she liked the material to be studied. Similarly, when the goal is to master a certain piece, instrument, or difficulty, adults may work hard and use more practice strategies than they do when they want to enjoy themselves or relax (Lehmann & Papousek, 2003). Thus self-regulation does not simply happen; it requires specific goals, feedback, and motivation. Most likely, high achievers have optimized their practice and can sustain the motivation to "do the right thing" most of the time (see also chapter 3).

Mental Rehearsal

Practicing is effortful, and fatigue is likely to lead to playing mistakes and useless practice. It is advisable to distribute practice time over several shorter practice sessions than to cram a whole day's work into one sitting (the same is true for studying academically). The reason is partly neurological: During rest and sleep, cognitive restructuring (consolidation) takes place, giving the brain time to digest the learning material. A good example of how your brain gets clogged with material occurs when you practice a passage and it deteriorates instead of improving (psychologists call this "proactive interference"). In short, the brain cannot sort out the different attempts because they are confusingly similar. Working on something markedly different in between passages releases this interference.

When a musician has physically practiced for some time, the body may be tired, especially when pain is present and rest is required; yet the mind might still be fresh. How could one practice in the meantime? This is where mental practice (also mental rehearsal) is helpful. When skilled musicians are thinking through music (in terms of its sound or movement), the same brain areas that are activated when hearing and producing music are stimulated. Movement areas are coactivated even when the piece is only heard! Although research on the topic is complex, mental practice does seem to work (Driskell, Copper, & Moran, 1994), especially when the cognitive aspects of the movement task prevail. When a student's technical skills are barely sufficient to master the piece, mental practice is less likely to show positive effects (see Williamon, 2004, chapter 12, for a review). However, practice away from the instrument is probably most beneficial for someone who is mentally fresh, who has the technical proficiency, and who possesses a vivid image of the piece. A review of existing research suggests that 20 minutes of mental practice provides the most benefits (Driskell et al., 1994, p. 488). Mental rehearsal with some degree of physical practice is best, probably because it reinforces the mental image and the motor programs. Sometimes our students claim that mental rehearsal does not work, but further questioning often reveals that their experience is based on a single try after a long day's work. Mental rehearsal is in itself a skill and requires a certain learning process just like other mental skills, such as yoga or relaxation (see chapter 8 on performance anxiety).

Automaticity

An established model of the stages of skill acquisition (Fitts & Posner, 1967; Proctor & Dutta, 1995, chapter 1, for a recent discussion) suggests a cognitive stage, an associative stage, and an autonomous stage. During the cognitive stage we use higher mental processes to acquire a task and develop motor programs; during the associative stage we practice the skill and focus on how the movements feel; and in the autonomous stage the execution of the skill requires little conscious effort, freeing up the performer's cognitive resources to deal with other matters than the skill itself.

The fluency of the autonomous stage that results from practice, the practice-based automaticity of sensorimotor skills, is a much-desired outcome. For example, fast runs and ornaments should be performed without thinking about them. By running unmonitored, those programmed movement sequences allow the performer to attend to more important aspects, such as shaping the performance, communicating with co-performers, or dealing with performance anxiety. When attention is directed to those self-reliant processes during performance, skilled performers may experience a sudden decrement in performance, whereas when attention is drawn away from them, performance may even improve (Beilock, Bertenthal, McCoy, & Carr, 2004; see chapter 5, the section on developing an explicit representational system). Novices, on the contrary, need to monitor their performance, and introducing tasks that compete for attention decreases accuracy. Does this imply that thinking about performance is bad? The answer is no; it simply means that the processes that are intended to run by themselves have to first be rehearsed using conscious thinking and that, once automatized, such processes should be left alone during performance. Given the musician's basic understanding of the music, problems during performance can be solved with recourse to the conceptual information. Conversely, motor processes that have become incidentally automatized during practice, or that have simply been rote-memorized and are thus not supported by mental representations, can become a liability during performance (see chapter 6 on memory). This effect can sometimes be observed among children who experience catastrophic memory lapses when they play at year-end recitals.

To conclude, practice can be viewed as a holistic behavior, comprising effortful striving for improvement along with more relaxing or enjoyable phases. But there is also a more restricted view, namely that which focuses on the skill-building components. The duration of practice is more important than previously assumed, but quality of practice is still central. Quality and quantity change as novices start to progress. To some extent, the suggestions regarding good, successful practice that psychologists can offer (e.g., Williamon, 2004, chapters 5–8) overlap with the true and tested wisdom of experienced teachers and performers. Most important, the mind and the body have to be fresh enough to work. Musicians have to learn to practice (often under supervision). Therefore, teachers should take great care to teach their students how to practice correctly (Barry & McArthur, 1994). The experts' strategies vary considerably but are all guided by effective self-regulation, that is, finding out what is needed and having the right tool to address the problem. This is the reason a large repertoire of practice methods is useful. The goal of practice is to establish mental representations that help the musician to understand the music. This deep understanding allows for smooth performance, as well as for all necessary problem solving—even on stage.

Study Questions

1. Why does practice have to be learned and what exactly is learned in the process?

2. Discuss whether or not retrospective estimates of practice durations are always true indicators of achieved level of performance.
3. What do the macro and micro perspectives of practice describe and how do parents and teachers influence them?

Further Reading

The following two reviews include helpful suggestions on how to improve one's practice.

Jørgensen, H. (2004). Strategies for individual practice. In A. Williamon (Ed.), *Musical Excellence* (pp. 85–104).

Barry, N., & Hallam, S. (2001). Practice. In R. Parncutt & G. E. McPherson (Eds.), *The Science and Psychology of Music Performance: Creative Strategies for Teaching and Learning* (pp. 151–166).

Part II

Musical Skills

5

Expression and Interpretation

Expressivity and Interpretation as Intentional Communication

The heavenly metaphor is etched deep into musical and artistic culture. We talk of performances as being "inspired," of performers as "playing like angels." Both listeners and performers can experience a sense of wonderment at the apparently unpredictable power of some performances. Listeners are not, of course, privy to the hours of deliberate work and shaping that performers can devote in preparation. But even performers sometimes surprise themselves and are unable to explain or predict why one performance is routine and the next performance of the same piece is "magic." Why is this so?

The crux of expressive performance is in nuance. Nuance is the subtle, sometimes almost imperceptible, manipulation of sound parameters, attack, timing, pitch, loudness, and timbre that makes music sound alive and human rather than dead and mechanical. It is a vital component of every musical genre, from the "swing" of jazz and pop to the uneven three-quarter beats of a waltz. We do not have very good everyday language for describing nuance, for capturing and notating it (Raffman, 1993). This is the reason that many aspects of music performance have to be "handed down" from teacher to apprentice through performance practice (i.e., demonstration and imitation). Our nuanced behaviors are also peculiarly susceptible to factors of which we may not be fully aware: our moods, our memories and associations as well as the subtle gestures and expressions of those around us.

Nuance is a subset of expression. Expression encompasses all changes in parameters that do not actually change the identity of the musical sequence. Expressive performance is also how performers display the deepest and most personal aspects of their work. It is the primary manifestation of their musical creativity and personality. Classical performers generally do not "own" the notes, because they were written by someone else. This means that judgments about the artistic worth of a performance are almost entirely based on the musician's ability to manage nuance in aesthetically significant ways. It can become a matter of huge personal significance, even financial survival, that one way of playing a well-known repertoire piece is unique and recognizable as quite different from another way of playing it.

Because of this, some performing musicians express unease when science attempts to analyze and understand expression. It can feel to them as though science is trying to encroach on the mysterious and personal core of their artistic being, even rob them of it. The fear is, perhaps, that if science could discover the "formula" for effective expression, then it could program computers to play expressively and do away altogether with human performers. A balanced assessment of the existing research renders these fears groundless. On the contrary, we believe that the kinds of analyses that science is now yielding can be of direct assistance to performing musicians in enabling new interpretational directions. Musicians have nothing to fear from the scientific assumption that human behavior, even the most apparently "magical," is rooted in concrete mechanisms in the brain, and the psychological processes they support are open to systematic analysis. As researchers of performance nuance, we can attest that analyzing these nuances does nothing to blunt our sense of wonder at a fine performance. If anything, our scientific experiences add layers of new richness to our listening and performing.

Expressivity and interpretation in music exist to communicate something from a performer to a listener. It is because listeners and performers share the same listening apparatus, from which understandings and representations can be constructed, that musical communication is possible. Communication is most effective in broad, basic emotional categories that have universal, biologically programmed modes of expression and that are, therefore, found in persons of all cultures. Four-year-old children can already distinguish an expressive character in music performance (Adachi & Trehub, 1998; see also Gembris, 2002, for a review). Although some reference is made in this chapter to the capacities of the listener, the main discussion of this is reserved until chapter 11. Listeners have the luxury of remaining intuitive and unfocused in their responses. A listener is perfectly entitled to say "this music excites (or calms, or saddens) me, but I do not know why." Performers are, however, missing a huge opportunity if their expressivity remains similarly intuitive. As the evidence suggests, a performer's effectiveness is greatly enhanced by developing explicit representations for performance that allow planning and conceptual memory for the details of an interpretation. Great performances do not just emerge spontaneously from intuition and impulse. They are always the result of much detailed work, even if, at the time of performance, many of these aspects can be experienced as automatic and effortless by the performer—and appear absolutely fresh and intuitive to the audience.

This chapter summarizes scientific research that demonstrates the following points:

1. Much of expressive behavior can be captured by relatively simple rules that apply to different performers and pieces of music. Such aspects of expression reliably communicate structural information (such as accent and metrical structure), as well as basic emotional information (happiness, sadness, tenderness, anger).

2. Many aspects of musical performance are rooted in expressive experiences outside music (e.g., the human body in motion, human speech and emotional vocalizations). Expression in music is powerful because it mobilizes biologically rooted instinctive brain mechanisms.

3. The management of expectancy and surprise is a key component of aesthetically powerful performances. Musical expression heightens and interacts with the way that musical structures play on our experiences of tension and relaxation, expectation and fulfillment.

4. Reliable and reproducible interpretations can be developed through deliberate learning and preparation activities. Although performances may appear "magic" to listeners, the wise performing musician (just like the stage magician) consciously calculates many key effects, using "tricks of the trade." Although interpretations are reliable and reproducible, they are also susceptible to last-minute changes, improvements, and even improvisation.

5. Interpretation, which is the selection and combination of expressive decisions across an entire piece, remains at its core an individual artistic and aesthetic enterprise. Although effective interpretations may have some shared general characteristics, the specifics of interpretation always depend on the performer's specific learning history, personality, and motivations.

6. The scientific study of performance has flourished in the last couple of decades due to the development of increasingly sophisticated and user-friendly means of recording and analyzing objective features of the performance, such as timing and pitch. The computer has transformed this research. In the earlier decades of the twentieth century, measuring performance was a laborious and error-prone process. With the advent of MIDI (Musical Instrument Digital Interface) and powerful analytical software, it is now possible to obtain in seconds what might earlier have taken many months (see Clarke, 2004, and Kopiez, 2002, for reviews of the development of techniques for analyzing music performance).

We suggest, if you are able, that you carry out the self-exercise for this chapter now. It could be more interesting to you to observe your own reactions before reading about research that shows how others react.

Self Study: Communication of Basic Emotions in Music

In this experiment you will produce your own performances of a simple song, play them to at least one other person, and compare the characteristics of your performances with the responses of the listener.

Part A. Making the Recordings

For this part of the experiment you will need (1) a quiet room, (2) your preferred instrument (this includes the voice), (3) a tape recorder to record your own performance.

In preparation, choose two emotions at random from the following list: HAPPY, SAD, ANGRY, TENDER, FEARFUL. Write each word on a different card, and write NORMAL on another.

Also choose a simple folk or popular melody. The melody should (1) be relatively short, (2) stand on its own without any need for accompaniment, and (3) preferably not have a very strong inherent emotional content. Play through the piece without particular expression enough times to ensure that you can play it accurately at a reasonable speed.

Shuffle the cards and deal them out on a table. The order in which you dealt these words will specify the order in which you make your recordings.

Switch on the tape and record three unrehearsed performances of the song, doing your best to communicate the emotion on each card. For "NORMAL," give a performance that you think might be similar to how it is normally performed. Write down the main aspects of what you do musically for each recording to distinguish it from the others by marking a score or writing a brief verbal description.

Part B. Assessing the Recordings

For this part of the experiment, find some friends. They do not have to be musicians. Write the six words—HAPPY, SAD, ANGRY, TENDER, FEARFUL, NORMAL—on a separate sheet of paper for each participant. Tell them they are going to hear three performances of the same tune and that afterward they have to guess, for each tune, which was the emotion (word) intended by the performer. Explain what "normal" means. Ask them to write the number of the piece (as they hear it in order) by the side of the word they think describes that performance best. Then play the tape recording of your performances once through. It is best if you leave the room while your friends make their judgments. Play it again if need be.

Look at how many of the performances your friends judged correctly. Now play the performances again, while you are all listening to them, and get your friends to describe what it was about the performance that caused them to make the judgments they did. Was it due to the speed, the pitch, the loudness, the rhythm, the way the notes sounded? Try to get them to be as specific as possible. Write down key things they said about each performance.

Compare what they said with what you wrote down about your intentions. Did the things they notice correspond to the things you tried to put into your performance? On the basis of this experiment, is there anything you can conclude about the reliability with which it is possible to communicate emotions through music performance?

Expression

Expression refers to the small-scale variations in timing, loudness, and other parameters that performers insert at specific points in a performance. An expressive gesture can often be completely contained within a sequence of a few notes. *Interpretation* refers to the way in which many individual expressive acts are chosen and combined across an entire piece to produce a coherent and aesthetically satisfying experience. Expressive devices are thus the basic building blocks of an interpretation, and our account begins with these.

One of the most important features of human musical performance is the fact that it is not, and can never be, free from note-to-note variation. This is what makes any human performance instantly distinguishable from a machine-generated performance, in which each note is played at exactly its notated duration and at the same loudness. So-called deadpan performances generally sound lifeless and unattractive to listeners. The variations found in human musical performance are of several distinct types, and performance research has identified different sources of variation. These are (1) random variation, (2) rule-based variations, and (3) idiosyncratic variations.

Stability and Random Variation

Seashore (1938/1967) showed that performers are very consistent with regard to expression in multiple reproductions of a piece and that variations present in one performance are also present in the repeat performance. The problem since has been to distinguish random variation from artistic spontaneity. It is difficult to obtain accurate measures of random variation from performances of meaningful music. The reason is that, even when asked to play evenly and without expression, musicians unconsciously retain small amounts of rule-based expression. Seashore (1938/1967) was one of the earliest researchers to ask performers to play without expression. He found that, although the degree of expression is reduced under these circumstances, it is never eliminated and that it retains the same general pattern that is observed when musicians are asked to play with expression (see also Palmer, 1992).

Random variation comes about because of the limitations of the timing and motor control systems of the human body. Even the most highly trained performers are incapable of playing a sequence of notes that have exactly the same sound characteristics (timing, loudness, timbre) from note to note. Studies of simple repetitive motor tasks, such as tapping, suggest that this variation is partly dependent on the speed of movement (the slower, the more variable; e.g., Wing & Kristofferson, 1973). It also appears to depend on experience. Repeated practice at a motor task can reduce the level of random variation (Gerard & Rosenfeld, 1995).

Shaffer (1984) showed that performers' consistency lasted over periods as long as a year. Figure 5.1 details the timing profile from three different performances of a Chopin étude by the pianist Penelope Blackie. The points on the line indicate durations of each successive note, and it is immediately apparent how similar the pattern of speeding up and slowing down is across all three performances. These types of findings are not confined to classical music. Ashley (2004) showed similar stability over even longer periods in repeat recordings by Paul McCartney of the same song.

Rule-Based Variation

The above-mentioned evidence for overall consistency in interpretation poses one of the major puzzles about performance that science needs to explain. How does a performer remember the thousands of subtle performance variations that allow almost exact reproduction from performance to performance? Why isn't the memory of the performer overwhelmed? Does the performer really need to memorize each of these individual values, as one might try to remember a very long telephone number?

Recent research shows that a great deal of performance variation can be accounted for by rather simple rules. The performer picks up these rules, or heuristics, either intuitively or by explicit instruction and then generates performances afresh each time by applying the rules. This hugely cuts down the memory load on a performer.

Although there are many individual rules, they fall into three major groups (based on the terminology suggested by Juslin, Friberg, & Bresin, 2002): *generative* rules, *emotional* rules, and *motional* rules. Generative rules are driven

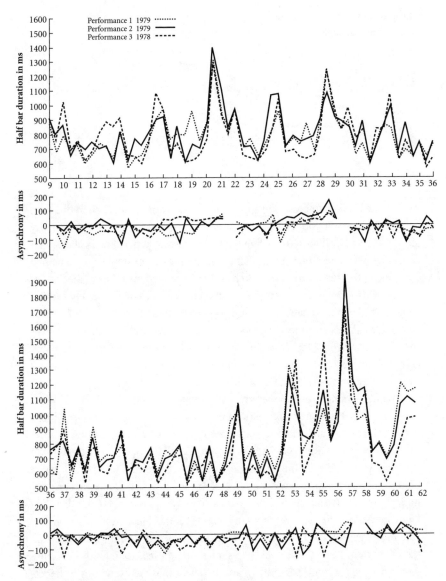

Figure 5.1. Beat duration in three performances of a Chopin étude by the same performer. From "Timing in Solo and Duet Piano Performances," by L. H. Shaffer, 1984, *Quarterly Journal of Experimental Psychology, 36*, 577–595. Copyright © 1984. Reprinted by permission of the Experimental Psychology Society.

by the structure of the music and help to make that structure clearer to a listener. For instance, *accenting* rules point out to a listener which elements are the most structurally important ones within a musical line. Sloboda (1983) showed that performers played the same melody differently if the metrical notation was shifted in relation to the note sequence (see the two parts of Example 5.1).

Music example 5.1. The identical musical sequence with two alternative metrical notations (from Sloboda, 1983).

This is one clear example of the application by performers of a generative rule. The performers in Sloboda's study tended to play the main beats slightly slower and louder than surrounding notes. Interestingly, performers showed no conscious awareness that the top and bottom lines of example 5.1 contained the same notes (they were separated by other, unrelated melodies in the test sequence). Also, performers were not specifically asked to play with any expression at all. They automatically changed their expression as a result of the visual metrical information. Listeners were able to judge which of the two notations was being played just by listening to the performances, proving that these variations really did have a significant effect on the way that listeners perceived the structure of the melodies.

Another example of a generative rule relates to *grouping* of notes (e.g., phrases). Such rules help listeners to understand which elements in a piece "go together" and are separated structurally from what precedes and follows them. For instance, Repp (1992) has demonstrated that performers tend to use a typical expressive timing pattern at the ends of musical phrases. Notes at phrase boundaries are played significantly more slowly than are their neighbors. This means that there is a greater time gap between boundaries than anywhere else. This gap perceptually segments the music; elements on one side of the gap appear to be grouped together, in distinction from elements on the other side. Repp (1998) has also shown that these durational patterns are so "ingrained" in both performers and listeners that they tend not to be explicitly noticed. He tested this by asking listeners to try to detect a small deviation from metronomic exactitude (a delay in the onset of a specific note) somewhere within a short musical performance. If the delay occurred at a phrase end, it was significantly harder for listeners to detect it than if it occurred in the middle of a phrase. The explanation for this result is that the delay at the end of the phrase is expected, whereas the same delay in the middle of the phrase is not, and so it is more noticeable. Even the most trained listener is often unable to switch off these "intelligent" mental processes that transform raw input into apprehended music. Listeners tend to hear the end result (a structure) much more directly than they hear the specific means by which that structure was communicated, and so performance research cannot rely on the judgment of expert listeners alone. Rather, we need technological assistance to study performance.

Examples of *emotional* rules are provided in a study by Juslin (1997a). He asked guitarists to play a familiar melody (such as "O When the Saints Go Marching In") in different ways to communicate different basic emotions (happy, sad, angry, and fearful). He then asked listeners to judge which emotion was present in each performance. Performers changed their performances in similar ways to communicate each specific emotion, and listeners were able to accurately judge which emotion was being conveyed. For instance, happiness is best communicated by a combination of fast speed, loudness, and a detached (staccato) articulation. Sadness is best communicated by slow speed, quiet dynamics, and legato articulation. However, in the study not all performers were equally effective at communicating emotion. Juslin and Laukka (2000) have shown that performers can improve their emotional communication by being given feedback on their communicative effectiveness. Another finding is that some emotions are less easy to communicate than others (Juslin, 1997b). For instance, tenderness is not as well communicated or recognized as the basic emotions of happiness, sadness, fear, and anger. Finally, Juslin and Laukka (2001) have proposed that particular performance cues so readily convey emotion because they are present in speech and vocalization. A happy person speaks faster, with staccato articulation, and louder than an unhappy one. Music borrows preexisting codes from language, which may be the reason it speaks so directly to listeners. It may also be the reason that some aspects of emotional musical expression appear to "come naturally" to many performers. They are transferring an already well-known code from speech into music. They do not have to learn everything from the beginning. At the same time, musical expression is not so universal as to be understandable to listeners of divergent cultures.

Motional rules are those that derive from naturally occurring movements, whether inanimate (such as the swaying of branches in the wind) or animate (such as the movement of the human body). When characteristics of these movements are incorporated into music performance, the expressive experience is one of naturalness or "humanness." Performances without these motional characteristics may sound inhuman or "robotic." Along these lines, Friberg and Sundberg (1987) showed that experienced classical musicians perform final slowings in a way that mirrors the deceleration of runners coming to a stop. Such slowing signals to us that the music is coming to a natural stop. Rules are specific to historical times. We intuitively sense this when listening to historical recordings (from the beginning of the twentieth century).

Idiosyncratic Variation

Although some subtle expressive factors may not be captured by such rules as the preceding, these rules (or others like them) can account in a quite satisfying way for a great deal of performance expression. Musicians tend not to differ from one another by ignoring these rules and creating new ones. Rather, they will differ from each other in the precise combination and relative emphasis of the different rules at their disposal or by the degree to which they apply the rules. One player may place more emphasis on articulation, another on dynamics (see, for example, Sloboda, 1985a). One may place more emphasis in emotional rules, another on generative, and so on. Even within these rules there is still practically infinite room for variability in the expressive repertoire. So discovering the rules of expression in no way limits the creative freedom of a performer, any more than discovering the rules of grammar limits the freedom of a novelist or a poet. On the contrary, we later argue that explicitly knowing and understanding these rules provides the performer with greater, not less, freedom to construct effective and musically interesting interpretations.

Giving prominence to some expressive rules over others is one example of the way in which expression can become idiosyncratic or personal to the performer. We know that such idiosyncrasies matter, and Repp (1997) has shown that, by and large, the more distinguished the performer, the more idiosyncratic the performance is likely to be. He analyzed the timing patterns in 24 performances of the beginning of Chopin's étude in E major. Fifteen of these performances were taken from commercial recordings by distinguished pianists (including Pollini, Ashkenazy, Cortot, and Horowitz), and the remaining 9 were provided by competent amateurs (students). The student performances were more similar to one another, and closer to the average, than were the professional performances, which tended to be more extreme in their use of timing deviations and more distinct from one another. Ironically, judges tended to prefer the average performance and thus rated many of the amateur performances as better than the professional performances. Repp provided the following conjecture as an explanation for his results:

> Perhaps most experts' timing . . . was indeed not as "good" as the students' timing. After all, the Chopin piece is extremely well known, almost hackneyed, and experienced pianists cannot stand any more hearing it played in a conventional way. Thus they deliberately distort its timing to give it a "new" shape that helps remove the staleness from the music and stimulates jaded listeners, *even though this new shape is less beautiful by conventional standards* (and the artists know it). (Repp, 1997, p. 442)

Whether or not Repp's speculations about performer motives are correct in this instance, he was surely right to emphasize the free and deliberate aspect of many performance decisions that performers make.

Other aspects of idiosyncrasy may be less free but constrained by some pre-determined feature. For example, performers differ considerably from one another in body size and shape, including those of the hand. This may influence the expressive outcomes in a range of subtle ways. For instance, a pianist with a very small hand may need to arpeggiate chords that span more than an octave, whereas larger hands would have no difficulty playing them simultaneously. There is no way around such differences, so a performer will develop distinctive performance styles that also reflect physical constraints.

Expressive Rules and Flexibility in Performance

How do we prove that an expressive performance is rule-based and not just the result of "blind" rote learning of a specific set of timing and dynamic nuances? One way is to ask the performer to provide an expressive performance of a piece he or she has never worked on before (by sight-reading it or rehearsing it for a few minutes). Here no premeditated interpretation is possible. And, in fact, expert accompanists manage to generate aesthetically pleasing interpretations on the fly which, given the real-time constraint, have to be rule-based. They approximate the final tempo and character of a piece by applying style-appropriate rules that the musical structure seems to call for (see chapter 6).

Another way of demonstrating that expressive performance is rule based is to put performers in situations in which they are required to change some aspect of their performances. Expert performers are generally capable of varying expressive aspects of their performances at will; for example, changing the amount of expression in a performance from minimal to normal to exaggerated expression (Davidson, 1993; Palmer, 1992). Other studies have shown that expert performers are capable of changing the emotional character from tender to aggressive (Askenfelt, 1986) or from sad to happy (Juslin, 1997a), again at will and on demand. There is evidence that such expressive rules are operating even in the song-singing of quite young children. Adachi and Trehub (1998) showed that 4- to 12-year-old children were able to modify their performances of the same song to effectively portray happiness or sadness to a listener.

A third source of evidence that expressive performance is rule based comes from studies in which performers have been asked to imitate the expression they heard in someone else's performance of a piece. Clarke and Baker-Short (1987) showed that musicians could imitate rubato more accurately when the rubato was applied in a context that was consistent with conventional rules for the application of rubato. When the rubato occurred in a nonconventional context, imitation accuracy was reduced. Woody (2003) showed that performers who were able to describe verbally an expressive device they heard in a short musical extract were more likely to be able to reproduce it correctly than those performers who could not describe it. Although this effect was stronger for what Woody calls "nonidiomatic" features (those not typical for the genre), it was also present with idiomatic ones. This suggests that when a performer can encapsulate expressive variations in a verbal description (which will inevitably be a rule-like conceptual abstraction from the actual sound), this variation is more likely to be incorporated into an imitative performance. Woody's study provided several examples of performers who were sure that they had heard an expressive device that was not present, in some cases even going in the opposite direction (e.g., they reported hearing a crescendo when the performance actually decreased in intensity). Another study showed that such difficulties were most pronounced when their own prior performances did not contain the expressive features that they were being asked to imitate (Woody, 2002). It seems as if their own prelearned expressive strategies were "getting in the way" of their hearing what was actually present in the models they were being asked to imitate.

These studies have clear educational implications. They suggest that imitation alone, without explicit conceptualization and verbalization, is likely to be less than optimal in assisting students to expand their expressive repertoires. Teachers who demonstrate what they want and then get the student to engage in discussion and description of what they heard may have greater impact on their students' expressive development than those who simply demonstrate or talk. Similarly, students who try to verbally characterize what they hear may be more effective at incorporating new expressive options into their toolkits than those who just copy without verbalization. Only what you consciously attend to can be effectively learned and transferred to other contexts.

Interpretation

Expression provides the building blocks for an interpretation. An interpretation is a more or less motivated and coherent set of choices about expression applied over an entire piece. Psychological research has rather more to say about the expressive palate than about how this palate is applied to an interpretation. The reason is partly that many interpretational goals will be unique to a specific performer, a specific piece, and a specific time. However, research findings do support at least two quite firm general conclusions about the nature of effective interpretations, namely that (1) interpretations impose patterning and structure that is evident across large-scale structures and (2) they happen on a global, as well as a local, scale.

Langner, Kopiez, Stoffel, and Wilz (2000), for instance, demonstrated the existence of regular and symmetrical structures that underlie dynamic (loudness) variations in expert performances of lengthy classical movements. One such structure is the "arch," which is characterized by a gradual increase in some quality (in this case, loudness) followed by a symmetrical decrease in the same quality. They showed that an important difference between expert and nonexpert performances of the same work was to be found in the degree to which hierarchically organized arches were found to span long musical structures (e.g., entire movements), as well as shorter musical structures (such as phrases). It is relatively easy to impose an arch dynamic on a single phrase of four measures. It requires far more skill to construct and control an arch that spans an entire piece lasting many minutes. Langner et al. (2000) found that expert performers could manage a hierarchy of separate, multiple arches embedded within the same piece. So, for instance, each 8-bar phrase could contain a dynamic arch simultaneously with a 64-bar structure that contains its own "meta-arch," in which the average dynamic of each phrase was also rising and falling in a controlled manner. The arches are hardly conscious and reflect more the deep structural understanding that experts bring to their interpretations. How this understanding is implemented in the performance is not clear to date.

Interpretations involve motivated decisions about expressive tactics at key structural junctions in a piece. Sloboda and Lehmann (2001) asked 10 pianists to prepare a Chopin prelude (No. 4 in E minor) for concert performance and, after the performance, interviewed each pianist about the main expressive decisions made. Every pianist spoke of specific locations in the music where particular expressive outcomes were intended. This was in addition to more global comments about the performance as a whole. Two clear characteristics of these moments were observed. First, expressive intentions generally resulted in objective differences in performance data at these points. These differences could be described either in relation to analogous material in the same performance (e.g., rubato more pronounced in phrase 2 than in phrase 1) or in relation to what other performers generally did at that point (e.g., the performer played more quietly at a point at which most other performers played more loudly). Second, listeners showed enhanced emotional responses to many of these moments, as signaled through relatively sudden rises in the perceived emotional impact of the music. Emotional impact was monitored by having listeners constantly adjust the position of a pointer on a scale while listening to the music.

The expressive events were not spread evenly through a performance. They tended to be clustered near the beginning and end of significant structural units, such as phrases (see Repp, 1992, mentioned earlier). This is strong evidence that intentional expression is particularly important in drawing the listener's attention to "architectural" aspects of a composition and in emphasizing or deemphasizing those structural features that are integral to the performer's conceptualization of the piece. Furthermore, expressive events tended to occur in more ambiguous or less engaging places at which the musical structure itself was not completely absorbing the listener's attention (e.g., the climax of the piece). In essence, performers display their most important artistic decisions in a conspicuous place in order not to waste them.

Key interpretational decisions are made early in the learning history of a particular piece and guide the rehearsal and memorization process. Learning a new piece of repertoire is, for most performers, a lengthy process that can require tens or even hundreds of hours spread over many weeks and months. A prevalent belief among music learners is that technical and interpretative rehearsals are separate processes that can be accomplished in sequence, first one, then the other. Students often talk of "learning the notes" as a process that must be completed, or at least that has significantly progressed, before interpretation is added, as if it were a final coat of paint. Detailed analysis of the actual behavior of expert performers has shown a different story. Experts appear to formulate key interpretational strategies rather early on in the practice period. Many world-class performers steep themselves in the music through listening, studying scores, and reading before they go anywhere near their instruments. Thus they already know much about the music, and how they want it to sound, before detailed rehearsal gets under way.

Chaffin et al. (2002) studied the way in which a professional pianist (Gabriela Imreh) put together a performance of Bach's *Italian Concerto* over a period of a year (see also chapter 4). Although interpretive decisions and detailed implementation of these in specific expressive and technical practice took place over the entire practice period, identification of key interpretive features took place rather early—within the first few hours of rehearsal at the instrument.

This research does not shed light on the reasons that the performer made her specific interpretational decisions. The performer's entire learning history would be needed to explain why she was attracted to this particular piece of music and the sources from which her ideas (either to emulate or deviate from other performers) came. The environments that educators create for advanced performers within the classical tradition are designed to ensure that students will be exposed to an appropriate set of ideas, traditions, and practices from which they can begin to develop their own individual interpretational voices—recognizable as falling within the norms of the tradition in which they are working, but also recognizable as something more than a mere copy of their role models.

One activity that many musicians undertake (and are encouraged to do so by many teachers) is to listen to different commercially available recordings of the same piece. Repp (1990) has demonstrated that such recordings are, indeed, measurably different in ways that have a direct impact on listener perception and judgment. He analyzed the timing patterns in 19 performances of the third movement of Beethoven's Piano Sonata op. 31, no. 3 (Minuet and Trio). Performers were all of the highest international renown (e.g., Claudio Arrau, Alfred Brendel, Emil Gilels, and Glenn Gould). The main performance measure was the inter-onset-interval (IOI), which is the time between the start of one note and the start of the next. A statistical technique called factor analysis was used to correlate the timing pattern of every performance with every other in order to discover independent features by which performances could be distinguished from one another. The factor analysis used only data from the Minuet (not the Trio) and ignored notes faster than quarter notes. Repp (1990) found

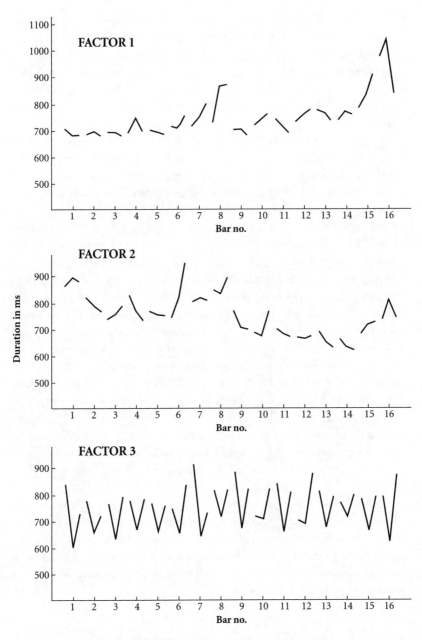

Figure 5.2. Factor timing patterns emerging from the principal-components analysis of 19 performances of a Beethoven minuet. From "Patterns of Expressive Timing in Performances of a Beethoven Minuet by Nineteen Famous Pianists," by B. H. Repp, 1990, *Journal of the Acoustical Society of America, 88*, 622–641. Copyright © 1990. Reprinted by permission of the Acoustical Society of America.

three main factors. Factor 1 represented the tendency to slow down at the ends of major phrases. Pianists differed in their tendency to do this, with Gould, Perahia, and Rubenstein making most use of this factor and Backhaus and Gieseking making little use of it. Factor 2 was characterized by a slow start to the minuet and a strong tendency for the second half to be faster than the first. Backhaus, Gieseking, and Ashkenazy scored highest on this factor, whereas Gould was lowest. Factor 3 represented pianists' use of what Repp describes as a "v-shaped" timing pattern for individual bars, in which the first and third notes are given more time than the second note, which has a significantly shorter duration. Brendel showed this pattern most consistently, whereas Gould and Schnabel showed it least (playing all three notes equally). Figure 5.2 shows the typical timing patterns for each of these factors.

In a second part of the study, Repp (1990) played all these recordings to nine professional pianists who knew this piece well and asked them to rate the performances on 20 bipolar rating scales (e.g., fast-slow, expressive-inexpressive, powerful-weak, serious-playful). Twelve of these scales were used quite consistently by judges, showing that there was the possibility of agreement on some aspects of the performance. Using the judges' ratings, Repp was able to divide the performances into five distinct stylistic groups. The largest group contained those which Repp characterized as "middle of the road," an average performance that represents a generally agreed way of performing this piece. Ten pianists were in this group (Frank, Davidovich, Perahia, Gulda, Bishop, Haskill, Solomon, Brendel, Ashkenazy, and Rubenstein). The other groups were much smaller and seemed to reflect more individual styles. Schnabel and Backhaus were in a group by themselves, as were Arrau, Gilels, and Kempf. The fact that these groups do not neatly reflect the distinctions found in the factor analysis of the performances can be explained as a consequence of concentrating on only one aspect of the performances—timing.

To fully capture the richness of these performances, a considerable number of additional objective analyses would have been required. However, this study offers a clear indication that, in principle, very specific judgments made by experienced listeners can be accounted for by objective expressive features of performances, easily measurable by mechanical means, and amenable to well-understood statistical techniques.

Learning and Improving Expressivity and Interpretation

Observation and Imitation

Because nuance is not fully describable, demonstration is always at the heart of musical skill. This situation is not unique to music. Almost every skill can be better learned by observing and imitating what experts do. Many classically trained musicians, however, have an irrational fear of listening to other people's performances, a fear that such activities will "contaminate" their own authentic interpretation. The data from Woody's (2003) study (described earlier in the chapter) suggest rather the reverse, namely, that a performer's own preferred interpretation may make it difficult to really take on board the differences present in another performance.

This fear of contamination seems very specific to the classical conservatory culture. The wider cross-cultural evidence suggests that masters of all genres generally study other people's performances intensively. In the development of popular and jazz musicians, exact imitation appears to be a universal primary stage in the learning process. Green (2002), in a thorough study of how 14 successful popular musicians developed their professional skills, observed that:

> By far the overriding learning practice for the beginner popular musician is to copy recordings by ear. It seems an extraordinary fact that many thousands of young musicians across the world adopted this approach to learning over a relatively short space of time—covering a maximum of eighty years since sound recording and reproduction technology began to be widespread— outside of any formal networks, usually at early stages of learning, in isolation from each other, without adult guidance, and with very little explicit recognition of the ubiquity of the practice across the world. (pp. 60–61)

Such tactics are obviously deeply "natural" in some sense and provide a bedrock of knowledge that can be gained in no other way. According to the culture, deviation from exact copying comes to predominate at different stages. For example, in Japanese traditional music, apprentice musicians place very high value on being able to exactly copy what their masters do. Only after they have perfected such skills do they earn the right to deviate from the master. In some types of popular music, exact imitation is a valued feature of highly expert performances (see the Cross-Cultural Perspective in chapter 10).

There is no evidence that avoiding the performances of others is a beneficial long-term strategy for a performing musician, and it is certainly not appropriate for someone not yet established as an independent professional. In the course of some recent research on young musicians, one of us was distressed to find that several young performers claimed that they had no time to listen to music and that they weren't particularly interested in doing so. We hope that students and those who teach them will generally reject such self-defeating attitudes and behaviors. Every performing curriculum must leave plenty of space for the developing performer to listen to a wide range of musical styles and performances.

Developing an Explicit Representational System

We have argued that expressive performance depends on the ability of performers to apply expressive rules to what they do. Without such rules, performers would be overwhelmed by the demands of thousands of arbitrary small differences

Cross-Cultural Perspective:
Self-Denial in Popular Music

Unlike classical performance, in which the aim is generally to spotlight the individuality and autonomy of the performer (or conductor) as interpreter, popular musicians very often try to be self-effacing. Green (2002, see pp. 49–53) documents two examples of this. One is the "cover" performance, an extreme example being the "tribute band," which, according to Green, often "aims for a precise replication of the original act, including not only every note of the music, but also the clothes, hair-styles and stage performances of the band they copy" (p. 49). The whole aim is to be indistinguishable from the original. Artistic success here requires the complete absence of any original artistic contribution of the performers. Their artistry is precisely in managing an exact imitation, good enough to deceive fans of the original band.

This is linked to a wider philosophy that underlies the way that many popular musicians approach their work. Session musicians "tend to have an attitude rather reminiscent of the pre-nineteenth-century position of the musician as a servant" (p. 50), One performer interviewed by Green said:

> I've always tried to be mindful of the fact that if someone hires me, because that's what we are, as freelance people we are allowing ourselves to be, we hire ourselves out to do a particular job of work. . . . When I get a job from somebody, I want to find out exactly what they want from me: not what I want from them, not what I want, not how I can do my thing in this—I think that's where some musicians go wrong is, you know, using a situation as a vehicle to do your own thing, when you are really serving, you are a servant of the person you are working for . . . (p. 47)

There are, of course, many situations in popular music in which originality and artistic creativity are valued and sought; these examples help to highlight how each genre and each performing tradition must be understood in its own cultural context. That can explain why some of the celebrated examples of "classical master meets pop/jazz master" or other "crossover" projects can sound somewhat awkward, for example, the famous collaboration of classical violinist Yehudi Menuhin with jazz violinist Stefan Grapelli in the 1960s or opera singers performing pop tunes. Regardless, there is certainly some artistic (and often economical?) benefit in trying to bridge musical barriers.

between performed characteristics of the notes they play. However, performers are not always consciously aware of the operation of such rules. Once performance rules are mastered procedurally, they become automatic and apparently spontaneous. At the beginning of learning, every action is accompanied by laborious conscious effort. Later, the details of individual actions recede, and the person is free to concentrate on higher-level aspects (see Sloboda, 1985b, for a more detailed account of the psychology of skill learning). In the case of musical expression, the experience of such automaticity can mislead the performer into believing that expression is truly intuitive and "best not attended to." It is certainly true that excessive conscious attention to an automated skill can sometimes disrupt a smooth flow and that an individual performance is best guaranteed precisely when one is able to leave many of the details to overlearned and automatic routines (see also chapter 4). However, this does not mean that the process of arriving at a secure interpretation should be similarly intuitive and unreflective. Sometimes habits acquired in one musical context (as appropriate to a particular genre or performing tradition) may need examining, adapting, or possibly even unlearning in a different context. For this reason, we believe that musical performers are best served by developing a rich and explicit set of concepts, ideas, techniques, and verbalizations for reviewing and developing interpretations.

We have already seen that students who are able to describe the expressive devices they hear are better able to reproduce them. Interaction with other musicians makes it much more likely that one will be forced to make explicit what is behind one's expressive and interpretative impulses. In a chamber group or another kind of ensemble, it is completely natural for questions to be asked, such as "What exactly are you doing in bar 50?" or "Why are you playing it like that?" We believe that this is the reason many educational programs require all students to join chamber groups in addition to developing their solo or orchestral performances. Teaching is another important means of encouraging a performer to make explicit (to pupils) what he or she is doing expressively and why. It is commonly observed that a good way of learning something is to teach it.

Performers may also need explicit conceptual systems because the expressive rules that become automated tend to be those that operate over short spans (of a few notes). The architectural and structural considerations required to hold an entire complex piece together are very unlikely to be of a kind that can be learned and operated on in a spontaneous or automatic fashion. For large-scale planning of expression and interpretation, something very much like a "story line" is needed (see Chaffin et al., 2002). The content of such a story line can take many forms. One device used by many performers is an actual story—they try to imagine a series of actions or situations to which the music would be an appropriate accompaniment. This could involve very specific imagery (of particular times, places, and people) or more vague imagery (of moods, atmospheres, feelings). Other devices involve conceptualizing parts of the music as shapes, arches, and other types of abstract structure, static, or motional. These devices can be very individual, both to the performer and the piece. What seems to matter most is that they provide a rich and multidimensional means of "knowing where you are and what is happening in the music" at any point (see chapters 4 and 6).

It is the common experience of many developing musicians that their attention is not appropriately focused during either performance or listening. They do not have a clear means of retaining a mental grip on the structure as a whole, so they concentrate either on the present moment (with the consequent shutting out of any significant awareness of how the present moment relates to past and future events) or let their minds wander away from the music altogether. Both of these tactics are unhelpful to expressive development. Attempts to provide training to performers that enhances their repertoires of explicit representations have wrought noticeable gains in expressive competence in the recipients of such training, when compared with control participants who did not receive the training (e.g., Sloboda, Gayford, & Minassian, 2003).

Obtaining Appropriate Feedback

In public performance, rather few opportunities exist for performers to obtain detailed feedback from audiences concerning the reception of their expressive intentions. Applause, enthusiastic or otherwise, is not very specific. It doesn't tell a performer whether the audience was able to hear that carefully planned transition from tension to calm in the second movement. For reasons we have already suggested, performers may not be in the best position to evaluate their own performances. They may hear what they want to hear, rather than what is really there. In other cases, they may introduce intended expression with insufficient magnitude so that listeners are unable to pick it up. One of the frequent observations made by teachers is that their students intend an expressive gesture, which they believe they have executed, but that the gesture is simply too small to be clearly detectable by a listener. Finally, it is quite difficult to set clear criteria for success, and a musician may be unable to assess a performance validly or reliably because little or no agreement exists about what constitutes a "good" performance (beyond the obvious criterion of being able to play the correct notes). Contrast this with competitive sports (such as tennis) or competitive games (such as chess). Performers get immediate and objective feedback—they either win or lose—and can work to increase the proportion of times they win.

Performance development thus depends crucially on the enhanced feedback provided to musicians by other professionals involved in their training and development (see chapter 10). Some feedback is provided by formal assessments (juries, examinations, etc.), although we should note in passing that some of the research on jury reliability does not inspire confidence (see chapter 11). Interpretational and aesthetic judgments are often unreliable, even when they are made by experts.

For these reasons, some researchers have been investigating means of more objectively enhancing the feedback available to performers (see Juslin, Friberg, Schoonderwaldt, & Karlsson, 2004). Such feedback, at its best, can be frequent, consistent, specific, and accurate, as has been demonstrated in the sports psychology literature (Singer, Hausenblas, & Janelle, 2001). By analyzing performance features with the aid of a computer, Juslin and Laukka (2000) were able to isolate the specific variations that effectively communicated individual basic emotions, such as happiness, sadness, or anger. In a situation in which the explicit performance goal is to communicate one of these emotions, it is possible to evaluate success in terms of the presence or absence of key features in the performance but also in terms of the communicative effectiveness of the performance, as measured by the proportion of listeners who reliably identified the intended emotion. Juslin and Laukka (2000) were able to show performers precisely what features of their performances were unhelpful or misleading, and they provided them with the opportunity to adjust their performances until they were reliably recognized as representing the desired emotion. Although this is a welcome demonstration that targeted feedback can enhance expressive performance, it is somewhat difficult to conceptually or practically extend such augmented feedback to more complex emotional messages or longer works.

Finally, a word of caution is needed about the social relativity of judgments of performance quality. Even within a coherent culture or tradition, people prioritize different things. The things that are most important for baroque performance are different from those that matter most in late Romantic music. Acquiring the specific rules of a new genre takes time, and acquiring the capacity to make appropriate judgments takes as much time. Conventional wisdom about a genre does not stay still, either. The way that Beethoven is played today in the West reflects a whole set of developments in historical research, modern performance practice, and conceptions of authenticity. The Beethoven performances of 50 years ago sound distinctly odd to the Beethoven proponent of today. When deciding how much weight to place on a particular judgment, it is always necessary to try to understand as much as possible about the social and cultural background and assumptions from which that judgment is being made. Only if these assumptions are consistent with those on which you and others you relate to are premising your activities will there be a good chance that following the specific advice will lead to beneficial outcomes all around.

Study Questions

1. What do you consider to be the strongest evidence that expressive performance is rule-governed? Evaluate the claims that a performance can be both rule-governed and creative at the same time.

2. What does research tell us about the role of conscious deliberate planning and verbal discussion and description in the construction of a musically convincing performance?
3. Can research tell us anything about the best ways to improve our expressive abilities?

Further Reading

The following are good and fairly comprehensive reviews of the literature on expressive performance.

Juslin, P. N., Friberg, A., & Bresin, R. (2002). Toward a computational model of expression in music performance: The GERM model. *Musicae Scientiae, Special Issue 2001–2002,* 63–122.

Parncutt, R., & McPherson, G. E. (Eds.). (2001). *The Science and Psychology of Music Performance: Creative strategies for teaching and learning.* See chapter 13, on structural communication, and chapter 14, on emotional communication.

Deutsch, D. (Ed.) (1999). *The Psychology of Music.* See chapter 14, on performance.

Kopiez, R. (2002). Making music and making sense through music. In R. Colwell & C. Richardson (Eds.), *The New Handbook of Research on Music Teaching and Learning* (pp. 522–541). Coding and decoding of musical expression, includes the sides of listener and performer.

6

Reading or Listening and Remembering

In this chapter, we discuss sight-reading, playing by ear, and recalling of memorized performance, because all three skills rely on our ability to store and retrieve information from memory, albeit in different ways. In classical music learning, reading music plays a role for sight-reading and provides a basis for acquiring new repertoire that will be performed from memory later. In jazz or popular music genres, as well as in most non-Western cultures, music is often handed down in oral traditions that by definition rely exclusively on memory.

Playing by ear and sight-reading both occur in the learning of a piece, whereas performance from memory follows later. Compared with sight-reading, playing from memory conjures for the listener the illusion that the performer owns the piece. Yet the demands with regard to perfection differ in many respects. When sight-reading, the musician can get away with some mistakes and a rather sketchy interpretation, whereas a memorized performance usually is note-perfect and conveys a unique interpretation. In sight-reading, which often takes place in the context of accompanying, the specific preparation for the performance is minimal, if not absent. Thus sight-reading happens "online," a fact that the performer has to cope with by using appropriate strategies. In contrast, memorized performances are extensively rehearsed "offline," allowing the performer more leisure to optimize the performance.

In Western music history, notation emerged with the advent of polyphony and the need for different singers or musicians to coordinate (see Sadie, 2001, "Notation"). Useful graphical representations of music have existed since antiquity and functioned as more or less precise memory cues. A common example may be tabulatures, that is, graphical notation that captures movements or hand positions and that were used for lute, guitar, or Chinese zither music. Our current music notation developed in the sixteenth century and was also used to

Table 6.1 Comparing sight-reading and playing by ear with recall of memorized performance

Unfamiliar music (SR: sight-reading; EP: playing by ear)	Familiar music (recall of memorized performance)
SR: Translate notation into performance in real time EP: Translate sounds and movements into performance	Retrieve music and motor programs from memory
SR: Produce expression on the spot, therefore less artistic EP: Copy expression, maybe modify later	Rely on carefully planned artistic interpretation
SR: Guess and infer EP: Trial and error	Everything is known in advance
SR: Continuous visual monitoring not always possible EP: Continuous visual monitoring possible	Instrument can be continuously monitored visually
Tends to be more flexible	Tends to be less flexible
Tends to be slower (initially)	Tends to be faster
Tends to be less accurate	Tends to be highly accurate

capture music for the purpose of codification and dissemination. For this it had to be very precise. Not all cultures or even all forms of Western music rely on notation to facilitate musical learning. Although Indian art music also possesses a notation, musical learning generally happens by oral transmission. Notation may be known but used only for scholarly purposes or to instruct nonmusicians about music. In jazz (and even more so in rock music), standard songs and their chord progressions (changes) are captured in lead sheets, but their execution is largely based on aural models—which often consist of recordings. In sum, music notation emerged under historical and cultural circumstances, in Europe or elsewhere, and is not part of all musical cultures. How heavily a musical community relies on it depends again on cultural factors (e.g., difficulty and stability of repertoire, philosophy, importance of literacy).

In the absence of external memory aids, such as notation or recording, musical memory becomes the only way to preserve a cultural heritage. When the performer is also the composer—for example, Beethoven performing his own works—memory is not an issue. Similarly, when an American Indian receives a song in the course of a vision quest, he presumably remembers the song well after a brief rehearsal. Some Far Eastern ensembles play from memory, whereas orchestral musicians in the Western tradition play from notation.

Throughout history, Western music saw a separation of the roles of performer and composer, along with tightening demands on faithfulness of the reproduction. With the availability of reference recordings today, everybody can know how a particular work is supposed to sound and will judge a performance based partially on its faithfulness to the score. A hundred years ago, soloists freely "improved" the works of others (some still do so today). Whereas memorized performance is expected of some instrumentalists but not of others, opera singers have always memorized their parts (see Aiello & Williamon, 2002). Franz Liszt and Clara Schumann were among the first virtuosi to amaze their audiences by playing from memory, and memorized performance is still favored by the audience (Williamon, 1999; see also chapter 9, this volume).

Outstanding memorization as well as playing by ear and sight-reading skills are often reported in the biographies of prodigies (e.g., Wolfgang Mozart, Felix Mendelssohn, Franz Liszt). Memorizing skills seem to signal to the outside world how attuned the child is to music. Equally admirable is an autistic child with exceptional musical skills (a so-called musical savant) who plays back a piece of music after only a few hearings. Sight-reading serves as proof that a young person is not simply a trained monkey performing one song by rote but has conceptually mastered the music system. We can imagine testing improvisatory skills for the same reason (e.g., Bach's visit to the court of Frederick II in 1747 and subsequent composition of the *Musical Offering*). Thus in our musical culture, (early) display of those skills is considered a sign of musical ability (see chapter 2). Often, several of these abilities occur at the same time. In fact, research shows that they are interrelated (McPherson, 1995; see chapter 1, this volume) and that, contrary to some musicians' subjective impression, better sight readers also tend to be better memorizers and better improvisers.

In this chapter:

1. We show that, although symbolic representations (music notation) are prevalent in our culture, some educators consider learning music by ear first to be a more natural way of learning music.
2. We introduce the notion that experts have acquired a privileged access to their long-term memory and that this is a crucial feature underlying sight-reading, ear playing, and memorized performance (recall).
3. We argue that reading is a reconstructive process that depends on previous knowledge and on the nature of the stimulus and that in this it parallels memorized performance.
4. We point out that sight-reading and memory skills can be improved through training.

Musical Symbol Systems

Symbol systems are an important part of our culture. Humans are intelligent because they can successfully invent and use symbol systems. We use one system—numbers—when counting and measuring, and we use another one—words—when speaking or reading. Obviously, music notation is also a symbol system that we acquire and use in music.

That symbolic representations change the way we think is exemplified in children's acquisition of notation (see figure 6.1). When young children were asked to notate a song so that another child might be able to play the song (Upitis, 1987), younger children resorted to drawing iconic representations in the form of scribbles, a hand, a drum, and so forth. Another kind of representation, called figural representation, is based on the perceptual closeness and number of events. A notation that preserves the number of events and ratios of durations is called metric representation, and only children familiar with music notation employed it. Apparently, knowing how to read music notation does not mean that we can use it to encode. Researchers asked a group of 12- to 18-year-olds to sing and notate the song "Happy Birthday" (see Davidson & Scripp, 1992). Among the participants were students who were entering the conservatory and who could perform the most difficult pieces on their instruments. Suffice it to say that the notations were rather deficient.

Most children do not learn to speak their native languages (mother tongue) by learning to read but by listening to the language spoken by significant others. As Sloboda (1978) puts it: "[N]o-one would consider teaching a normal child to read while he was at a very early stage of learning spoken language. Yet it seems the norm to start children off on reading at the very first instrumental

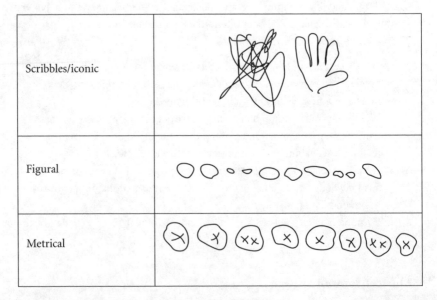

Figure 6.1. Different representations of rhythms (see text for details). From "Children's Understanding of Rhythm," by R. Upitis, 1987, *Psychomusicology*, 7, p. 50. Copyright © 1987 by *Psychomusicology*. Adapted with permission.

lesson without establishing the level of musical awareness already present" (p. 15). This is precisely why some music educators, notably among them Shinichi Suzuki in the second half of the twentieth century, have developed methods to teach children music without the initial help of music notation (similarly Mainwaring in the 1940s; see McPherson & Gabrielsson, 2002). Evidence is slowly emerging that it is preferable and more natural to move from "sound to symbol," from doing or participating to reading and writing (McPherson & Gabrielsson, 2002; Rogoff, 2003). We therefore agree with McPherson and Gabrielsson (2002, p. 113), who advocate a more integrated approach "where performing music by ear serves as preparation for literacy development in the beginning stages of musical involvement, and where performing with and without notation is encouraged during all subsequent levels of development." It encourages novices to rely on and train their internal musical representations instead of merely cueing motor programs through visual input.

The Core Mechanism of Sight-Reading and Memorization

We leave out the basic perceptual processes involved in viewing black dots on the page and recognizing them as music notation or in listening to sounds and recognizing them as music. Such processes are the same as those involved in recognizing all other surrounding visual or auditory information. They are commonly referred to as visual or auditory perception and dealt with in textbooks on perception and sensation. Instead, we enter the stage at a later point in the processing hierarchy, namely, when the musician has recognized the visual input as notation or the auditory input as a rhythm or melody and is supposed to make sense out of it and act on it.

An important psychological concept for our discussion is called "chunking" and has to do with how humans process information. Rather than processing information bit by bit, humans tend to search for patterns that allow them to process several units of information at the same time. For this, perceptual input is grouped into meaningful units (chunks). Look at the following array of letters and try to remember them: "g-s-n-i-i-g-d-h-a-t-e-r." Presumably they appear to you as a random string of letters, difficult to remember. You possibly saw the word "hater," which could facilitate later recall. Obviously, if the same 12 letters were presented to you in a different order, say "s-i-g-h-t-r-e-a-d-i-n-g," grouping and later recall would pose no problem. Similarly, it would be quite difficult to remember the individual notes "c-d-e-c-c-d-e-c-e-f-g-e-f-g" (the first two bars of "Frère Jacques"), or the sequence d-f-a-c (a D-minor 7 chord) if they did not "mean" something to us. Our knowledge, speech, and movements are organized in chunks. If you divide up a piece of music into smaller units during practice, for example of several measures each, this is not chunking as psychologists understand it. Chunks are

---

Self Study: Musical Structure and Cognition

First, get some staff paper and read the following instructions. In this exercise, you will briefly see two musical examples that you will try to notate from memory on your staff paper.

Look at Example A, page 125, for only 2 seconds, then cover it quickly and start to write. Do the same with Example B, page 126. Follow the instructions in the paragraph below once you are done.

Now count the number of correct pitches by comparing your notation with the original. You probably noticed that one example was much easier to remember and transcribe than the other, because it was more conducive to chunking. In the first example (A), your mind most likely grouped the triad and the short run but was less able to chunk the notes of the second example (B) in a similarly meaningful way. Experts have extensive knowledge and can find meaningful units in almost every note sequence. However, when their system of attributing meaning is challenged (e.g., with completely atonal music), their ability to memorize fails, too.

---

smaller meaningful units, and a musical section is likely to contain several chunks (see the self-exercise).

The size of chunks is variable and depends on the level of expertise, as experiments with chess players have shown (Simon & Chase, 1973). In these experiments the size of chunks could be judged by the number of pieces that experts recalled without pauses, suggesting that each burst of recall represented a chunk of jointly stored information. Better chess players differed from lesser players primarily in the larger number of pieces that belonged to a chunk. Later on, we discuss in more detail a similar finding from sight-reading research, namely, that better sight readers recall longer sequences of notes than less skilled sight readers after brief exposure.

The ability to group and make sense out of information depends on previous knowledge, be it procedural (knowing how) or declarative (knowing what). For example, to understand the preceding example of "sight-reading," we have to know English; the equivalent German word (*Vomblattspiel*) would not mean anything here regardless of the order of letters. Somewhat similar to the grammar of a spoken language, musical meaning is also enabled by the regular and predictive structure of music. The sequence and probability of certain events help us establish meaning—for instance, that a dominant-seventh chord resolves in the tonic, that most melodies are four to eight bars long, or that certain tactile patterns on the keyboard form chords. Chunking is in essence a memory mechanism that links our perception to previously stored knowledge.

Based on thousands of experiments, psychologists have developed sophisticated models of how information is perceived, processed, and stored. A common model of memory assumes three distinct stages (see any introductory psychology textbook). The first stage is assumed to be a sensory short-term memory that lasts only fractions of a second. If the information is unattended at this stage, it is lost forever. Scientists agree that deployment of attention is tantamount to learning (and recalling). Conversely, the information that is selected enters short-term memory (STM), where it can reside for varying amounts of time. STM contains currently relevant information for further processing and manipulating. If its content is meaningfully rehearsed and actively grouped, it can be transferred to long-term-memory (LTM). As the name suggests, information in LTM can be retrieved even after a very long time. An extension of the STM idea is the *working memory concept* (Baddeley, 1986), which views working memory as a sort of workbench on which items are held and operated on. We can compare this type of memory to the random access memory in computers that loses its content when the computer is turned off.

A real challenge for any theory of memory are the achievements of experts, including musical experts, who can recall large amounts of material, even incidentally or after being interrupted while working. To explain the data, Ericsson and Chase (1982) developed the concept of *skilled* or *expert memory* (lately elaborated as the *long-term working-memory theory* by Ericsson & Kintsch, 1995). Skilled memory theory states that experts develop a privileged access to information stored in LTM by using so-called retrieval structures that reside in STM. Think of it as pointers from STM to relevant knowledge in LTM. These retrieval structures are very much shaped to suit the task that experts habitually engage in. For example, a track athlete who was investigated in a now famous experiment was able to recall two-, three-, and four-digit random numbers by recoding them into running times. All those times were then arranged in a tree structure with lower and higher level nodes (Ericsson & Chase, 1982). We could speculate that someone who plays popular music by ear would have generic slots to store melodic lines with their corresponding chord changes using a schematic outline of the structure with 4-bar or 8-bar phrases.

Interestingly, the superiority of the memory skills has been found to be domain-specific, meaning that unfamiliar material or structurally incoherent material is less memorable. A math whiz might be able to recall and compute multiple-digit numbers but still forget where he put his keys or important papers. We know from our own experience that memorizing or sight-reading unconventional (e.g., nontonal) material can be extremely frustrating because memory skills are so specific. This effect is due to the breakdown of our chunking mechanisms, and instead of coding larger meaningful units (tonal melodies and harmonies), we have to group individual notes or intervals. This was shown for musical memory by asking expert musicians and nonmusicians (novices) to memorize notated melodies that were either tonally and harmonically traditional

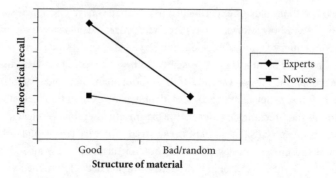

Figure 6.2. Schematic representation of the skill-by-structure effect on memory.

or rather random (Halpern & Bower, 1982; see figure 6.2). The authors found that experts did better on the whole but that they performed only as well as non-experts on the random melodies. This differential skill-by-structure effect has been shown in other domains of expertise as well.

Coping with Performance Demands

Having mentioned the important memory mechanisms that enable us to store and recall material, we now discuss how sight-reading and memorizing work in real life and how this functioning corresponds to demands imposed on the performers (see Aiello & Williamon, 2002; Chaffin et al., 2002; and Ginsborg, 2004, for reviews on memory; Lehmann & McArthur, 2002; Sloboda, 1985b, chapter 3.2; and Thompson & Lehmann, 2004, for reviews on sight-reading). Stated simply, the goal of expert performance is to circumvent limitations of the human information-processing system (see also chapter 4). Whether this is done by intelligent anticipation, a hallmark of expert performance in all domains, and problem solving or by creating long-term working memory structures will depend on the specifics of the task at hand.

Sight-Reading

To value sight-reading and the cognitive tasks associated with it, we have to understand how the eye works. When we look at music notation, or any object for that matter, it seems perfectly static and part of a larger, coherent picture. Yet it surprises most people to learn that our eye does not work like a snapshot camera in which the entire picture is captured simultaneously; rather, it focuses on one small area at a time. It operates like a camera that has zoomed in on a small detail, and in order to get the entire picture, it takes many successive snapshots.

At normal reading distance from a book (30 cm), the area in focus may be about two words (10 letters) long. This focal point of our vision cannot be enlarged by training. It is only possible for expert readers to make more sense out of partially perceived information in the periphery of this area. To view a larger scene, our eye has to jump from one point to the next about three to six times per second, while the brain constructs an image that we experience as a coherent whole. These small jumps are called *saccades*, and their sequence is neither random nor fixed but rather depends on (1) where in the visual field things are happening, (2) where we expect things to happen, and (3) what information we are trying to extract. Our expectations, as well as the nature of the stimulus, both determine where the next saccade will go. The pauses in between these movements are called *fixations*, and this is the only time that our visual system can actually gather information. By recording fixations and saccades with so-called eye-tracker equipment and later plotting the locations of the glances, we can study how people deploy attention when recognizing faces, pondering a chessboard, or reading (Goolsby, 1994; Kinsler & Carpenter, 1995; Rayner & Pollatsek, 1989).

The results obtained from registering a musician's eye movements while he or she is sight-reading vary greatly depending on the study and methodology used, but there are some general findings. Sight-reading (or sight-singing) musicians are looking forward and backward from a midway point where they are currently gathering information. Put differently, they are looking ahead, as well as back to the point of execution, because the eye is always a little ahead of the hands (or voice). The musical structure influences how music may be scanned by the reader (Weaver, 1973, cited in Sloboda, 1985b). For example, it was found that eye movements for homophonic music often followed vertical patterns such as chords, whereas polyphonic music with its horizontal structure invoked zigzagging horizontal scans. Also, fixations became longer as the material became more difficult.

The exact locations of eye fixations are dependent on the sight reader's experience (Goolsby, 1994). Goolsby studied the eye movements of musicians (skilled and less skilled sight readers) while they were sight-singing unfamiliar music. More skilled readers peeked around, searching for information, backtracking to places they did not identify at first, whereas less skilled musicians looked at every consecutive note (and still made mistakes). Unlike the less skilled musicians, the skilled ones also scanned expressive/dynamic markings.

That the eyes are not simply moving about but actively extracting information can also be shown by covering up the score unexpectedly while a person is playing and asking her to play from memory whatever she can still remember. The distance between the current point of performance and the farthest point ahead where the eye is looking is called perceptual span; the distance between the current point of performance and the last note played when the score is covered unexpectedly is called the eye-hand span (or more generally an eye-performance span). Sloboda (1974, cited in Sloboda, 1985b) found that better sight readers had larger eye-hand spans (roughly seven notes) than poorer readers (roughly four notes). The existence of those spans and the fact that superior performers generally had larger spans suggest that information is being stored in more or larger chunks. Note that the number of eye movements or fixations is not equal to the number of chunks in the sense that each eye fixation brings in one chunk of information. Rather, a chunk is constructed internally in response to information that may be gathered with several fixations. Being able to construct larger chunks faster during time-critical activities has the advantage that the performer gains time for translating the visual input into motor programs.

Not only the eye movements but also the entire eye-hand span adapts to the musical structure, again pointing to the intricate interplay between expectation, knowledge, and performance. And we can safely say that the musician is not aware of, nor can he or she consciously influence, the shrinking and expanding of the span described in the following. Sloboda (1974, cited in Sloboda 1985b) presented pianists with short music examples using a slide projector. The participants sight-read the music until, at a point unknown to them, the projector was turned off. The pianists continued to play whatever they could recall from the score. As mentioned, the better sight readers remembered more, but astonishingly, the eye-hand span often corresponded with the distance from the current point of performance (when the projector was turned off) to the next phrase boundary. For example, when the phrase boundary was much farther away (say 12 notes) than the average eye-hand span, the pianists played only as many intermediate notes as their individual eye-hand span would allow for. However, when the phrase boundary was at a reachable distance (say 6 notes), even those participants whose average range of eye-hand span was only three to four notes reached the boundary. Conversely, readers with a larger modal eye-hand span might also get no farther than this phrase boundary, displaying a shorter than typical span. A similar phenomenon of shrinking and expanding spans had been previously observed for the eye-voice span in reading (cf. Rayner & Pollatsek, 1989).

Pieces of music are not random arrangements of notes but rather coherent entities that we identify as being in a certain style or by a certain composer and containing a fair amount of redundancy (e.g., recurrence of thematic material). This fact allows us to build up certain expectations about upcoming sections, which cuts down on the amount of information we have to process at one time and helps us direct our attention to the relevant places in the score. For example, if we see the start of a scale, we will not hunt around for notes anywhere on the staff but rather in close proximity to the previous note, most likely on the same diagonal. This is where experts can take advantage of blurry information in peripheral areas of the fovea as a basis for inferences or guesses.

General reading research shows that text readers do not actually read all the words or letters but omit short and common words such as *a* and *the*; they also focus more on word boundaries than on the center of words (Rayner & Pollatsek, 1989). This has also been shown in music. Sloboda (1976, cited in Sloboda, 1985b) conducted a sight-reading experiment with pianists in which errors were introduced in excerpts of classical music. The original scores were modified by moving a note up or down a whole step, resulting in a violation of traditional rules of harmony, and pianists were asked to play the music *as written*. Altered notes were played as written most often in the right hand and at the beginning of a phrase, somewhat less correctly at the end, and most poorly in the middle. Otherwise, pianists inadvertently "corrected" some of the altered notes to what they apparently thought should have been notated. The number of falsely corrected notes even increased when the pianists played the piece a second time, suggesting that their expectations of harmonic context had strengthened.

In Sloboda's 1976 experiment, the musicians' inferences were tested using performance errors, whereas another experiment addressed voluntary guesses (Lehmann & Ericsson, 1996). First, sight-reading pianists were asked to accompany a prerecorded solo track. On the second attempt they saw the same score, but some notes had been omitted and had to be filled in from memory. A similar procedure was repeated with a different score in which notes were omitted already at the first trial. Better sight readers recalled significantly more correct notes in the first task and inferred (improvised) more appropriate notes in the second task, although they had not even seen the original. These results clearly indicate the reconstructive (i.e., "make it up as you go along") process that underlies sight-reading. But how does this reconstructive process work?

To be able to infer, the sight reader has to rely on pattern recognition. Assuming a fast access to long-term memory, as we explained earlier, the skilled reader will identify patterns and swiftly respond. When musicians were asked to compare pairs of presented note patterns by judging their sameness, significant reaction-time differences were observed between groups that varied in sight-reading skill (Waters, Underwood, & Findlay, 1997). Not only were skilled sight readers faster compared with less skilled sight readers, but they were also more sensitive to disturbances from randomizations of tonal and rhythmic parameters. This handicapping effect of expertise underscores how strongly experts rely on the patterned nature of the stimulus. Also, experts used fewer fixations to compare the two stimuli and needed less time to decide. Here, we can also suspect that experts constructed larger chunks.

This all suggests that a sight reader is not merely engaged in a mechanical process of translating visual input automatically into motor programs (see chapter 4, section on automaticity). Rather, skilled readers reconstruct in their heads what the music should sound like based on the perceptual information, no matter how scarce it may be due to the time constraints. In the process, expectations and knowledge are integrated. What eventually feels for the performer like "intuition" and allows for quick and accurate guessing is really access to knowledge of style, performance practice, and music theory.

Memorization and Playing by Ear

Much of what we have said so far about chunking and the reconstructive nature of human problem solving has to do with memory skills. Musical recall requires the reconstruction of sounding objects for motor production (singing, playing, and writing). We can assume that if something has not been encoded correctly in the first place, reproduction will be impossible (such as an incorrectly *remembered* phone number). But even if a correct internal representation exists, false execution may still be possible (such as a wrongly *dialed* phone number).

Musical memory comes in two variations: one that happens more incidentally as a by-product of practice and one that requires great deliberation and effort to establish (see figure 6.3). When a musician repeatedly plays a piece of music, interconnected sequential chunks are created (this is called forward chaining). In this case, each chunk functions as a cue to the next; thus playing one chunk will trigger the next (see figure 6.3, top). This is the way that our "muscle memory" (kinesthetic or rote memory) works. Unfortunately, when the connection between two chunks breaks down (e.g., due to anxiety), the following chunk cannot be retrieved anymore. Novice performers, when performing from memory, sometimes encounter the problem that their hands miraculously know how the music continues, but their heads do not. Even restarting the piece from the beginning may not help to overcome a sudden memory lapse. Therefore, relying on this type of rote memorized performance alone is unsuitable for a serious stage performer (Aiello & Williamon, 2002; Chaffin et al., 2002).

Instead, experienced performers go a different route. These musicians learn to establish a clear mental image of the piece that is rather independent of—but may include—tactile cues. Memorization strategies include writing down parts of the piece, analyzing it away from the instrument, starting in different places, or singing one voice while playing another (for pianists). This work leads to storage of meaningful units (chunks) in a way that we can metaphorically picture as a tree-like structure in our heads. Chaffin et al. (2002) studied a professional pianist learning the Presto movement from J. S. Bach's *Italian Concerto*. The authors recorded all the practice on video. Although initially some automatic memorization took place as a by-product of practicing the interpretive and technical aspects of the piece, the pianist deliberately learned the piece a second time by establishing so-called performance cues, places in the score that will be attended to during performance. Such cues can be of an expressive (e.g., "this is the sunrise part"), interpretive (e.g., "make sure the crescendo yields to a sudden pp"), or technical (e.g., "watch that jump now") nature. The performer creates a sequence of those cues that lead him through the piece. Those cues are nested within a hierarchical structure that contains structural information about the parts of the piece (see figure 6.3, bottom). At will, a performer can change vantage points during a performance and move from overall artistic goals

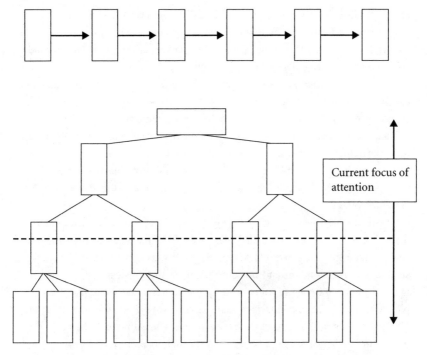

Figure 6.3. Top, schematic drawing of a forward chained representation of a piece of music. Individual elements could be movement sequences that cue each other. Bottom, schematic drawing of a hierarchical memory structure with detailed information at the bottom and higher order nodes that could represent phrases, sections, and performance cues. The current focus of attention is variable.

(at higher levels of the tree) to detail-oriented attention at the keystroke level (at the bottom of the tree; cf. Chaffin et al., 2002, chapters 4 and 9). The advantage of performance cues over a simple forward-chained performance is that the performer can jump from one point in the piece at will to the next meaningful point in case of a problem—provided that this moving around was also practiced. Another piece of evidence for the importance of those performance cues is that music at or near those cues can be more accurately recalled than other places in the piece, even years after initial memorization (Chaffin et al., 2002).

Serious musicians and master teachers have always tried to give advice about how to commit music to memory, considering musical meaning and instrumental demands alike. Teachers generally advocate a multiple coding system in which ergonomic considerations, such as hand positions, visual and tactile patterns, musical analysis, and metaphorical associations work together to build a rich mental representation of the piece (e.g., Gieseking & Leimer, 1932/1972). Singers are advised to memorize music and words together, giving them two possible entry points for retrieval (Ginsborg, 2004). Eventually, consecutive chunks and sections are interconnected on different levels, and when one level fails during performance, another one can take its place. This does not preclude the artist's allowing the automatic pilot to take over (or run in the background), but the performer can always take over command.

In a study in which pianists were asked to memorize a short piece, Lehmann and Ericsson (1997a) found that those participants who tried to memorize note by note were slower in committing the piece to memory than those who conceptualized the piece in terms of its harmonic and melodic structure. In a later task, participants were asked to alter their performances by transposing the piece or by playing hands separately. Again, the faster memorizers could adapt their performances better to the new demands than could the slower note-by-note memorizers.

When playing pieces from memory, we do not simply turn on an internal recording, but we truly "re-create" the piece. This has been demonstrated by analyzing performance errors. If a tape recorder were turned on, such mistakes should be rather random and not dependent on the musical context. Instead, musical memory is highly influenced by the context, and when playing polyphonic music, voices can interfere in systematic ways (Palmer & van de Sande, 1995; see chapter 8, this volume, section titled "The Situation"). Moreover, although the audience tends to believe that musicians perform flawlessly, MIDI recordings of several performing concert pianists showed that performance errors did occur quite often (Repp, 1996). Those errors, however, were well hidden in inner voices or involved plausible alternate notes (e.g., "E" instead of "C" in a C major chord).

Although some memory is created by first reading notation, other memory is based on auditory presentation. Remembering things from a few repeated hearings (i.e., through oral tradition, ear playing) usually imposes different demands on the degree of verbatim reproducibility. Research on Yugoslavian epic singers (Lord, Mitchell, & Nagy, 2000) clearly showed that these performers did not recall the same word every time but that they used formulas that allowed them to generate very similar epics over and over again (see the Cross-Cultural Perspective feature). The same is true for stage actors. When the singer or actor knows why a character is acting a certain way, in what setting, and in what mood, this is enough to generate an appropriate line. Whether a greeting is uttered using the expression "Hi," "Hi, there," or "Hello" is not critical, as long as the friendly tone is maintained. However, contrary to common conceptions, extensive verbatim memorization can also occur, and it is impressively documented for gamelan (Bali) and steelband (Trinidad) ensembles (Bakan, 1994; Helmlinger, 2005).

Outstanding playing by ear is a feat displayed by some musical savants and blind musicians. Musical savants, that is, persons with deficits in some areas of mental functioning who often possess extremely well-developed memory skills, also rely on the grammar and redundancy of music (Miller, 1989).

Cross-Cultural Perspective: Yugoslavian Epic Singers

Yugoslavian oral epic singers can narrate epics of up to many thousands of lines from memory—at least it seems so (Lord et al., 2000). This narrative poetry is handed down orally from generation to generation, and it has been claimed that the singers of tales memorize the texts. The scholar Albert Lord set out to show that the known poems by Homer were likely a notated version of an oral literature that was still ongoing in twentieth-century Europe. In his extensive research using dictated and recorded songs, he proved that the epics were not memorized but recreated using a plot and a large number of formulas, that is, "group[s] of words which [are] regularly employed under the same metrical conditions to express a given central idea" (p. 4). Based on a general outline of the story, each singer elaborates in traditional ways on details or exchanges characters and settings, adapting to his audience regarding mood, length of song, and dramatic buildup. Sometimes performers claim that two versions are identical, yet the transcriptions of such renditions do not support those claims. Here is an example of four versions of "Marko and Nina" by Petar Vidic (Lord, 2000, p. 236):

- Marko is drinking wine with his mother, his wife, and his sister.
- Marko arises early in his stone tower and drinks raki. With him are his mother, his wife, and his sister Andelija.
- Marko arises early in his tower in Prilip and drinks raki. With him are his mother, his wife, and his sister Andelija.
- Marko arises early in his stone tower. With him are his mother and his wife.

The transcriptions display similarities and a common story (same characters, etc.), but they are not identical in words or sense. Lord also showed that circulating written versions can influence subsequent singers who use parts of them or even memorize them entirely by rote. Thus what superficially looks like memorization is in fact recomposition. What we mean to show by this example is that the concept of memorization is different in different musical cultures and that musical performances are always reconstructions, either from notation (published transcriptions) or from memory.

Although some of them can play back a piece of music after hearing it only a few times, their performance errors are similar to those of nonhandicapped expert musicians. It was found that for short pieces composed in traditional Western harmony, they were surprisingly accurate, whereas when the structure did not adhere to the grammar of tonal Western music, they played rather haphazardly and did not extract the possible underlying 12-tone building principle. Thus even high-level playing by ear is again a reconstructive process, and only if the incoming material can be chunked and encoded meaningfully is recall possible.

How Reading and Remembering Can Be Improved

Having discussed the nature of reading and remembering, we now have to consider the obvious remaining questions: Why are some people better at it than others? And how are these skills related? Most people will memorize the music they are currently rehearsing, but they will play by ear or sight-read pieces of lesser difficulty. Unlike jazz musicians or some blind musicians who often play by ear, many classical musicians are weak by-ear players. Sight-reading is somewhat stronger, because learning increasingly difficult repertoire from notation for performance is accompanied by heightened notational complexity. Finally, memorizing for performance will come more or less easily, depending on the person's experience with the task.

Although many musicians readily state that they are either superior "sight readers," "memorizers," or "by-ear players," the statistical evidence suggests otherwise. Good sight readers are not necessarily bad memorizers, and vice versa. Among other studies, McPherson (1995) found a positive, moderate correlation among all skills. One possible explanation is the underlying common cognitive mechanisms that have to do with how a person processes (chunks) and stores musical information. It is likely, then, that training one skill yields a positive transfer to others.

We previously stated in chapter 4 that amount of practice could be used as a rough indicator of level of performance and that students who had accumulated more hours of practice tended to play better than those with fewer hours. Can we find a similar measure for sight-reading, memorizing, or playing by ear? Unfortunately, most musicians do not practice those activities as systematically as they rehearse repertoire for performance. Research on playing by ear is conspicuously lacking in the psychology literature, whereas much has been said about it in ethnomusicological literature.

Lehmann and Ericsson (1996) studied the sight-reading ability of advanced student pianists. The authors believed that it should be possible to identify and quantify beneficial training activities that may foster the development of sight-reading skills. Therefore, participants in the study were asked how much time they had spent as piano accompanists working with a choir, a soloist, or playing in church. In addition, the participants enumerated all the pieces in their "accompanying repertoire"—that is, those pieces they would feel comfortable accompanying on very short notice. Indeed, better sight readers had spent more time in accompanying activities and had a larger accompanying repertoire than less skilled sight readers.

In the Lehmann and Ericsson (1996) study just mentioned, the amount of repertoire was predictive of how well musicians sight-read. But simply doing more of the same thing is not likely to improve performance (see chapter 4, this volume). Rather, the pianists actively sought out challenges and learned more and more complicated pieces specifically for the purpose of accompanying other people. One of the first sight-reading researchers, Bean (1938, p. 3), noted that the "successful learning of the skill of efficient reading seems to involve a trick of which neither teacher nor pupil is conscious." As we now know, having enough opportunities to gain experience but also deliberately imposing challenges may be this trick (more on improving sight-reading and memorizing skills can be found in Williamon, 2004, chapters 7 and 8).

As we know from general psychology, memory is context-specific; that is, we not only learn a specific content but also remember the learning environment, physiological state, and so forth, associated with it. Practicing exclusively in one setting and always at the same time may therefore harbor the danger of a decrement in performance when performing under changed conditions (e.g., evening vs. mornings, hungry vs. full, in bright stage lights vs. cozy lighting; see Mishra, 2002). Also, passages that usually run on autopilot may become shaky when the performer suddenly decides onstage to understand the harmonic progression underlying the passage. Such changes should not be done during performance (see chapter 4). Instead, practice should, despite all regularity, contain some variability closer to performance time in order to help prevent memory lapses.

The trainability of memory and the use of mnemonic techniques have been demonstrated repeatedly in relevant literature within and beyond the realm of music. Sharpened memory for domain-related material results from engagement in the domain. It is likely that strategies for implicit memorization are subject to training, as are practice skills in general (see chapter 4). However, in the case of musicians, or actors for that matter, explicit memorization is necessary for stage performance because incidental (implicit) memory is not secure enough.

Is there one right way of memorizing? Because memory relies on previous knowledge and meaningful encoding of material, and because everybody has a different learning history, strategies for memorization will have to differ somewhat among performers. As pointed out earlier, explicit memorizing is a skill that may require idiosyncratic ways of training. One of us knew a guitarist who had great difficulties with a new teacher who wanted her to memorize music using visual mental images of hand positions, although she was used to memorizing using musical analysis. The student became frustrated and started to have memory problems during performance, which had never occurred prior to working with this teacher. We would speculate that people who cannot account for how they memorize are very much in tune with their functioning strategies, whereas people who struggle with memorization are probably using less efficient strategies.

In summary, this chapter has discussed sight-reading, recall, and ear playing, focusing on the shared mental mechanisms that enable these skills, namely, memory. Whereas in sight-reading visual input has to cue inferences and pattern recognition, memorized performance relies on cueing successfully and in sequence chunks from a (hierarchical) retrieval structure. The data on eye movements in sight-reading, on performance errors by professional performers, and on ear playing of artistic savants indicate clearly that these processes are accompanied by active search for relevant information and a heavy reliance on the familiar structural properties (grammar) of the music. Highly effective memory mechanisms (long-term working memory) are acquired through training and are therefore very domain-specific. To understand and improve memory and recall, we have to consider individual learning histories.

Study Questions

1. What evidence can you point to that would explain how experts can process information faster?
2. Explain why some individuals believe that photographic or tape-recorder memory is possible and discuss this view from a scientific perspective.
3. Describe how and why sight-reading, memorizing, or playing by ear can be enhanced.

Further Reading

The following are overview chapters with much application to everyday life.

Williamon, A. (Ed.) (2004). *Musical Excellence: Strategies and Techniques to Enhance Performance.* See chapters 7 on memorizing and 8 on sight-reading and improvisation.

Parncutt, R., & McPherson, G. E. (Eds.). (2002). *The Science and Psychology of Music Performance: Creative Strategies for Teaching and Learning.* See chapters 7 on learning music, 9 on sight-reading, and 11 on memory.

Chaffin, R., Imreh, G., & Crawford, M. (2002). *Practicing Perfection: Memory and Piano Performance.* A detailed and fascinating account of memorization in the context of practice.

Example A

Example B

7

Composition and Improvisation

W hen you are writing, editing, or rephrasing an e-mail, a card, or a short poem for a festive occasion, you are in fact composing. When chatting with a classmate in the hall, doodling on a notepad, or dancing at a party, you are really improvising. Hence, improvisation and composition are common behaviors in our daily lives, activities we generally enjoy doing, as can be seen in children's spontaneous vocal improvisations during play. They happily make up songs as they go along or modify existing ones in clever and funny ways. If we are comfortable and able to improvise and compose with words and art, why are many adults not able to do so with music? Many classically trained musicians cringe when asked to improvise or compose, whereas for jazz and rock musicians these skills are common.

We often associate great musicians of the past with the term *creative* and are reluctant to use it in reference to our own activities. A more neutral term to use would be *generative* to indicate that new material is being generated in the process of improvising or composing. However, we sometimes forget that composers in J. S. Bach's times were also performers and improvisers. Considering the thousands of small churches with their musicians whose names we will never know, we can estimate that the existing musical inheritance is but a minuscule fraction of what was actually produced. What has come down to us are works by composers highly esteemed in their own time, or chance discoveries of works that only later became known.

Gardner (1997; see also Sternberg, 1999) distinguishes between persons who master or perfect certain domains (e.g., Mozart), those who make new domains (e.g., Freud), those who influence others (e.g., Gandhi), and finally those who reflect on their own psyches (e.g., Virginia Woolf). The really famous ones among them are often referred to as "geniuses." The focus of this chapter is not on the genius type of accomplishment but rather on everyday musical generativity (creativity), simply because we cannot predict which works or people will become canonized and why.

The benefit of learning to improvise and compose is that those activities deepen our understanding of the musical structure. This awareness is likely to benefit music performance because it improves structuring of the piece during rehearsal and because the performer might discover things that invite a certain interpretation or help during preparation (practicing, memorization). Some people even claim that improvisers also transfer their spontaneity to rehearsed performance. Finally, it is likely that acquiring generative abilities will benefit musicians in the area of sight-reading, as it demands problem-solving skills. This chapter explains the following:

1. Our rather strict contemporary division between creating and re-creating music has historical reasons and denies the fact that generative musical behavior is widespread. Furthermore, composition and improvisation are very much related and often cannot be readily distinguished.
2. The creative undertaking appears to take a trial-and-error route with certain regularities. The fact that it can become automatized renders it mysterious to outsiders and insiders alike.
3. Children first engage in creative processes and then have to acquire the idea of an "aesthetic product" through formal training. Even top musicians have to hone their generative skills over many years.

Improvisation and Composition as Everyday Activities of All Musicians

Having mentioned earlier that people engage in generative processes on a regular basis in nonmusical domains, we now describe such activities in a musical context. It may be surprising to discover that music notation is incomplete; most of what we do with it is interpreting it. Because it only specifies the mathematically correct timing, the approximate pitch, and some vague expressive markings, performers have to add complex expression, interpret ornamentation signs, and often amend the score in other ways. An obvious situation in which classical musicians explicitly become "creative" is in the cadenza in solo concerts or certain works in twentieth-century music. Also, in sight-reading we engage in problem solving that often results in simplifying the score, or, when we arrange a piece for ourselves or students, we are small-scale composers/ arrangers. Music theory lessons also provide situations in which we turn into composers, writing four-part or counterpoint, among other things. In sum, the overwhelming majority of musicians—even classically trained ones—engage in generative processes akin to composition and improvisation.

Historically speaking, today's specialized performer who plays exclusively pieces composed by others is a recent phenomenon. Up to the late nineteenth century, many musicians (though not necessarily orchestral musicians) were composer-performers playing mainly their own works. Clara Schumann, for instance, was one of the first performers who played pieces by many different composers, specifically promoting her husband Robert's works. Today we play pieces by Liszt and Paganini, who were actually touring virtuosi, improvising a great deal and often playing variations of then popular opera melodies. There are well-known works in music history that are said to have emerged from or to reflect the improvisational practices of a given historical time, such as baroque fantasias or classical variations. J. S. Bach's *Musical Offering* from 1747 is said to have been strongly inspired by his performance in front of Frederick the Great in Potsdam. Improvisational practices remained active in classical music well into the twentieth century, when famous performers still changed the score at will to suit their artistic goals.

What can be gathered from the previous paragraphs is that the distinction between improvisation and composition is not as clear as one would think. For example, when a composer improvises in a certain style and then writes pieces that are rooted in this improvisational practice (as did Beethoven and Liszt), the connection between both types of generative processes is obvious. The twentieth-century composer Giacinto Scelci is known to have recorded his improvisations, then to have had his assistants transcribe the tapes and publish the transcripts after a final editing. Scelci's music, therefore, consists largely of his improvisations. Earlier we mentioned how our music notation allows for certain interpretations. In jazz music, the degree of freedom of the performer is even greater when only a melodic line and chord changes are given as referents. Extreme demands on the generative powers of the performer are often imposed by contemporary art music when the score contains only nonstandard notation. Some performers may even wonder where the "work" is, and different renditions of the piece are likely to sound very different. The degree of improvisation necessary in different art forms varies considerably (Pressing, 1984; see figure 7.1).

Because some types of music are transmitted through music notation and others aurally, notation is not a sufficient indicator to distinguish composition from improvisation or to establish true authorship. Ethnomusicologists face the problem that most of the music they are interested in is not written down and often has no author; other music consists of a static repertoire (e.g., Japanese court music, Balinese gamelan music). Sometimes the author (composer) is known, and sometimes there are multiple authors or versions of a piece. Whereas in Western music authorship is mostly ascertained in classical music, jazz music knows many so-called "traditionals."

It is almost impossible for listeners to know whether music is composed or improvised, as the following anecdote from the nineteenth century exemplifies: The

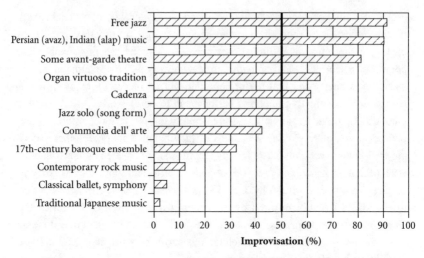

Figure 7.1. Estimated degree of improvisation in different musical genres. From "Cognitive Processes in Improvisation," by J. Pressing, 1984, in *Cognitive Processes in the Perception of Art,* edited by W. R. Crozier & A. J. Chapman, 1984, pp. 345–363. Amsterdam: Elsevier. Copyright © 1984 by Elsevier. Adapted with permission.

famous pianist Kalkbrenner visited the music theorist A. B. Marx and improvised for him a piece of roughly 15 minutes in length. Marx was extremely laudatory of the performance. A few days later his admiration transformed into anger when he received a printed score in the mail that contained this very same "improvisation." It turned out that the work had long been composed and printed and that Kalkbrenner had actually deceived Marx (Gerig, 1974, cited in Lehmann & Ericsson, 1998a, p. 76). If this difference is hardly noticeable to an expert, how much more difficult would it be for an average listener to spot such a distinction in an unfamiliar type of music?

Generative processes in music may look quite different, depending on the historical time and culture under consideration (see cross-cultural box). Even if they do not recognize it as such, virtually all musicians engage in some sort of generative activities. We have spent much time talking about the problematic distinction between improvisation and composition because we will suggest later that they are very similar—if not in fact the same process—and that our perception of difference emerges chiefly because they are typically associated with different musical genres.

The Creative Process

If it were a straightforward matter to research creative processes, they would not have been an ongoing topic of interest for such a long time. But why are

Cross-Cultural Perspective: North American Indians' Song Quest

North American Indians believe in the supernatural power of music. Consequently, each song has its unique power, and it is of utmost importance that rituals are accompanied by the correct song: "The right way to do something is to sing the right song with it" (Nettl, Capwell, Bohlman, Wong, & Turino, 1992, p. 270).

Some songs are given to humans in the course of visions, that is, they are caught out of thin air (e.g., Densmore, 1926; Nettl et al., 1992). It is, therefore, not the receiving human who is credited with inventing the song but the guardian spirits or other supernatural powers. People who generate songs more frequently do so as part of their role as medicine men or healers, a partly religious function. The particular power of a song can be intentionally shared, inherited, or traded. The body of existing songs can be viewed as the currently known repertoire of personal songs of which the owners may or may not be known today.

New "compositions" come into existence when young men undertake a vision quest by going to a remote place, fasting, or preventing sleep. Some might also make use of certain psychogenic substances (herbs). Either by falling into a state of exhaustion or by reaching a heightened mental awareness, the vision seeker receives his dream or vision song. By repeating the song, the young man secures it and makes it his most personal possession. Later, more songs can come to the Indian in similar or other situations (Eagle, 1997).

Thus, in the Native American belief system, every man (what about women?) has the potential to receive songs. The aesthetic qualities or inventiveness are of secondary importance, as the song is sung because of its magical powers. Only a close study of different songs, of the musical ability of individual creators, and of the exact circumstances of the composition could reveal how a generalized psychological theory of creativity could be applied to this type of generative process.

they so hard to understand? One reason is that artists often have difficulties verbalizing how they go about creating something and the resulting product does not always show all the traces of its manufacturing. Another reason is that generating music is an ill-structured problem, and there are so many unknown constraints that the outcome is difficult to assess, as the opposite judgments of music critics and teachers readily attest (see chapter 11). A final argument is that some artists may not want to tell us accurately about the creative process because they fear that this could destroy some of the mystique associated with musical creativity. Psychologists call this impression management, and it is quite common, not only in music.

In spite of these problems, researchers have tried to investigate composing and improvising. The method of choice is to watch someone do it and ask the person to think aloud concurrently while working (obviously, in improvisation this has to be done retrospectively). The resulting verbal protocols are then transcribed and analyzed for emerging patterns. Similarly, one can try to analyze written accounts of musicians about their generative processes.

Composition

In a postal survey study, Bahle (1947/1982; see also Rasch, 1981) asked composers of his time to set given poems to music and to reflect on the generative process, of which they then gave a written account. Bahle's delicate analysis offered a theoretically interesting and empirically grounded distinction between composers whom he called "working types" and others who were labeled "inspirational types." Those two types differed in how they found and solved musical problems, what methods they employed when working, and how they assessed their products. The inspirational types were less conscious about their work and experienced the source of their ideas and solutions as relatively random and coming from the outside, while the working types toiled systematically and experienced the product as a direct result of such efforts. The author suggested that the latter type was more represented by composers such as Beethoven, Stravinsky, and Brahms, while the former type followed a pattern found in Schubert, Tchaikowsky, and Berlioz (Bahle, 1947/1982, p. 346). Consequently, the inspirational type, being controlled by the process, cannot really verbalize much about it, whereas the working type would be a better source of data for a psychologist. It is interesting to read interviews or self-reports of musicians to determine what category they might belong to.

A more recent account was published by Colley, Banton, Down, and Pither (1992), who studied 3 novices and 1 expert composer working for 1 hour on 9 bars of a four-part chorale to a given soprano line. The participants' think-aloud protocols were recorded and a brief structured interview conducted. Analysis of the protocols revealed that the novices solved technical problems on a chord-to-chord basis, consciously applying rules and checking for rule violations. The expert, however, was concerned with how the different parts moved, what was ahead, and whether or not the solutions were typical of Bach's style of composition. Apart from the fact that the expert seemed to have automatized the basic procedures and accessed relevant knowledge more easily, he also had a strategy and constrained the task by limiting his options at certain points, such as cadences, by using typical patterns or working out modulations.

An often-cited model to describe the creative process was originally developed by Wallas in 1926 (based on Pointcare). It contained several stages (preparation, incubation, intimation, illumination, and verification) and paid tribute to the historical period of its origin by assuming some contribution of the unconscious (Sternberg, 1999). Here we present an amended model that includes the trial-and-error, working-it-out phase observed in most generative processes.

1. A person must have acquired enough knowledge, skills, and attitudes during a phase of *preparation* to be fully functional in a domain. Only then can one identify relevant problems, know how to solve them, and even be intentionally innovative.
2. Following the posing of an aesthetic problem comes a phase during which not much observable behavior occurs but during which somehow solutions are sought. This phase is called *incubation* or gestation and requires little awareness.
3. An act of *illumination* (Eureka!) ends incubation, when the creator will experience a sudden rush of ideas for a solution. This phase is often reported later in anecdotes with regard to discoveries in science (e.g., Archimedes in his bath).
4. The next phase is the *elaboration,* during which trial-and-error work becomes important. Trials with subsequent evaluations repeat until an acceptable solution has been found. This phase is often accompanied by considerable work and effort. It is entirely conceivable that as the elaboration progresses, new problems emerge, which in turn follow recursively the phases outlined here.
5. The final phase is that of *verification*, in which the creative product is assessed by a third party, often an audience. Some composers dread this phase because they have no control over the processes involved here. This phase can even have a historical dimension—for instance, when once-neglected composers who might even have died in utter poverty become highly fashionable at a later time, with no monetary benefit to them, of course.

Because the first solution is not always the best, most composers (and writers) edit more or less extensively what they write. This trial-and-error process is commonly referred to as sketching and provides an important source of evidence concerning generative processes (cf. Sloboda, 1985b, p. 102). Beethoven is probably most well known for his extensive sketching activities, but other composers have also left us with telling materials from their workshops. Many people believe that W. A. Mozart did not draft at all (this claim can also be found in Gardner, 1997). Recently it was discovered that the myth regarding Mozart's lack of sketching was unfounded and was due to extensive loss of evidence—and also to the deliberate obscuring of related facts (Konrad, 1992).

Thus we can safely assume that all known composers do sketch, albeit to varying extents. By using such cultural techniques as writing and sketching, similar to making a shopping list, composers free up their cognitive resources, especially if they fear forgetting an important detail. Sometimes a composer will put a piece aside for a while and return to it later. Psychologically speaking, this time away will break the mental set and allow the creator to have a fresh look at it; the same thing happens to performers preparing a piece for performance. The notes can then be evaluated and reworked independently from any constraints of time and locality. The likely result is a more coherent and possibly more complex work. Eventually comes the big moment when the brainchild is presented to the world and exposed to verification. Either the audience likes and remembers this version, or it is scrapped temporarily—or forever.

Improvisation

Unlike composers who can talk while composing, improvisers can only report on their thoughts after improvising. In his book, Sudnow (1993) describes in a sometimes amusing fashion his learning to play jazz piano. One of the striking aspects was his initial attention to technical details, the gradual move to more stylistic and aesthetic aspects, and the ultimate discovery that the music seemed to happen automatically while he almost became a detached onlooker. In fact, it may be exactly this eerie experience of automaticity that makes it difficult for experts to report in much detail on what they are doing at a given point.

An interesting attempt at tapping into the cognitive processes during improvisation was undertaken by Hargreaves, Cork, and Setton (1991) in a controlled study with professional and semiprofessional jazz pianists. The pianists were asked to improvise melodies with the right hand to a given accompaniment (acoustic bass with left-hand voicings). Immediately after their performances they were asked about the thoughts they had had while playing. The novices either could not provide much information or had concentrated on individual musical parameters, such as the harmonies. Strategies and plans were hardly mentioned. On the contrary, the experts referred to plans and strategies that were characterized by technical, melodic, or even metaphorical ideas (e.g., "It should sound like a cathedral"). Their plans emerged even prior to playing, and the musicians appeared more relaxed during their improvisations compared with the novices. Here, we are very much reminded of Colley et al.'s (1992) results regarding composition.

Whereas the phase model of the creative process described previously is easy to spot in the works of composers and poets, we can only speculate on how it might apply to the improviser. Imagine a typical creative problem involving a musician who wants to play a new song (referents are a melody adorned with a chord sequence). First, a rather ready-made melodic solution is retrieved from memory or generated according to rules. As the first phrase unravels almost without conscious effort (incubation), the musician has an unusual idea of how to continue (illumination), which she proceeds to play (elaboration). If she and her comusicians like it, she repeats it and makes minor alterations (further elaboration). During this elaborative phase, different options will be tried and tested, rejected or accepted. For a composer, this process is mainly done behind closed doors (with sketchbooks bearing witness), while for rock or jazz musicians some of it will happen in public on consecutive renditions of a chorus or on different occasions. Because the jazz musician has only a few chances at a time to try the new pattern, the elaboration process can take a long time, depending on how often the piece is played (or practiced alone), but the conditions for verification are good, because an audience is often present. Monson (1996) shows that in jazz ensembles this process of verification happens in a language-like, discursive manner, whereby approval, irony, and disapproval are being "voiced" in the group using the instruments. In contrast, composers have more opportunity for solitary elaboration but fewer chances for verification. That verification is important as quality control can be judged from the instances in which composers such as J. S. Bach amended their pieces between performances or even between printings (Breig, 1997). By and large, the verification is done by the peers and the audience, but also by the imponderability of history. It happens in retrospect that the esteem of history for individual pieces or musicians changes—for better or worse.

Because the most important phase in the generative process is the elaboration, we need to look at it more closely in the context of the complicated improvisation model of Johnson-Laird (2002). Of course, every musical genre may require a specific generative model, but there are some generalities to learn from the one outlined here. Johnson-Laird criticized the common misconception that jazz musicians operate in a simple pattern-based manner, chaining one stored pattern to the next in a clever way. Instead, we have to assume a complex generative process somewhat akin to that used in speech production. Despite the fact that the author did not discuss composition explicitly, the model could also apply to it.

If all possible solutions that come to mind for a given musical problem were admissible, we would call the underlying generative process "neo-Darwinian." However, and this is more realistic, composers and improvisers constrain the possible output, thereby establishing what theorists call a "neo-Lamarckian process." As a result, all obtained patterns are reasonably good and can be evaluated in a second step. Good examples for the different results can be heard on rarely published alternative takes on jazz recordings. If initial constraints were strict enough, what criteria would be left to apply to the output? In fact, the initial rules are not completely deterministic and allow for some choices, which may prove more or less appropriate. Imagine that a certain finger movement is easier for a bass player than another movement and is therefore frequently chosen over a less entrenched one. The result may sound less interesting and may

---

Self Study: Musical Generativity in Your Own Biography

1. Write a short account of a memorable instance on which you have composed or improvised music. What led or encouraged you to do it? Try to remember how you felt afterward.
2. If you play a musical instrument, try to compose (with or without notating it) or improvise a simple piece for your instrument. Think aloud and record your thoughts as you proceed or afterward. Once you have finished, listen to the protocol and identify the different stages you went through (problem, idea, elaboration, evaluation).

---

not be cherished by the audience ("Oh, here he goes again!"). More important, the criteria that operate during generation may be different from those that operate during verification. Obviously, while playing and making choices, the improviser (or composer) does not know what the audience or critics will say until they cheer in delight. Moreover, at least in improvisation, the choices have to be made so fast that a conscious decision is much less likely than an algorithmic one; this implies that most of the time the performer will have to work on autopilot in order to save up cognitive resources for particularly important decisions (see also chapter 6). According to Johnson-Laird, the rhythmic distribution of notes is done by using prototypes and their variants, whereas the selection of pitches is constrained by one's knowledge about the currently possible notes (for a given harmony).

Contrary to what many classically trained people seem to believe, it is not the case that jazz musicians reinvent everything they play every time they perform. This would be a complete waste of effort. Instead, researchers have started to show that what jazz musicians, as well as rock groups, engage in is a sort of collective memory composition (Berliner, 1994). They start with some version that is being refined and then starts to crystallize with repeated performances or rehearsals. Eventually, they have a piece that forms a rather fixed representation in the minds of the musicians. This is the reason that amateur groups especially tend to sound quite similar on consecutive performances and can produce well-coordinated renditions of pieces. However, this does not preclude deliberate deviations from a fixed rendition.

In sum, the generative musical processes that underlie composition and improvisation are rather similar in that they constitute iterative stages in which a product is refined successively. That they operate on different time scales in composition and improvisation has certain consequences. Composition is not time-critical, so the composer can think at length about solutions, write them down to avoid forgetting, and come to highly complex, unusual works. In improvisation performers have to cope with real-time constraints, making it necessary to automatize a number of processes that would otherwise hinder them from seeing the overall context or from finding ways to collectively compose the piece to some perfection.

Altered States and Creativity

Drugs, alcohol, or specific pathological states are sometimes thought of as increasing creativity. However, more often than not, the short-term gains that may come from an altered mental state do not transform into outstanding products, as Boyd (1992) found out from interviews with famous musicians. Psychogenic substances can break the mental set and thereby allow innovative solutions, reduce inhibition (especially in shy personalities), or increase mood and motivation, resulting in possible benefits for the generative processes. However, those altered states also tamper with the critical mind and the conscious efforts of elaboration and verification, which are necessary to solve creative problems. Musicians may find that they overrate the quality of a product while under the influence of certain substances (see Bahle, 1947/1982, for classical composers; see West, 2004, for a review). The fact that some successful musicians were unfortunately addicted to drugs does not imply that taking drugs increases creativity. The goal should be to live a long and healthy life, as well as being musically creative throughout.

Learning to Be Musically Creative

Our respect for musical geniuses is so great that we might even conceive of them as a race apart, endowed with a completely different genetic makeup from everybody else. And although we have today no scientific way of proving this assumption to be wrong, we can at least look for patterns in their lives and learn from them (Gardner, 1997). If the genetic makeup of famous creators had been the sole source of their success, they would not have had to learn their trade in an effortful fashion. Rather the opposite is true.

In research on chess players, Simon and Chase (1973) found that it took about 10 years for even the most gifted chess players to gain international reputations. This suggests that, in this domain, long phases of training and practice are necessary to reach high levels of performance (see chapter 4). Would a similar rule of thumb hold for music? Hayes (1989) demonstrated that composers also need about 10 years from the start of training to entrance into the profession, regardless of their starting age. As in all theories of creativity, W. A. Mozart serves here also as a touchstone. Hayes went on to show that Mozart's earlier works, that is, those falling within the first 10 years of his career, were less famous and hardly ever performed compared with the later ones. Moreover, some of Mozart's earlier works were arrangements or adaptations rather than genuine masterworks. Weisberg (1999) also described learning trajectories of generative musicians, among them the Beatles. For the Beatles he concluded that many early songs were not recorded because of quality considerations but that their real contribution to the history of popular music occurred between the years 1965 and 1967, which was roughly 10 years after John Lennon started in 1957. Thus all musical genres require long-time immersion in the discipline as a prerequisite to producing innovative works.

What happens during the formative years? There are obviously two things that need to be considered, namely, knowledge and skill. Both of those are acquired through deliberate practice and instruction. Classical music composers, for example, are known to have studied the old masters by literally copying, paraphrasing, and imitating them. We can read about this in many biographies of famous classical composers from J. S. Bach to G. Ligeti. In our days, film music composers and music theorists alike would be able to produce an adequate copy of any past or contemporary style. Popular musicians, including the Beatles, have started by copying (covering) songs of successful bands before attempting to write their own (e.g., Green, 2002). Jazz musicians like to listen to other jazz musicians' recordings and even try to imitate them. They study famous musicians by transcribing their solos or patterns (see also commercially available transcriptions of solos played by famous musicians) and sometimes by rehearsing them like compositions. The mastery of existing knowledge, such as counterpoint techniques and orchestration in classical music and patterns, idioms, and so forth, in jazz, seems to be a prerequisite for inventing new things. Only when we know what already exists can we intentionally invent something new or at least recognize that we just did.

Sometimes composers will emulate past styles for aesthetic purposes, such as the American composer Rochberg, who wrote a few pieces in a classical manner. Rosemary Brown, a spiritual medium, claimed to communicate with long-dead composers such as Liszt, Beethoven, and Debussy, who allegedly dictated to her new compositions from the other world. Musicologists believe that this gifted amateur composer was essentially manufacturing decent stylistic copies (Vetter, 1998). Such imitations for purposes other than practice often elicit criticisms because they are considered less innovative than the developing of new musical styles. But Gardner (1997) points out that creativity also consists in perfecting a given domain. The discussion about epigones is rather philosophical and culture-specific because other cultures do not value innovations that much but instead prefer the stability of a given style. Even in the Western classical tradition some epigones achieve their special claim to fame.

In classical music performance, formal instruction with a teacher plays a vital role (see chapters 2 and 10). Virtually all composers have taken theory or composition lessons with a teacher at one point or another. In jazz, rock, and popular genres, musicians can also informally teach each other during jam sessions or rehearsals. In such settings, learning from modeling, experimenting, and obtaining feedback from other musicians take the place of formal one-on-one instruction. This process is more entrepreneurial in the sense that the learners have to take charge of the learning situation with the result that they feel as though they are largely self-taught. Many participatory musical cultures rely almost entirely on such informal types of instruction. Some things about composition and improvisation can also be learned simply from playing an instrument. Surely after playing a lot of classical piano music, any amateur would know how to play a simple idiomatic left-hand accompaniment. We can learn by mere exposure, and not only in music. There are always opportunities for informal learning, but many musical cultures also offer formal instruction for reaching higher and more specialized levels of performance.

Listening to music is also a central activity that fosters generative abilities through the formation of aural skills. Before the advent of recording equipment, musicians had to physically attend performances in order to listen to music. For instance, the Mozart family traveled to Italy to familiarize themselves with Italian opera, and probably most well-known composers, including Haydn, Verdi, and Berlioz, avidly listened to music, even quite analytically studying scores (e.g., Bahle 1947/1982, pp. 6–10). Louis Armstrong hung out at the local places where jazz music was played, even though these places were not exactly in the best sections of town. Musical apprentices in India accompany their master to every musical event and wait for him, thus gaining ample exposure to his musical style. Today musicians have it easier, because they can listen to recordings, thereby exposing themselves to the achievements of recognized experts in the field. Children also learn their language by primarily listening for more than a year, and some music teaching methods (e.g., Suzuki) take advantage of this type of learning process. Listening creates expectations, and these expectations can in turn be used to produce music. After all, composers and listeners have to use a common language (see chapter 5).

By studying the masters analytically and finding out how to produce certain rhythms, sound effects, or musical structures, the aspiring composer develops the ability to internally generate similar structures. This aural imagery that many composers mention in their writings can be rather vivid. By using noninvasive methods to look at what happens in the brain while people listen to music or image it, researchers have found that the right side of the brain is particularly active, especially the areas farther to the front and subcortical areas, such as the thalamus, that are connected to memory functioning. When words are added, typical regions of the brain engaged in language processing may also be activated (Halpern, 2003, for a review). Thus thinking in music has an observable physiological basis (see chapter 11).

Formal instruction in a new musical genre is not available right after the genre is invented. For example, at the height of the swing era, one had to go to Minton's Playhouse in New York to hear the members of Benny Goodman's big band jam after their official performances, and it was there that bebop started to develop (Broadbent, 1996). Today, bebop techniques are taught at conservatories or can be studied using published jazz methods and play-along recordings. All of this is seconded by knowledge about the history of jazz music and its greats. Jazz has, like other types of music before and after it, become part of formal music education at all levels.

A musician who has acquired all the necessary knowledge and skills has a chance to produce something new—maybe even outstanding. Some people believe that a composer just has to work long and hard at a single piece for it to become the *magnum opus*. This view might have to be replaced with the *constant-probability-of-success theory* (see Simonton, 1997, for a review). Simonton's theory posits that the probability of writing something notable is constant for a given person. Also, the person's entire output will conform to a bell-curve-like distribution, with the majority of works being of medium quality, few being of very high, and few of very low value. This means that by increasing the output, the composer will most likely produce more notable works (but also incur more failures). Furthermore, the life-span curve of the output of creative people typically follows a function that can be described as a backward upside-down J (see figure 7.2), rising sharply at first and then tapering off slowly toward the end of the career. This life-span trajectory, together with the aforementioned constant-probability-of-success idea, predicts the peak performances of composers and other creators. In countless publications, covering different domains (arts, sciences, politics), Simonton has convincingly demonstrated his theory.

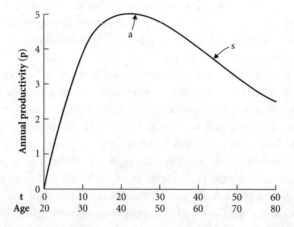

Figure 7.2. The life-span trajectory of artistic productivity for a particular domain can be mathematically described and predicted. The maximum of the apex (a) as well as the slope of descent (s) depend on personal factors and career age (t) (adapted from Simonton, D. K., 1984, *Genius, creativity and leadership,* Harvard University Press, p. 111). Used by permission.

Earlier research regarding age and peak performance (Lehman, 1953) had already shown that those performance peaks fall at different ages for different musical genres: Symphonic composers, for example, tend to peak at 30–34 years of age, earlier than operetta composers, at 40–44 years. In brief, the expected success is influenced by the musical genre, the typical life-span trajectory for this genre, and the output of the individual composer. This does not mean that late successes are entirely impossible, but they become less probable, as do extremely early ones.

Nevertheless, enough researchers have argued that people differ in their innate creative potential (e.g., Gardner, 1997; Simonton, 1997). One researcher even suggested that, based on a longitudinal study in which musically creative children were followed from childhood through adolescence, there might be a hormonal basis for musical generativity that favors males (Hassler, 1992). Yet none of the researchers negates the tremendous importance of a nurturing environment and teachers for the development of creative skills (see chapters 2 and 10). Obviously, such an environment will allow the person to acquire the relevant knowledge and skills at an early age. This does not happen without frustrations, and the budding composer or improviser will have to learn to cope with failures. Interestingly, self-efficacy plays a role here, too (see chapter 3), and musicians who have already successfully contributed ideas to a compositional process (e.g., in a rock band) are likely to continue to be musically creative because they know they can (Rosenbrock, 2002; see chapter 9, section on social processes of collaborative rehearsing and creating). This biographical development might lead to a typical personality profile of composers that has been described as more self-sufficient, expedient, introverted, radical, and imaginative compared with nonmusicians (Kemp, 1996).

Researchers have studied not only how famous composers or improvisers developed, but educational researchers especially have also looked at the creative products of ordinary children to find out how generative abilities evolve (e.g., Bamberger, 1991; Kratus, 1989; Swanwick & Tillman, 1986; see Webster, 1992, and Hickey, 2002, for reviews). Children are creative in the sense that they invent new material, but their creativity is not what we would consider professional creativity. The results of their generativity arise from the goal of learning to master the domain and are often not driven by the urge to produce some output (see the spiral model in figure 2.4). Instead of only collecting final products of compositional and improvisational processes, Kratus (1989) observed the generative process of children between the ages of 7 and 11. The children worked for 10 minutes on a musical invention task ("make a song") using a keyboard, and their efforts were tape-recorded. Later, the recordings were analyzed by coding the extent to which the children had exhibited certain behaviors over time, namely, exploration, repetition, development, and silence (pause). The author found that younger children tended to continuously explore the material until they ran out of time (see figure 7.3). Repeating and developing the material

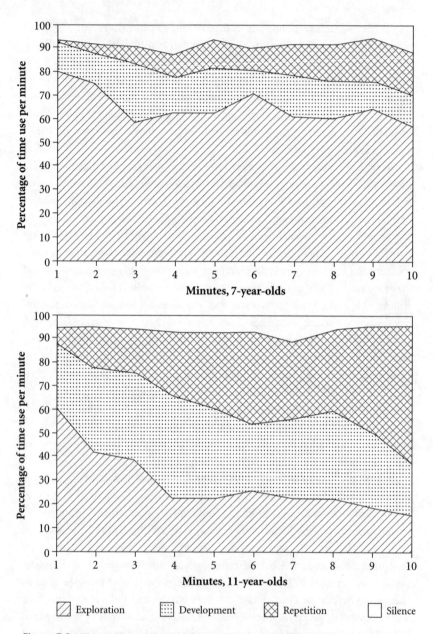

Figure 7.3. The time use analysis of the composition period for the 7- and 11-year-olds shows that exploration is the main activity for the younger ones, whereas older children engage in activities that lead to stable products. From "A Time Analysis of the Compositional Processes Used by Children Ages 7 to 11," by J. Kratus, 1989, *Journal of Research in Music Education, 37,* 5–20. Copyright © 1989 by MENC: The National Association for Music Education. Reprinted by permission.

did not play an important role. Conversely, older children started to explore the material but soon began to develop it and to repeat certain portions. In fact, these older children's behavior resembled that mentioned earlier of composers. Children with formal musical training showed an accelerated transition from playful explorations to a more outcome-oriented way of working. Even younger children with formal musical training showed patterns that were more typical for older kids, regardless of training.

Kratus also recorded two consecutive renditions of the final "song" at the end of the 10 minutes, which allowed him to compare the similarity between renditions. When looking only at children whose renditions were very similar, he found that their time use was dominated by activities that would ultimately lead to a secure and reproducible product (short exploration, subsequent development, and final repetition). Children whose renditions were dissimilar were on average younger and had been exploring practically all the time. Thus the development of musical generativity in children—and possibly in all novices—goes from a process to a product orientation, and the desire to produce a stable and reproducible output accompanies certain behaviors, namely, elaboration and memorization.

Based on previous research, Kratus (1991) postulates an interesting progressive model in seven stages of how novices learn to improvise (p. 93):

> Level 1: Exploration. (The student tries out different sounds and combinations of sounds in a loosely structured context.)
> Level 2: Process-oriented improvisation. (The student produces more cohesive patterns.)
> Level 3: Product-oriented improvisation. (The student becomes conscious of structural principles such as tonality and rhythm.)
> Level 4: Fluid improvisation. (The student manipulates his or her instrument or voice in a more automatic, relaxed manner.)
> Level 5: Structural improvisation. (The student is aware of the overall structure of the improvisation and develops a repertoire of musical or nonmusical strategies for shaping an improvisation.)
> Level 6: Stylistic improvisation. (The student improves skillfully within a given style, incorporating its melodic, harmonic, and rhythmic characteristics.)
> Level 7: Personal improvisation. (The musician is able to transcend recognized improvisation styles to develop a new style.)

This model bears some resemblance to the model by Swanwick and Tillman (1986), discussed in chapter 2, and shows clearly the path from exploration to product orientation with further refinements regarding stylistic aspects and innovation of the domain. Thus generative abilities develop with knowledge and skills.

Study Questions

1. Explain the problems associated with the traditional distinction between the concepts of composition and improvisation.

2. How do generative products of professional composers or improvisers differ from the ones made by children? Include a discussion of the developmental model by Kratus (1991).

3. Use this chapter as a basis to describe the biography of a well-known composer/improviser, and try to focus on aspects of skill acquisition.

Further Reading

Kenny, B. J., & Gellrich, M. (2001). Improvisation. In R. Parncutt & G. E. McPherson (Eds.), *The science and psychology of music performance: Creative strategies for teaching and learning* (pp. 117–134). A very informed description of improvisation.

Pressing, J. (1998). Psychological constraints on improvisational expertise and communication. In B. Nettl & M. Russell (Eds.) (1998), *In the Course of Performance* (pp. 47–68). Application of expertise theory to improvisation.

Webster, P. (1992). Research on creative thinking in music: The assessment literature. In R. Colwell (Ed.), *Handbook of research on music teaching and learning* (pp. 266–280). A comprehensive review for the field of music education; the same author maintains an extensive annotated bibliography on the Internet.

Sternberg, R. J. (Ed.) (1999). *Handbook of Creativity.* Various aspects of creativity; however, most of them cover music only in passing.

8

Managing Performance Anxiety

M ost musicians choose their line of work based on a love of music and a desire to share it with others. Considering only this, one might believe that musicians enthusiastically welcome all opportunities to perform for people. Alas, this is not always the case. Being a performing musician involves pressures of different kinds. Often the greatest stress is felt when musicians take the stage to perform. Instead of sensing excitement in sharing their music with an audience, they feel apprehension and distress. This anxiety, commonly called "stage fright," is a serious and debilitating performance problem for many musicians.

Unfortunately, performance anxiety may start early in the lives of musicians. Although parents and teachers provide children with the encouragement and assistance they need to develop as music students, they can also place such an emphasis on achievement that their young musicians feel pressured. Research has shown that adolescent musicians share the same experiences of performance anxiety as older performers (LeBlanc, Jin, Obert & Siivola, 1997), and we can assume that even younger musicians are susceptible to it when thrust into adult-like performing situations. In a survey of junior high and high school music students, roughly 55% of them reported having suffered from performance anxiety (Shoup, 1995).

Similar incidence is found in adult populations. Based on research, we estimate that around half of all performing musicians are affected to some degree by performance anxiety. Wesner, Noyes, and Davis (1990) found that 61% of students and faculty at an American school of music reported either "marked" or "moderate" distress when performing and that 47% blamed anxiety for their impaired performances. A survey of professional orchestra members showed 59% reporting past incidents of performance anxiety (Van Kemanade, Van Son, & Van Heesch, 1995). Other research has suggested that this problem is prevalent among all sorts of musicians (Cooper & Wills, 1989; Fishbein, Middlestadt, Ottati, Strauss, & Ellis, 1988). Noted sufferers include virtuosi Artur Rubenstein and Vladimir Horowitz, as well as hugely successful popular musicians Barbra Streisand and John Lennon. That even successful musicians struggle with performance anxiety attests to the fact that it is fundamentally unwarranted; that is, it does not stem from being untalented or unequipped to perform.

It is much easier to identify a case of performance anxiety—you know it when you have it—than to write a textbook definition. Usually it is defined by the physical and mental sensations experienced. Common symptoms are excessive sweating, trembling hands, and a loss of concentration, but many others can occur. Psychologists attempt to look beyond these physiological symptoms to define performance anxiety by its causes and the conditions that produce it. Wilson (2002) has identified three sources, which we will call the person, the situation, and the musical task. The following sections correspond to these sources:

1. *The symptoms*: The physiological responses of performance anxiety are similar to what the body does when feeling threatened or afraid. The activation of the body's emergency system produces physical and behavioral symptoms that can be treated through bodily training and medicinal remedies.

2. *The person*: One source of anxiety is within musicians themselves. Whether the underlying cause is a general predisposition for anxiety or unrealistic thinking about performing, musicians can benefit from cognitive treatment approaches.

3. *The situation*: Another source to consider is situational stress, which relates to the environment and circumstances of a particular performance. Identifying stress-inducing aspects can lead to incorporating helpful strategies into performance preparations.

4. *The musical task*: Because a sense of control is needed to perform confidently, another source of anxiety is a musician's level of mastery of the music to be performed. The music must not challenge performers beyond what they know their skills to be.

The Symptoms

When a person perceives a threat—whether real or imagined—the body reacts naturally. Sometimes called the "fight or flight" defensive mechanism, the brain activates the body's emergency system, the sympathetic branch of the *autonomic nervous system*. The nerves stimulate the adrenal glands in the abdomen to release certain hormones into the bloodstream. These hormones, commonly referred to as adrenaline, affect organs throughout the body in characteristic ways. Table 8.1 shows how the changing functions of the organs result in abnormal feelings within the person.

Table 8.1 How the Physical Changes of Arousal Translate into Physiological
Symptoms of Anxiety

Adaptive bodily function	Sensation felt
Heart beats vigorously to increase oxygen supply to muscles	Pounding chest
Glands in the skin secrete perspiration to lower body temperature	Excessive sweating, wet palms
Lungs and bronchial airways open to supply more oxygen	Shortness of breath
Saliva flow decreases	Dry mouth, lump in the throat
Digestive system is inhibited as blood is diverted from stomach to muscles	"Butterflies in the stomach," nausea
Pupils dilate to sharpen distance vision	Blurring and focusing problems
Muscles tense in readiness for increased physical exertion	Tension, shaking hands, muscle tremors

These *physiological symptoms* constitute the physical state of arousal, which is also marked by increased brain activity. Although most musicians more readily identify too much arousal (or anxiety) as a problem, too little arousal would also make it difficult to perform well. Imagine just waking up in the morning, when you feel you have no energy. Your heart rate is slow, your breathing is shallow, and your mind is anything but alert. Certainly in this state of low arousal, you are in no condition to carry out the physical and mental challenges of performing music. Psychologists who work in areas such as the performing arts and sports point to "optimal arousal" as a condition for high-quality performance. Athletes and performing artists alike talk about the need to get "psyched up" or "pumped" for an event, in effect drawing on an *adaptive anxiety* that actually facilitates better performance.

How the Symptoms Can Affect Performance

Named after two psychologists, the *Yerkes-Dodson Law* depicts the relationship between arousal and performance as an inverted U (see Figure 8.1). As arousal increases from low to moderate levels, performance quality improves. Performance is at its highest when arousal is at a moderate level. Additional arousal amounts to *maladaptive anxiety*, being detrimental to performance quality. In reality, what constitutes optimal arousal depends on several factors, including the nature of the task to be performed. Greater manifestations of physiological arousal are probably more enabling for a rock and roll set drummer than for a flutist in a Baroque chamber ensemble. An accelerated heartbeat and amplified muscle readiness match the physical exertion required to play a drum set, but

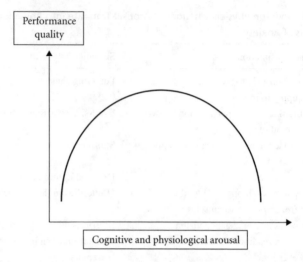

Figure 8.1. Yerkes-Dodson inverted U model of the relationship between arousal and performance quality.

these symptoms could interfere with carrying out the fine motor skills and breathing control required to play the flute. Thus the same bodily changes of arousal that are facilitative for some people can be debilitating symptoms for others.

The problem with these physiological symptoms is that they can lead to deterioration in performance quality. Visual disturbances caused by the dilation of the pupils can interfere with reading printed music, especially under bright stage lighting. Additional muscle tension and shaking will negatively affect the physical production aspects of performance. The end result might be inaccurate pitch production (e.g., finger placement, arm movement) and rhythmic timing. High arousal often influences the choice of tempo, which tends to become faster in performance than during practice, adding technical difficulties. Certainly a combination of these physical sensations can make musicians feel so strange that they are unable to concentrate or to execute the expressive aspects of the music. The manifestation of symptoms is likely related to the physical demands of different instruments, meaning a greater prevalence of shortness of breath and dry mouth in wind players or sweaty palms and finger tension in string players. It could be, though, that these are just the symptoms that the players notice most often or find most bothersome.

In addition to directly producing performance mistakes and hindering expressive control, these physiological symptoms may cause musicians to change how they normally and correctly go about performing. For example, a trumpet player who normally uses strong breath support to produce higher pitches on the horn may suffer from shortness of breath, and he may try to compensate by using excessive force of the mouthpiece against the lips. The latter method is much less effective and will result in fatigue more quickly. Such undesirable adaptations, as well as the performance mistakes that result, are sometimes referred to as the *behavioral symptoms* of performance anxiety.

Some psychologists have also made note of *cognitive symptoms*. While on stage, musicians may be mentally preoccupied with negative thoughts about their performance. They may feel tense and worry about making mistakes, such as forgetting things, being unable to play expressively, looking foolish, hyperventilating, or even blacking out and fainting on stage (Steptoe & Fidler, 1987). Afflicted musicians often engage more in this mental "catastrophizing" before, rather than during, performances. Such thoughts are more a source of performance anxiety than a symptom. Negative thoughts tend to intensify in the minds of performers as they are on stage struggling with other symptoms. Satisfying the different cognitive demands simultaneously leads to a narrowing of attention regarding performance, and instead of taking in all relevant cues for performing, attention becomes selective and, unfortunately, not always aimed at the correct cues (for example, performers stop listening to themselves).

Clearly the physiological, behavioral, and cognitive symptoms are interrelated and can occur simultaneously. For example, musicians' worries (cognitive) going into a performance may cause them to tremble, sweat, and tense up (physiological) on stage, resulting in performance mistakes and poor technique (behavioral), all of which increases their negative thinking (cognitive). This kind of vicious cycle has led some psychologists to believe that the inverted U is not the best model to illustrate the deterioration in performance that occurs

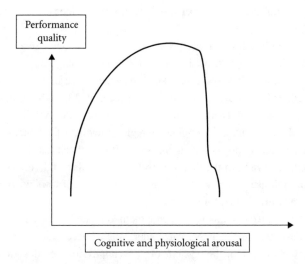

Figure 8.2. The catastrophe model of the interaction between arousal, cognitive anxiety, and performance quality.

once moderate arousal is surpassed. The *catastrophe model* of anxiety and performance replaces the gradual tapering in performance (of the inverted U) with a sharp downward plunge. According to these researchers, the key to predicting the course of deterioration is the cognitive components of performance anxiety. With a performer who is suffering only from the physiological responses to stress, the gradual decline of the Yerkes-Dodson model is apt. However, as more cognitive anxiety is introduced into the equation, the more catastrophic the loss in performance quality will be. The catastrophe model has received empirical support mainly in the realm of athletics, but psychologists have readily applied it to the realm of music performance as well (Wilson, 1997; Wilson & Roland, 2002).

Treating the Physiological Symptoms

Sometimes the most expedient course of action is to target the physiological symptoms for treatment. One such approach is the use of *relaxation techniques*. Among musicians, it seems that the most common of these are deep breathing and muscle relaxation exercises (Wesner et al., 1990). Deep breathing before and during performance may be the most popular coping strategy of any kind (Roland, 1994; Shoup, 1995). Slow, deep breathing ensures that the body takes in the amount of oxygen it expects in its state of arousal. Another approach directed at physiological symptoms is progressive muscle relaxation training. In these exercises, a person proceeds through areas of the body, alternately contracting and relaxing the muscles, one at a time. Often the procedure starts with extremities such as fingers and progresses inward to larger muscles, such as those in the shoulders. Research has shown this training to be effective in reducing several measures of performance anxiety in musicians (Sweeney & Horan, 1982).

In some clinical tests of performance anxiety treatment, relaxation techniques have been supplemented with *biofeedback training*. Using monitoring devices with visual displays, musicians are made aware of the physiological responses their bodies are exhibiting (e.g., accelerated heart rate, higher skin temperature, increased tension in muscles). When they successfully employ relaxation techniques and other coping strategies, they have the benefit of seeing the positive results in physiological measures. Biofeedback assistance has been used to reduce tension in the thumb muscles of violinists and violists, forearm muscles of violinists and clarinetists, and facial muscles of woodwind and brass players (see Lehrer, 1987, for a review).

The *Alexander Technique* is a specific method related to relaxation and bodily awareness. Its creator, F. M. Alexander, was a successful Australian actor who went on to develop his system of "psychophysical re-education" in response to performance-related health problems. The technique has a distinctly philosophical component, emphasizing the unity of body and mind, but it also offers solutions to "misuse" of the body through enhanced sensory awareness and physical training. Exercises largely focus on proper bodily posture, position of the head, and use of muscles when moving. The Alexander Technique was not developed with stage fright in mind, but it is widely used by musicians to reduce unnecessary tension that accompanies anxiety. Some research attests to its effectiveness in improving heart-rate variance, self-reported anxiety, and positive attitude toward performance (Valentine, 2004).

Despite the potential help offered by these relaxation approaches, some musicians have turned to medications to deal with the symptoms of performance anxiety. The most common drugs used are *beta-blockers*. Surveys of classical musicians suggest that in certain circles, approximately one-quarter of performers use beta-blockers (Fishbein et al., 1988). Beta-blockers impede the physiological symptoms that stem from adrenaline being in the bloodstream. Normally, the adrenal hormones in the blood bond to the beta receptors of organs throughout the body, causing them to change their function. When a beta-blocking medication is taken, its chemical agents in the bloodstream also bond to the organs' beta receptors, in effect blocking out the adrenaline. Research has confirmed the effectiveness of beta-blockers in relieving the physiological symptoms of anxiety and has linked their use to improvements in performance (Nubé, 1991). There is some evidence, however, that beta-blocking drugs can have negative side effects in performers, especially if taken in large doses (Nubé, 1994). Improper dosage is a real concern given that some performers use beta-blockers without a doctor's prescription (Fishbein et al., 1988). Another concern raised is whether the lowered sensitivities to anxiety provided by beta blockage also results in reduced sensitivity to the expressive aspects of music performance. Although a feeling of "detachment" has been reported by some musicians while using beta-blockers, it would be difficult to say whether this is an effect of the drug itself or simply a cognitive symptom of performance anxiety that previously went unnoticed amid more debilitating physiological symptoms.

Although our attention thus far has been mainly on the physiological side of performance anxiety, it should be pointed out that because of the interrelated nature of physiological, behavioral, and cognitive aspects, it is likely that the treatments discussed here also have some benefit beyond physiological symptoms. For example, relaxation techniques can likely affect the cognitive processes of musicians, such as refining a performer's powers of attention and concentration. Or maybe performers just become more at ease knowing that they have done something to alleviate the physical symptoms that bothered them in the past.

The Person

For many musicians, merely treating the physiological symptoms does not completely eliminate the experience of performance anxiety. The brain activates the body's emergency system only when a person perceives some sort of threat. This points to the importance of the cognitive realm. How musicians think— their attitudes, beliefs, judgments, and goals—determines in large part the extent to which they perceive a performance as threatening. Consider the following example of how a musician might describe struggling with stage fright:

> I'm normally an anxious person anyway, and before a recital it gets worse. I guess I get obsessed with preparing because I want everything to be perfect. I rarely even get to bed at a decent time since I'm practicing so late. I keep thinking about how disappointed my family would be if I bombed on my recital.

Trait Anxiety

Performers themselves are the first source to be considered in explaining performance anxiety. As professionals, musicians show a stronger disposition toward anxiety than do people who are not performing artists (Kemp, 1996; see also chapter 9). A person's cognitive makeup is a collection of "hardwired" biological and genetic factors, as well as many learned traits. A predisposition to be anxious (in all aspects of life) makes one susceptible to performance anxiety. Although some view *trait anxiety* as an inherent characteristic, research also suggests that an anxious personality results from an accumulation of certain life experiences (Kemp, 1996, p. 86). Nevertheless, a number of research studies have shown a correlation between measures of trait anxiety in musicians and the prevalence of performance anxiety (Cox & Kenardy, 1993; Hamann, 1982). Craske and Craig (1984) provided evidence that in musicians who are generally less anxious (low trait anxiety), the performance anxiety experienced is limited to physiological symptoms of arousal. Highly anxious performers, however, can struggle with increased thoughts of worry and behavioral symptoms during performance.

Although there is certainly great diversity among the personalities of musicians, research has identified several personality traits that are common in the profession and often associated with anxiety. One such characteristic is *introversion* (Kemp, 1996). Introverts have an inward-looking personality. They maintain relatively few close friendships, prefer to be cautious and plan ahead, and usually keep their feelings to themselves. Greater introversion may be associated with higher performance achievement in certain music specializations, such as composing; more extraverted characteristics have been found among music teachers and popular musicians. In addition to introversion, musicians have also scored high in measures of *neuroticism*, or emotional instability. This would describe a person who regularly experiences a wide array of emotions (mood swings) and also shows instability in relationships and interactions with others. Both introversion and neuroticism have been found to correlate with performance anxiety in musicians (Steptoe & Fidler, 1987).

Self-Handicapping and Perfectionism

A combination of extreme introversion and neuroticism can lead to social phobias. This type of anxiety is marked by a preoccupation with how others will judge the performer. Research with musicians has established a link between social phobia and performance anxiety, suggesting that those who suffer from stage fright tend to feel apprehension in other social contexts, as well (Cox & Kenardy, 1993; Steptoe & Fidler, 1987). Wilson (1997) pointed out that some performers' overconcern about the opinion of others can lead to a particularly destructive behavior called *self-handicapping*. In this condition, people try to preserve their standing in the eyes of their peers by setting up excuses for failure in advance. Before a performance, musicians might start to complain about feeling sick or publicize reasons for not being able to practice as much as they wanted. Their desire to have an explanation for a performance failure may even escalate to the point of actually sabotaging their performance ability, perhaps through excessive drinking or damaging their own instruments.

Finally, *perfectionism* is another mental source of anxiety. Perfectionism is defined by unrealistically high expectations, especially of oneself. It is often manifested as inordinate concern about minor mistakes and inconsistencies and a tendency to notice what is wrong instead of what is right. It is easy to see why this trait is relevant to musicians; although awareness of performance errors—especially in individual practice—is necessary in order to improve one's skills, a perfectionist viewpoint is irrational. Minor performance mistakes in and of themselves usually will not ruin the experience for most audiences, but musicians' preoccupation with them can prevent them from accomplishing more expressive performance goals. Pianist Artur Rubinstein seemed to understand this:

> Never mind if I miss one or two notes. The big line is the thing, and it seems to convey the right thing to the audience. Otherwise I would have been pushed from the concert podiums years ago. The public wouldn't stand for it. I think I am the champion of playing wrong notes, but I don't care. And the public doesn't seem to care much. (Elder, 1982, p. 3)

Dispositions such as introversion and perfectionism are considered personality traits, but they may not be firmly set attributes beyond a person's control. These traits manifest themselves in the thought processes of musicians as they practice, prepare for a performance, and eventually take the stage. There is reason to believe that musicians have been conditioned to be introverts and perfectionists as performers, perhaps despite larger personal values that they hold. The faulty appraisal of perfectionism and preoccupation with audience members' judgments lead to mental catastrophizing. Performers can come to believe, for instance, that they might forget everything they've practiced, throw up on stage, and otherwise make complete fools of themselves in front of everyone who is important to them. These are cognitive problems, or breakdowns in realistic thinking.

Cognitive Treatment Approaches

Cognitive restructuring is a treatment strategy that targets a person's thought processes. Musicians learn to identify thinking that is unreasonable and counterproductive, replacing it with thoughts that are realistic and more task-focused. This is usually accomplished through self-talk, in which musicians mentally recite statements to themselves. For example, one team of researchers provided highly anxious pianists with "attention training," in which they were taught to replace hypercritical thoughts with self-statements such as "I've learned the music thoroughly and am well prepared" or "I need to concentrate on maintaining a constant tempo" (Kendrick, Craig, Lawson, & Davidson, 1982). After 6 hours of instruction (three 2-hour sessions) and 5 weeks of trying to implement the training into practice performances with family and friends, the pianists significantly reduced their symptoms of performance anxiety. Similar methodology and results were reported by Sweeney and Horan (1982). Constructive self-talk can help musicians learn to accept the physical and emotional responses that naturally accompany a public performance and come to appreciate this kind of arousal as potentially facilitating. The most prevalent cognitive coping strategies among performing musicians involve some form of self-talk (Roland, 1994). Although not research based, a number of books written by musicians promote the use of self-talk to correct excessively critical thinking. Green and Gallwey's (1986) *The Inner Game of Music* is perhaps one of the most popular.

Wilson and Roland (2002) have suggested that another cognitive aspect of performance anxiety involves *goal setting*. Drawing on research in sports performance and academic achievement, they contend that a musician's goals are either process oriented or outcome oriented. Process-centered goals relate to what a musician hopes to carry out during performance. They tend to be more immediately attainable, such as proper intonation or a wide range of dynamics usage. On the contrary, outcome goals are more definitive accomplishments, such as winning a competition or a position in a select ensemble. Whereas a process goal can enable skill development and even foster the enjoyment of performing, an outcome-goal orientation can promote perfectionist thinking.

As shown in this section, the mental makeup of a performer is a primary source of performance anxiety. Anxiety can manifest itself in troublesome thought patterns such as perfectionism, catastrophizing, and faulty appraisal of other performance aspects. Paraphrasing Wilson (2002), we may summarize the most effective cognitive strategies as follows: (1) learning to accept a degree of anxiety and some minor errors during performance; (2) appreciating the process of performance rather than dwelling on the audience's evaluation; and (3) using self-talk to supplant overly critical thinking with more realistic and task-oriented thoughts.

The Situation

A second broad source of stage fright is the situation of a performance. Anything in the environment or circumstances surrounding a performance that intensifies a performer's sense of threat will increase the level of anxiety experienced. The most significant element of a performance situation is the presence of an audience. The intimidation posed by anonymous faces in a packed concert hall can be equaled by a smaller audience consisting of more significant listeners—loved ones, music experts, adjudicators. Consider this fictitious musician's description of stressful performance conditions:

> Auditions are the worst. You're all alone up there, usually without an accompanist or anything. And the judges are just sitting there listening for every little mistake, trying to find a reason to eliminate you. I think they make the situation uncomfortable just to see how you handle the pressure.

Social Contexts of Performing

Performing music is not stress inducing per se, but doing it in front of people seems to be. Many musicians who experience performance anxiety before audiences show no symptoms when performing alone—even when they know that their heart rate and other physiological signs are being monitored (LeBlanc et al., 1997). We've already seen how a fear of negative evaluation can stimulate performance anxiety. The state of affairs may be exacerbated by the social context of our Western concert tradition, which is marked by strict observance of performance conventions and great psychological separation of the performer from the audience. Due to this formal environment, classical artists may suffer more from performance anxiety than musicians in the jazz genre, which can include more informal performance venues (Kaspersen & Götestam, 2002). In the concert tradition, the performer on stage is not just sharing his or her art but is viewed as a specially skilled expert to be considered "from afar" by the people in the audience, some of whom are adoring fans and others critics. In this context, beginning musicians might feel themselves inadequate to fill such a role, and experienced performers may fear that their past successes have set a standard that they might fail to maintain.

In terms of public performance, anxiety is greater when performance conditions put a musician "on the spot." Situational stress has been shown to increase with larger audience sizes (LeBlanc et al., 1997). A related factor would be the degree to which musicians "feel" the presence of the audience, suggesting the importance of the audience's proximity to performers. An even stronger determinant of felt anxiety, however, seems to be the number of co-performers who occupy the stage. Cox and Kenardy (1993) studied adult music students in group and solo performance conditions and, not surprisingly, found greater levels of

Cross-Cultural Perspective: Performance Anxiety among Jazz Musicians

The musical experiences of jazz performers can be quite distinct from those of their classically oriented counterparts. In addition to the performance conventions associated with each style, the musical subskills required and the means by which they are developed also differ. In a survey study of conservatory students, Kaspersen & Götestam (2002) found that those in the jazz-oriented program reported substantially fewer problems with performance anxiety than did classical specialists. Many of the jazz students described playing in front of an audience as exciting and motivating. This reflects a different attitude toward public performance than that often expressed by classically oriented student performers.

Certain characteristics of jazz likely contribute to a lesser incidence of performance anxiety. Most forms of jazz include much improvisation. This personalizes the act of performance and may cause musicians to focus more on emotional expression. Indeed, the pedagogy of jazz emphasizes expressing oneself through the music as the highest priority. This comes in contrast to training and performance practices of classical music, which traditionally requires precise technical and "note-perfect" performance, often performed from memory.

Also, jazz musicians have historically relied much less on isolated practice to acquire their performance skills. Much of their skill development takes place in real performance situations, in the presence of other musicians ("jam sessions"), if not an actual audience. Again, this is in contrast to classically oriented musicians, who log much time in individual practice. For them, isolated practice can feel like their natural musical environment, making public performance seem all the more formidable.

performance anxiety in the solo situation. The combination of a large audience size and few co-performers can produce a situation in which performance anxiety is most likely to occur.

To some musicians, the size of the audience they're performing for is not as important as *who* the listeners are. Added stress can come when the audience includes a person of special significance, such as a friend or family member or a musical expert. Imagine telling an aspiring cellist that Yo-Yo Ma happened to be passing through town and decided to catch the recital! The presence of an audience contributes situational stress because of a performer's worry about how he or she will be evaluated by others. Certain people's judgments carry

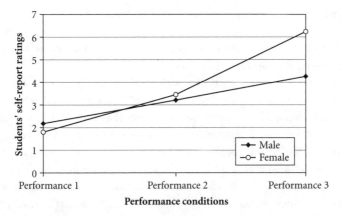

Figure 8.3. Graph from LeBlanc et al. (1997) showing measures of self-reported anxiety in three performance conditions: Performance 1, alone in a practice room; performance 2, in a practice room with a researcher present; and performance 3, in a large rehearsal room with four researchers and a small peer-group audience present. Students reported their levels of anxiety on a 1–10 scale. From "Effect of Audience on Music Performance Anxiety," by A. LeBlanc, Y. C. Jin, M. Obert, & C. Siivola, 1997, *Journal of Research in Music Education, 45,* p. 487. Copyright © 1997 by the Music Eduactors National Conference. Reprinted by permission.

more weight than others, which is why auditions, juries, and performances in competitions are among the most stressful (Craske & Craig, 1984; Hamann & Sobaje, 1983). Clearly, a musician's perception about the importance of a particular performance affects the anxiety with which he or she approaches it. Certain personality and cognitive traits can interact with situational factors to produce exaggerated beliefs about the significance of some performances and about the consequences of success or failure. For example, in Cox and Kenardy's (1993) comparison of group versus solo performance conditions, social phobia was found to be a critical factor. In group settings, performers with social phobias were no more anxious than those without. However, in a solo performance situation, the musicians with social phobia experienced significantly greater performance anxiety.

Dealing with Situational Stress

Musicians who are susceptible to performance anxiety must appreciate the influence of situational factors, but they should also realize that they often have much decision-making power over the conditions of performances they give. Collegiate music students, in particular, are usually in charge of making the arrangements for their recitals. If they have a choice in the venue of their performance, they may choose according to the size of the auditorium and the physical layout of the stage area and audience seating. Also, because the presence of co-performers on stage tends to reduce felt anxiety, musicians may benefit from including duets or small chamber works on their programs instead of performing solo pieces exclusively.

Unfortunately, many aspects of a public performance occur *only* in a public performance. In the practice room, for example, you typically have no audience, you're dressed comfortably, you can take breaks as desired, and you don't have to deal with bright lighting and the openness of a stage. One strategy for dealing with performance anxiety is the use of *mental rehearsal*, in which performers try to vividly imagine what they will experience in an upcoming performance. Mental rehearsal is intended to program the body and mind for the special conditions so that they may automatically behave as desired during the actual performance. It also serves to occupy a performer's thoughts in a more constructive, rather than destructive, way.

One step better is engaging in *practice performances*. It is, of course, common practice for ensembles to hold dress rehearsals in order to acclimate to the conditions of the performance hall. Practice performances for solo musicians are probably not as routine, but they are a good idea. The success of a simulated performance depends on how well it includes the elements of a "real" performance that differentiate it from a typical practice session, such as the presence of an audience, more formal performance attire, and playing straight through the music without stopping. Practice performances for supportive audiences, such as family or friends, have been a part of effective therapy for stage fright (Kendrick et al., 1982). In fact, in one large study students who performed more often were found to report less performance anxiety than others (Linzenkirchner & Eger-Harsch, 1995). Based on his review of research, Lehrer (1987) concluded that more frequent performing should be a part of any treatment approach, because "widely spaced exposure to anxiety-provoking situations may lead to increased anxiety" (p. 149).

When working with performers whose anxiety is particularly crippling, some psychologists have employed the behavioral approach known as *systematic desensitization*. In this type of therapy, which has been used to treat all sorts of phobias, a person attempts to maintain a relaxed state while being exposed to conditions that are increasingly stress-inducing. This process may be carried out by having the person either imagine the situations or actually encounter them live. For example, after achieving a relaxed state, a musician might first think of an "easy" performance situation, such as playing a familiar piece for a friend in a practice room. If still feeling relaxed, the musician might then imagine an additional person in the room and then playing for the two people in a larger rehearsal room. The situations steadily intensify in terms of the elements that provoke anxiety. Of course, systematic desensitization can also be carried out with real performances, instead of imagined scenarios.

Self Study: Creating a Personal Anxiety Hierarchy

Wilson and Roland (2002) suggested a self-directed strategy for carrying out systematic desensitization called *anxiety hierarchies*. For this exercise, assume that you'll be giving a solo performance of a piece of music you already know.

First, list as many different performance situations as you can imagine. You may want to enlist the help of other musician friends in order to come up with a good-sized list. Also, it might help to consider some of the varying conditions that define performance situations (and performance anxiety), such as size of the performance venue, proximity to audience, size of audience, significance of audience members, and time of performance.

After you've got a good list, you'll then need to rate each situation to indicate how stressful it would be for you to give a performance under those conditions right now. Use a scale of 0=no anxiety to 100=extreme anxiety. Then relist your situations in order of increasing anxiety. Consider using this hierarchy in the coming weeks and months; imagine yourself being in those situations or actually giving performances in these progressively anxiety-inducing situations.

The Musical Task

A third source of stage fright is the performance task itself. Musicians often go into performances questioning whether or not they really have the skills to play the music on the program. We're often led to believe that in order to improve ourselves, we must push our limits, to try to exceed what we think we're capable of. For some performers, however, the weeks leading up to a big performance can include nightmares, such as drawing a complete blank when trying to play a piece from memory. Mastering the technical demands of a piece can consume all their practice time such that they feel unable to prepare an expressive interpretation of it. Ideally, they would go onstage with confidence in their abilities, but sometimes it seems that the music is just too hard. Consider another example of how a musician might describe an episode of stage fright:

> The first thing I think when I'm standing on stage is that I should've practiced more. I know the exact parts of the music that I'm going to mess up. And while I'm waiting for those spots, I end up making other mistakes too. You'd think that by now my teacher could pick music that I'd do well with.

When musicians are driven by the fear of things "going wrong" in a performance, they will logically think that thorough preparation is the key to success.

Task mastery, referring to the level of a musician's skills for carrying out a performance task, is an important factor in performance anxiety. Obviously, increased practice and training generally lead to improved performance skills. But the idea here is that greater mastery of a musical task will allow that task to be performed more successfully under anxious circumstances. In two studies with college musicians (Hamann, 1982; Hamann & Sobaje, 1983), the student performers with more years of formal study, indicating greater skill levels, demonstrated superior performance under enhanced anxiety conditions. These researchers equate task mastery with strength of performance behaviors, which musicians rely on when under the duress of a performance. Further, their research suggests that for musicians with high task mastery, the anxiety of a performance is a motivational factor that actually enhances performance quality (see also chapter 3).

Rising to the Challenge

Why is it that some musicians seem to perform better onstage before an audience than in a practice room? Often their general level of musicianship exceeds the challenge presented by the music itself, and only with the challenge of a public performance are they motivated to give their best performances. These musicians are not debilitated or even distracted by the arousal of a performance; they thrive on it. Performing is a rewarding experience for them.

Performing will most likely to be an "optimal experience" for musicians, when the challenge posed by a performance matches their level of skill. The term *flow* describes the experience of being fully engaged in an intrinsically rewarding activity (Csikszentmihalyi, 1993). Flow experiences can happen while performing music. According to flow theory, the first requisite for such an experience is a balance between the task challenge and skill level. When a musician's skill level exceeds the challenge of a performing task (e.g., playing simple music alone in a practice room), boredom prevails. On the other hand, as previously discussed, when the challenge is higher than a musician's skill level, the result is anxiety. Experiences of flow while performing music—with or without an audience—likely contribute to young people's excelling in music as a career. O'Neill (1999) found that among teenagers at a specialized music school, higher achieving performers reported significantly more flow experiences while making music, as compared with lower achievers. A person feels flow when she or he approaches the performance with focused goals in mind and applies great concentration to them while performing. A large portion of performers' mental energy is devoted to monitoring feedback related to performance (e.g., what they hear of themselves and other performers). The performers who experience flow have little opportunity for self-consciousness or worry about others' perceptions. Some performers describe it as being "totally absorbed" or "lost" in the music. If the music being performed is too difficult, musicians will expend much attention to physically producing the music—especially those "trouble spots" in a piece—and not have the mental resources available to monitor feedback. Wan and Huon (2005) provided evidence that the performances of novice musicians deteriorate under pressure due to exhausting their attentional resources to step-by-step control of skill processes.

Even when entering an anxious performing situation, musicians can gain confidence in their abilities through adequate practice and preparation. The term *self-efficacy* refers to people's belief in their ability to accomplish something (see chapter 3). Self-efficacy theory states that when people believe they can control potential threats, they do not engage in apprehensive thinking nor experience the physiological symptoms of anxiety (Bandura, 1991). Self-efficacy is a cognitive factor, but in many ways it is more closely linked to acquired skills than to a person's feelings about him- or herself. To have strong self-efficacy, you must first possess the skills and then come to realize that they are adequate to meet the challenges you face. Proper self-efficacy is based on a realistic appraisal of task mastery and possession of the means to achieve a goal.

Aside from the obvious problem—not being competent to begin with—there are other things that can undermine a performer's self-efficacy. Certain disabling personality traits and cognitive factors can leave a musician without a sense of control. In one experiment with collegiate pianists, those with high trait anxiety showed a measurable drop in self-efficacy when performing in front of an audience (Craske & Craig, 1984). In a study of professional performers, Mor, Day, Flett, and Hewitt (1995) found that the perception of personal control was an important variable in explaining stage fright, especially when jointly considered with the personality trait of perfectionism. Their research attributed debilitating performance anxiety to the combination of a perfectionist attitude and a low sense of control. Although practicing and preparing will normally increase musicians' sense of control as they enter performances, there is also a danger for perfectionist personalities. These musicians may attempt to manage their performance anxiety solely through excessive practicing, growing more frustrated as the perfection and control they seek elude them. This kind of overpractice can result in physical symptoms of overuse, which are another reported source of stress among musicians (Wilson, 2002).

Finding the Balance

For musicians, balancing the challenge of the task with skills they possess is largely done when deciding what music to perform. Unfortunately, musicians may not recognize this point of decision making as a critical factor in performance anxiety. Choosing music to perform is different from choosing music to practice, especially for those who have struggled with performance anxiety. Here, the performer must be realistic in choosing music to perform and factor in the time and effort it will actually take to prepare it. If musicians are looking for a motivational hook to practice, they should consider performing music that they personally like. All too often, music students relinquish the decision making to a teacher, or they feel compelled to choose from a list of established repertoire. However, student musicians (and their teachers) should strive for a balance between working on pieces they "should perform" and making music they actually enjoy. LeBlanc et al. (1997) theorized that when student musicians choose their own music, they are provided with an added incentive for excelling in its performance. They may invest themselves more into preparing it and, consequently, enter the performance with greater confidence in their ability.

Study Questions

1. Within the three broad sources of the person, the situation, and the performance task, what specific sources of performance anxiety fall within the control of musicians? In what ways do outside forces (e.g., other people, performance conventions) sometimes usurp that control?
2. Review the physiology of arousal. What determines whether the body's physiological adaptations of arousal become debilitating symptoms of performance anxiety?
3. In what ways could music students adapt their practicing to better prepare themselves for the anxiety-inducing aspects of public performance?

Further Reading

Connolly, C., & Williamon, A. (2004). Mental skills training. In A. Williamon (Ed.), *Musical Excellence* (pp. 221–245). Practical recommendations for relaxation techniques, mental rehearsal, preperformance routines, and concentration development.

Roland, D. (1994). How professional performers manage performance anxiety. *Research Studies in Music Education, 2,* 25–35. Survey of the many performance anxiety coping strategies.

Wilson, G. D., & Roland, D. (2002). Performance anxiety. In R. Parncutt & G. E. McPherson (Eds.), *The Science and Psychology of Music Performance: Creative Strategies for Teaching and Learning* (pp. 47–61). Research on performance anxiety, including treatment approaches and management strategies.

Part III

Musical Roles

9

The Performer

I f you are a performing musician or training to be one, you likely realize how important individual practice is for developing your skills. Perhaps you have tried to make your practicing as thorough as it can be by making a list of the various types of performance skills you need to work on regularly. Most musicians might list technique, sight-reading, and interpretation; some might also include playing by ear, improvising, or memorization among their target skills. But how many musicians' practice routines include time for improving their expressive body movement and facial expression? Although these things are certainly extramusical and need not be addressed in practice sessions as other musical competencies are, they are, nevertheless, important skills. In fact, they may be critical to performance success.

There are still other performance skills that cannot be addressed in individual practice because they relate to group music making. A great deal of music training is delivered through one-on-one instruction and directed almost exclusively at solo performance. In this context, musicians focus solely on themselves, thinking about what is needed to perform on their instruments, monitoring the sound they are producing, and making adjustments as they go. In an ensemble setting, however, they must do all this *and* pay close attention to the music being made by others in the group. The challenge presented here is the reason we have rehearsals. Of course, the process of coordinating an ensemble performance is more easily accomplished when the participants relate well with one another and share a commitment to the success of the group. Unfortunately, this is not always the case.

Clearly, a successful performing musician must possess certain skills that fall outside the core of musical abilities covered in this book's second part (chapters 5 through 8). It is obviously the first priority of musicians to develop the musical skills (e.g., sight-reading, improvisation, playing expressively) that are necessary for the performing they wish to do. These by themselves, however, are not enough to ensure success as a performer. Many musicians find their early years as full-time performers to be a "crash course" in all the extramusical skills required to succeed.

This chapter considers research that has examined aspects of being a performer that are sometimes overlooked. The results of these studies suggest the following:

1. What an audience *sees* in a live performance can heavily influence what it *hears*. A performer's physical appearance and stage behavior can affect listeners' judgments of the musical quality produced.
2. Musicians' bodily movements while performing have important communicative purposes. The most noticeable gestures often occur at key expressive moments in the music and can be more effective than sound for informing an audience about a performer's emotional intent.
3. Like any other group of people working together, musical ensembles are subject to powerful interpersonal dynamics and social processes. The success of a group can ultimately hinge on how the musicians handle leadership, individuality, and collaborative problem solving among themselves.
4. Ensemble performance also requires specialized musical skills. The coordination of multiple parts into a unified musical whole is accomplished as musicians engage in some rather sophisticated perceptual and attentional processes.
5. In order for a music career to be most rewarding, performers must learn to deal with the sources of stress within it. Failure to adapt to the pressures can contribute to serious problems, including depression, substance abuse, and performance-related injuries.

Taking the Stage: The Performer-Audience Relationship

You can probably think of a famous musical entertainer about whom you would say, "He's not the strongest musician, but he's a great performer on stage." Or perhaps you have been at a large social event, carnival, or fair and come across a live musical performance. Although the music might be a style that you would not listen to on your own time, the live performance may be so engaging that you feel compelled to take it in. Although musical skills may be the most important criteria on which musicians are judged (see chapters 1, 4, and 5), visual aspects of live performances are also very influential on audiences.

First Impressions

In many social settings, people make judgments about other people based on how they look. This is true when audience members observe musicians in a performance. Research has shown that listeners' opinions about the musical quality of a performance are influenced by performers' physical appearances. For example, North and Hargreaves (1997b) had college students listen to original pop music while, for each excerpt, viewing a picture of a musician who was presented as the composer and performer. The listeners responded more favorably to the same music when they believed it was created by a physically attractive musician than by an unattractive one. Pieces allegedly by attractive performers were better liked and judged as reflecting greater artistic merit, sophistication, and intelligence. Similarly, Davidson and Coimbra (2001) documented the importance of physical appearance in the assessment of singers in a music college setting.

Wapnick and colleagues (Wapnick, Darrow, Kovacs, & Dalrymple, 1997; Wapnick, Kovacs Mazza, & Darrow, 1998, 2000) conducted a series of studies that used musicians as evaluators (see also chapter 11, section on music critics and jurors). These studies also expanded beyond physical attractiveness to consider other factors of what is commonly called "stage presence," namely, dress and stage behavior. The performers being judged—singers, violinists, and pianists, respectively—showed great variability in the formality of their attire, despite their being instructed to dress for a recital or audition. They also exhibited diverse body language and stage mannerisms. In general, these studies reported higher appraisals of music performance for musicians who rated high in the categories of attractiveness, dress, and stage behavior. These findings suggest that how musicians take the stage is as important as the quality of their music. Performers may "win over" an audience, at least in part, based on their physical appearance and on their ability to signal confidence through body carriage, smiling, and eye contact with the audience.

Of course, the types of stage behaviors and appearance valued by judges and audiences vary depending on the musical genre and cultural context. Performance etiquette is determined in large part by sociocultural norms. Within Western classical music the expectation is formal attire, such as a dark coat and tie for men and an evening dress for women (black if they are playing in an orchestra; see figure 9.1 for a different approach). When walking on stage, a soloist is expected to greet the audience through facial expression and by bowing to its opening applause. Although it is not often practiced, audiences seem to appreciate it when performers speak comfortably and warmly to them during a concert, perhaps introducing pieces, providing interesting background information, or sharing anecdotes. The formality of the classical conventions is not found in all performance traditions, such as jazz, folk, and other popular music, in which the people on stage are not as psychologically separated from those in the audience.

Figure 9.1. In addition to their superb performance skills as instrumentalists, the Canadian Brass members are known for their unconventional dress and stage practices, which include wearing white tennis shoes (and other costumes) and moving around the stage while performing. Photo from the Canadian Brass website, http://www.canadianbrass.com/picoftheweek/051704.html.

Bodily Gesture and Movement

Research has also established that the bodily movements made by musicians while performing are an important part of the expressiveness of performance as experienced by audiences. This should not come as a surprise, given the close relationship between music and movement. Consider how people use movement terms to describe the expressiveness of musical sound, such as calling staccato tones "bouncy" or saying that a repeated rhythm propels the music forward. People likely learn to connect music and motion from the earliest stages in life, as seen when a father bounces a young child on his knee while singing play songs or when a mother gently rocks an infant to the sounds of a lullaby. This basic connection of music and movement is further seen in the prominent role physical gestures play in expressive music performance (Davidson & Correia, 2002). Franz Liszt was known for supplementing the musical communication of his piano performances with effusive bodily gestures (see figure 9.2).

There appear to be several functions and meanings of the body movements used by skilled performers. First is the production of musical sound itself. Obviously the demands of the instrument (e.g., the slide mechanism of a trombone) and the music being performed (e.g., sixteenth note scalar runs at a fast tempo) define the context within which a musician's body will move. In other words, performers' movements will reflect what they believe is the best way of achieving the desired sound in terms of rhythmic accuracy, timbre, and intonation. But beyond that, successful performers tend to use bodily movement to

---

Cross-Cultural Perspective: Defying the Performance Etiquette Conventions of Classical Music

The social etiquette of classical music performance has remained largely unchanged for many generations. Performers wear formal attire (e.g., suits and ties, evening dresses), greet the audience with a bow, and sit or stand in place while performing. Audiences are also subject to certain "rules" of etiquette, sometimes observing a dress code themselves and almost always sitting silently in a dimly lit hall during performance and applauding at the appropriate times (not between sonata movements, please!).

Although many people have come to appreciate classical music in part because of its formal performance etiquette, surely such conventions serve to put off other potential audience members. Davidson (1997) has suggested that the appeal of some popular classical performers can be attributed to their nonconformity to performance etiquette. In describing a successful British string quartet, she explains:

> [T]hese men do not wear dinner jackets and bow ties. Rather, they wear colourful silk shirts and casual trousers. Nor do they simply acknowledge their audiences through sequences of bows and nods; they can often be seen during concerts chatting informally with their audiences, or exchanging comments to one another between pieces. (p. 213)

Other research has supported the positive effect of greater interaction between performers and the audience in a classical music context (Davidson & Coimbra, 2001). It seems that more and more musicians are challenging the conventions of formal performance etiquette, perhaps in efforts to attract new followers to their music (see figure 9.1).

---

enhance their communication of expressive information. One general principle is that the more emphasis a musician intends to place on the music, the larger the movements will be. In fact, the visual cues provided in a performer's physical gestures may be the only way to communicate certain expressive ideas in a live performance. Davidson (1993) video-recorded musicians performing in three manners: deadpan (no expression), normal projected expression, and exaggerated expression. A group of musicians evaluated the performance recordings, working in sound-only, vision-only, and sound-and-vision conditions. Adjudicators relying on sound only were largely unable to distinguish between the normal and exaggerated expressive manners of performance. However, both the vision-only and sound-and-vision conditions allowed differentiation between the levels of expression.

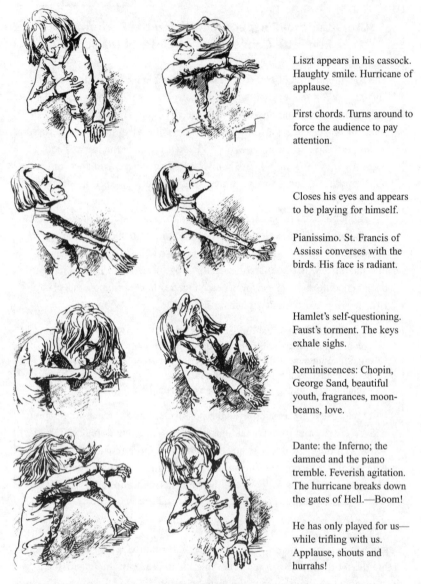

Liszt appears in his cassock. Haughty smile. Hurricane of applause.

First chords. Turns around to force the audience to pay attention.

Closes his eyes and appears to be playing for himself.

Pianissimo. St. Francis of Assisi converses with the birds. His face is radiant.

Hamlet's self-questioning. Faust's torment. The keys exhale sighs.

Reminiscences: Chopin, George Sand, beautiful youth, fragrances, moon-beams, love.

Dante: the Inferno; the damned and the piano tremble. Feverish agitation. The hurricane breaks down the gates of Hell.—Boom!

He has only played for us— while trifling with us. Applause, shouts and hurrahs!

Figure 9.2. Caricatures of Liszt at the piano, drawn by János Jankó in 1873. From *Virtuoso* by H. Sachs, 1982. Copyright © 1982 by Thames & Hudson. Reprinted by permission.

Because a musician's expressive intentions are shaped by the musical structure of a piece, it follows that physical gestures during performance can be linked to structural features (see chapter 5). Clarke and Davidson (1998), in analyzing the movements of a concert pianist's performance, associated different types of head and body swaying with particular locations within the form of the piece and with instances of a recurring motif. Other research with clarinetists similarly linked bodily gestures with stipulations of the music (Wanderley, 2002). Changes in posture tended to mark the beginnings of phrases, quick movements of the clarinet's bell coincided with staccato articulations, and circular bell movements occurred during slower legato playing (see figure 9.3).

Other types of performer movements are not as easily accounted for. The bodily rocking common among pianists has been of particular interest to some researchers (Davidson & Correia, 2002). Although it surely can communicate expressive intentions to an audience, it has likely other functions, as well. A pianist may carry out this movement for the comforting sensation it provides. This may put the musician at ease during the performance situation or engender what is believed to be the right mood for playing the music properly.

An alternative explanation of performer rocking is simply that it is a learned behavior. That is, musicians, sometime during their development, have observed it in more experienced performers and taken it on for themselves, believing it is just what a performer should do. Much movement on the part of musicians surely falls under the category of learned behavior. This type of physical gesture is perhaps most common within popular styles of music known for their strong sociocultural links. A popular image of the lead singer of a rock band usually includes active full-body movement during performance, such as jumping, kicking, and energetic dancing. The specific gestures used are largely culturally defined. For example, music with a sexual message is often performed with suggestive pelvic movements. Performers of American rap and hip hop music often use punching and jabbing arm motions reminiscent of boxing, thought to be related to the origins of the musical style (Ramsey, 2000).

Although the Western classical concert tradition usually prescribes a quiet and still audience, in other popular genres, musicians prefer to perform before a more active audience. Thus some gestures from performers act as signals designed to elicit physical responses from those in attendance, perhaps clapping along to the music, dancing, and other kinds of movement. Finally, performers in all styles of music are known to use physical gestures to communicate with co-performers (see the section on ensemble performing later in the chapter).

Other Presentational Factors

When preparing for a concert or recital, many musicians do not spend a lot of time working on their performance body movements or considering how their physical appearance will affect the audience's impression of their musical skills. After all, musicians face enough challenges in adequately rehearsing the music to a performance-ready standard. How musicians prepare for performance not only affects the musical quality but also other presentational aspects

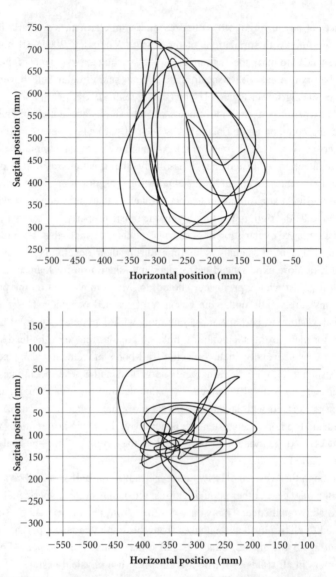

Figure 9.3. Circular movement patterns of the clarinet bell during the opening bars of the Brahms *Clarinet Sonata No. 1.* The graphs show the movements of two different clarinetists. From "Quantitative Analysis of Non-Obvious Performer Gestures" by M. M. Wanderly, 2002, figure 5. In I. Wachsmuth & T. Sowa, Eds., *Gesture and Sign Language in Human-Computer Interaction: Revised Papers* (pp. 241–253). Copyright © 2002 by Springer Science and Business Media. Reproduced with permission.

that will determine the audience's concert experience. Of course, the degree to which performers are prepared and feel confident when the curtain rises is usually readily perceived by spectators.

Musicians will be most successful when they feel mastery over the music they are performing (see chapter 8). If they take the stage with excessive concerns about merely executing the technical demands of the performance (e.g., "getting the right notes and rhythms"), it is unlikely that they will realize the expressive potential of the music. A performer possessing the skills to match the challenge posed by the music may approach the optimal state of flow, or be fully engaged in a rewarding musical experience (see chapter 8). It is likely that audiences are impressed by musicians who are "into it" while performing.

Facial expressions are effective indicators of emotion, some being universally identifiable across cultures. Whether smiling to signal delight or furrowing one's brow to show consternation, a performer's use of facial expression and body movement can enhance the communication of emotional intent. As alluded to in the previous section, one explanation for pianists' rocking is that they do it to heighten *their own* emotional connection to the music, which would then be evident to an observing audience (Davidson & Correia, 2002). Recognition of this may be why many musicians use mental imagery and memories of felt emotions in order to evoke a state of mind they believe is suitable for a particular piece of music (Persson, 2001).

One type of facial expression, namely, closing the eyes while performing, necessitates special preparation on the part of musicians. In the case of performing composed music in the Western classical tradition, memorization is required. Williamon's (1999) study has suggested that performing from memory affords a number of benefits to musicians. First of all, preparing for a memorized performance requires greater practice, which likely improves many aspects of the musical quality. In his study, people evaluated the qualities of an expert cellist's performances in several memorized and nonmemorized conditions. Because of the cellist's general mastery over the instrument, technical performance was rated high across all conditions, but musical and communicative aspects were judged to be higher with memorization. Most of the advantage is likely due to the absence of a music stand that obstructed audience members' view of the performer. The lack of any visual obstruction may permit a more "direct psychological connection" with the audience (Williamon, 1999, p. 92). This adds to the perception that the performance is coming from (owned by) the performer, as opposed to coming from the printed page. Finally, Williamon's research also suggests that some observers of performance, especially those with greater musical training themselves, may simply be impressed by the fact that a performer expended the effort to memorize a piece. Before even hearing a note, the listeners may be predisposed to like the performance

Self Study: Describing Your Ideal Performer Self

From the perspective of a newspaper music critic, write a concert review of a perfect performance given by your ideal performer self. Try to be as specific as possible in giving an account of this concert. Include some information about the impressive repertoire performed and the wonderful musical sounds that the performer (the ideal you) produced, but emphasize in your review all the extramusical performance skills responsible for thoroughly captivating, affecting, and/or entertaining the audience. Do *not* consider any realistic appraisal of your actual performance skills, but imagine—as vividly as possible—what it would be like if you had ideal skills in terms of stage presence, bodily movement, and overall audience appeal. Otherwise, write a similar review of a performance that impressed you because of the stage behavior of the performer (e.g., famous musician, fellow student).

based on an admiration for the musician's diligence and authority shown through memorization.

Clearly, there is more to carrying out a successful live performance than being able to play the music (even from memory). It seems that many aspiring musicians fail to acknowledge the visual contact in the way they go about their craft. Relatively little instruction within music performance training is devoted to these extramusical performance factors that strongly affect how listeners judge someone's musicianship. Most of these, including aspects of physical appearance, stage behavior, bodily gestures, and use of printed music, are under the control of performers themselves. They amount to skills that can be developed with proper training and practice. Davidson and Correia (2002) have summarized teaching methods for improving music students' use of the body. These include increasing awareness of muscular tension and postural habits and identifying dramatic physical gestures that match phrases within a musical work.

Sharing the Stage: The Skills of an Ensemble Performer

Whereas solo performing can offer a special satisfaction to some musicians, virtually all enjoy the rewards of group music making. In some cases, the group effort begins at the compositional level, as several musicians collaborate in creating music to be performed or recorded later. In other settings, a group of musicians who have never before worked with one another may be assembled together for the first time on stage to present a coordinated ensemble performance with no prior rehearsal. Group music making presents many specialized challenges to musicians and involves a variety of social factors.

Social Processes of Collaborative Rehearsing and Creating

Most of the time, the public performance of an ensemble is preceded by rehearsals. In these rehearsals musicians coordinate their multiple parts into a single musical product and create some interesting social dynamics. Music ensembles bear out some of the findings of general research into group processes (often conducted in workplaces, schools, and social organizations). For example, the productivity or quality of work produced by a group can be related to individual members' feelings of affiliation and cohesion. Also, leadership and status are important issues that affect a group's activities.

Some musical ensembles, such as professional orchestras and school bands, have a conductor or teacher as the designated leader. Although many other musical groups have no official authority structure, even chamber groups or rock bands may have an informal leadership structure (Rosenbrock, 2002; Ford & Davidson, 2003). Regardless, successful collaboration depends not only on the musical but also on the social coordination between members. "Ensemble performance is about teamwork," one researcher has written, "Half the battle of making music together (and ultimately staying together as an ensemble) is fought on social grounds" (Goodman, 2002, p. 163). In rehearsals, interpersonal dynamics between players take shape through social exchanges around the music. As a newly formed group rehearses and discusses their music making, leadership tends to emerge. In a study of musicians' roles in wind quintets, Ford and Davidson (2003) found that although all group members endorsed democratic decision making and shared responsibility, most were still able to identify a leader. Exactly who emerges as a leader can sometimes be linked to the personnel makeup of the group and performance demands of the music. Musicians who are known to possess superior individual performance skills may hold special status. In the informal group practices (or "jam sessions") of popular musicians, oftentimes a more experienced player will assume a leadership role by sharing with others previously unfamiliar chords, progressions, or "licks" (Green, 2002). The instrument played by each person can affect social roles within the group. This may relate to social stereotypes attached to particular instruments, such as the inferior standing of the second violin within a string quartet, the presumed subservient role of the piano accompanist, or the drummer in a major rock group. Related to this is the way an instrument is used in a composition. Because the higher pitched instruments within ensembles are often the most prominently heard (e.g., flutes in woodwind quintet, trumpets in brass ensembles), those players may be more likely to assume a leadership role (Ford & Davidson, 2003). Yet other research has suggested that gender is an important factor, with males generally being more direct when sharing opinions (Berg, 2000; Davidson & Good, 2002).

In many performing groups, the leader role shifts among the players. This exchange may sometimes correspond with the music being rehearsed. Different pieces of music can feature different instruments; for each work, the player whose part is most prominent or who composed the song may be expected to head up the rehearsing. Exchange of leadership may also occur according to the expertise of group members. For example, a player known to have the best "ear" in terms of intonation may take charge of all the group's tuning concerns. As far as improving individual musicianship, a group that shares leadership responsibilities and values each member may be most advantageous to musicians. Based on her research of peer-managed high school chamber music ensembles, Berg (2000) concluded that those members within a group who contribute to the decision making (e.g., on matters of interpretation) are more likely to grow musically from the ensemble experience.

An especially critical time in rehearsal, during which musicians' roles within a performing group are perhaps clearest, is when musical problems are encountered. Depending on the music being rehearsed, the ensemble members may face problems coordinating tempo, articulation, dynamic balance (loudness), and harmonic intonation, to name but a few aspects. Success in solving such performance problems depends largely on how well a group identifies and deals with individual performer idiosyncrasies (Davidson & Good, 2002; Rosenbrock, 2002). Thus, with musicians' egos potentially on the line, the group cohesion felt by members is an important factor. Ford and Davidson (2003) advance the idea that a group can better achieve its goals when all members feel free to address issues in rehearsals. This may be more likely to occur in ensembles whose members have been working together for some time. In such settings, the musicians can more wholly devote their energies to solving musical problems, as opposed to establishing or exercising social identity and status (Berg, 2000). Groups in which members do not feel a strong sense of affiliation are less likely to be successful and risk having some members discontinue their involvement (Ford & Davidson, 2003; Murningham & Conlon, 1991).

Because the functioning of the group is so dependent on sociocultural factors, it follows that group music making enterprises are affected by traditions related to musical genres. Allsup (2003) has provided evidence that truly collaborative music making and "community making" can be difficult within a classical music context but perhaps more readily attainable within jazz and popular music styles. In this study, high school band students formed two small groups (four or five members each) and met regularly to make original music together. One group decided to put aside their primary concert band instruments and instead work with a rock band instrumentation of electric guitar, bass, keyboard synthesizer, and drums. The other group, rejecting rock music as too easy and formulaic, chose to create music for their concert band instruments. The groups' collaborative sessions were observed and the music students interviewed. The creative sessions of the rock band were characterized by peer learning, collective generation of ideas, and productive peer critiquing (see also Green, 2002; Rosenbrock, 2002). As one music student said, "One person would come up with an idea, and we'd just kinda like work off the idea. . . . If someone didn't like it, they'd say so right away. It works pretty well" (Allsup, 2003, p. 30). The classical group, however, struggled with what they believed the compositional process should be, debating issues of form, tonality, and historical style. In this group's session, the students often separated from each other to work individually, usually notating their ideas on paper. The researcher concluded that once ideas were on paper, students were even more reluctant to change them to accommodate the contributions of others. The frustration faced by the students in this group ultimately led them to abandon the classical style in favor of jazz, at which point they began to experience greater collaboration.

Processes during Group Performance

As discussed, influential social factors come into play in group music making. Although they are extramusical, to be sure, the development of certain interpersonal skills seems to be a prerequisite for successful ensemble participation. There is also a set of musical skills unique to group performance. After all, the many musicians of a large band or orchestra may sound great playing their independent parts while in individual practice, but they can still fail to "put it all together" to form a whole ensemble work. The skills required to do this center around musicians' abilities to coordinate the aspects of their own performing (e.g., pitch, rhythm, articulation, loudness) with those of other performers. Multiple psychological processes are involved as performing musicians monitor, evaluate, and anticipate their own parts while simultaneously doing the same with the music being produced by others.

Because music occurs across time, synchronization of performance is perhaps the most important effort undertaken by an ensemble. Coordinating the timing of performed music involves several cognitive mechanisms (Goodman, 2002). First is what could be called the *ensemble's clock*, referring to the performers' shared awareness of a main tempo for a piece of music. Although many conductors surely want their beat patterns to be considered the absolute point of reference, the ensemble's clock is really an internal pulse generated within each musician. The movements of a conductor's baton merely indicate his or her conception of the clock and may or may not match the performers' internal tempos. While the ensemble's clock acts as an underlying framework, the rhythmic precision with which musicians play the notes of their parts depends on their *timekeeping skills*. Based on the feedback gained by hearing other performers' parts and perhaps watching a conductor's gestures, a musician anticipates how the others' rhythmic timing will occur and attempts to execute his or her own part with it. To put it simply, a musician might think, "On the basis of the previous note, when is the next note of a fellow performer going to sound?" (Goodman, 2002, p. 154). Anticipation is also required as performers consider the amount of time needed to get notes to "speak" on their particular instrument. When musicians in a group are all employing these timing skills effectively, their collective performance will sound rhythmically "together." Of course, the precise synchronization we hear is merely an auditory illusion, as playing notes at the exact same time is beyond the capabilities of human perception and performance (for a sophisticated explanation of ensemble timing, see Rasch, 1988).

Similar processes occur as musicians work to fit other qualities of their individual performing with those of a group, such as bringing their own single pitch in tune with the chord created by the ensemble or balancing the loudness of their note with the production of the rest of the ensemble. It becomes clear that skilled ensemble playing is a sophisticated cognitive activity. As pointed out by Keller (2001), ensemble performance requires complex "multitasking" of musicians who are limited in how much attention they can devote to simultaneous tasks. The two general tasks involved are the primary task of paying attention to one's own part and the secondary task of knowing what is concurrently happening in the aggregate structure (i.e., all parts). Dealing with one's own performance alone involves (1) retrieving relevant musical knowledge from memory, (2) executing the motor programs needed to produce the desired sounds on an instrument, (3) monitoring that musical production, and (4) mentally representing it in order to make judgments about it (see chapters 1 and 4). Additionally, tracking the aggregate structure of the ensemble requires similar processes (Keller, 2001). Problems in coordinated ensemble performance frequently arise when musicians are forced to devote virtually all their attention to their own parts (due to the difficulty of the music) and are unable to attend to the aggregate structure. Thus it is helpful for musicians to come to rehearsal with their individual parts already well practiced. If they can rely on some degree of automaticity in their own musical production, then they can allocate more attention to processing other musicians' parts and the aggregate structure. Attentional strain is further exacerbated when musicians are unmotivated or suffering from anxiety. Such conditions diminish the total "resource supply" that musicians have to allocate to the multiple performance processes (see chapter 8).

The attentional resource demands of ensemble performance are less for an expert musician who possesses an extensive generalized musical knowledge base to draw on. This information can allow more immediate mastery of one's own part and a more efficient understanding of the aggregate structure. This explains how certain advanced musicians are able to effectively perform together as groups with only a few or even no rehearsals. Bastien and Hostager (1988) examined a public performance by a group of four accomplished jazz musicians (saxophone, piano, bass, and drums) who had never before played together. This "zero-history" group was able to deliver a high-quality performance largely because of the shared information and performance expectations among its members. They could rely on the mutually known song repertoire, structural conventions, and performance practices of jazz. In other words, these musicians knew that on a "gig" like this one, they would play songs they all knew and that the performance of each would follow a standard form, such as (1) piano introduction, (2) the song's melody, or "head," played by the saxophone, (3) improvised solos, and (4) restatement of the "head." Also underlying shared information are established social practices, such as that the soloist at any given time has license to determine certain qualities of performance for the group (e.g., overall loudness level, style and texture, rhythmic complexity) and that the other musicians are expected to follow. Performers usually communicate such musical decisions in real time using nonverbal means. Sometimes this communication is completely musical, that is, it is done aurally through performance (Murningham & Conlon, 1991; Williamon & Davidson, 2002; Monson, 1996). Bastien and Hostager's (1988) jazz performers often signaled the end of their improvised solos with "winding down" cues, such as lowering the loudness of their playing.

Eye contact is also critical in the communication of co-performers. It may be used to supplement musical communication cues. One musician might look at another as if to say, "I'm expressing a certain musical idea. Try to match it". Eye contact is common at points in the music that are important as far as coordination, such as entrances and exits of individual parts (Bastien & Hostager, 1988; Williamon & Davidson, 2002). Clayton (1985) found that when musicians were not able to see one another during a group performance, their musical output was less coordinated in terms of timing and dynamics.

Furthermore, the importance of eye contact is related to musicians' prevalent use of physical gesture to communicate with each other. Sometimes the way a musician is carrying out the movements needed just to play an instrument can serve as a visual cue to co-performers. The height of a pianist's hand lifts or the size of a violinist's bowing motions can indicate how the music should sound. Otherwise, musicians may add to their performance body movements to convey information to others. Davidson (1997) has categorized communicative physical gestures between performers as *illustrators* and *emblems*. Illustrators are self-explanatory gestures that can serve various purposes. For example, in order to coordinate a synchronized group attack at the beginning of a piece, one performer might nod his head to signal the downbeat (some wind players commonly use the bells of their instruments). Emblems, on the other hand, are more like gestural symbols whose meaning must be learned. Consider, for instance, a jazz combo like the one mentioned earlier. Improvised solos do not have a set length, as individual soloists can decide how many times they wish to play through the chord changes of a song. Another musician who thinks that the current solo may be "winding down" prematurely might make a repetitive circular gesture with a finger as if to say, "Keep playing."

Instructors within formal music education do not always explicitly teach the principles of ensemble performance to their students. It is even less common in formal training to address the social skills that facilitate collaborations between musicians. Music students often learn these things through the enculturation provided by participation in school performance classes, community youth ensembles, and informal music-making ventures with friends.

Off Stage: The Psychological Demands of a Musician's Life

Most musicians wear many "hats" in their professional lives, reflecting their diverse roles and responsibilities. Few musicians as young adults are able to work *exclusively* as performers, composers, or music teachers (see chapter 10). It is common for musicians to find themselves doing a little of all of these things. Especially early in a musician's career, when he or she is trying to "make it" as a performer or composer or songwriter, time spent rehearsing and writing music may not directly result in any income. In order to make a living, some musicians may seek employment in music merchandising (e.g., as a salesperson at a local music store) or may establish a private teaching studio. Other times, aspiring performers hold down nonmusical jobs while simultaneously trying to further their music careers. As musicians diversify, they may not fully appreciate that different lines of work—even within the broader field of music—require the development of specialized skills in order to be successful. Even when a person is able to work exclusively as a performing musician, there are still important extramusical skills involved in having a successful career. Oftentimes, performers must be their own agents, publicizing and promoting their music and handling legal issues of copyright law, licensing, and contract negotiations.

Throughout their lives musicians deal with expectations and psychological demands that are quite different from those in the rest of the population. As young children, musicians are put on a track toward full-time involvement in musical experiences and receive special attention (see chapter 2). Research suggests that, compared with people in other walks of life, musicians more closely identify with their chosen profession and find it more difficult to detach themselves from their work (Spahn, Strukely, & Lehmann, 2004). For many musicians, life never arrives at any real place of stability. For example, it is common for a classical musician, after making a living for decades exclusively as a performer, to make a transition later in life to working primarily as a teacher.

The Performer Personality

Because of the distinctiveness of the job, one might wonder whether only a certain kind of person chooses to pursue a career in music or whether a person is shaped by the pursuit itself and takes on personality characteristics similar to those of other musicians. The many studies conducted on this topic have taken a variety of approaches and sometimes have offered seemingly contradicting results; Kemp (1996) has done the best job of synthesizing and interpreting this body of research (see chapter 10 for the personality of teachers). He acknowledged that a person's behavior is a product of environmental influences, but he has maintained that the musician's conduct also depends on "the kind of person that he or she is" (Kemp, 1996, p. 15). It is likely impossible to know to what extent personality traits are set predispositions, as opposed to consequences of life experiences. Regardless, the research has shown a number of personality tendencies among populations of musicians.

Musicians as a whole tend to score higher in measures of *introversion* and *neuroticism* (emotional instability; see chapter 8). Consequently, one might think that musicians' personalities only serve to make them more vulnerable to personal problems, such as anxiety, depression, and relationship conflicts. On the contrary, as young people develop into skilled musicians, they likely benefit from facilitating personality traits that accommodate the demands of musical involvement. A combination of introversion and *independence*, another trait found to be strong among many musicians, can be manifested as self-sufficiency, a sense of personal control, and an ability to perform tasks that are perceived as boring or monotonous. In other words, they may be well suited to carry out the individual practice that is expected of aspiring music performers. Musicians also tend to have higher levels of *sensitivity*. Taken together, sensitivity and independence have been linked to personal qualities such as creativity, intuition, and an aesthetic orientation, all of which can be very important in music. Finally, musicians tend to be less conforming to societal gender stereotypes. This psychological *androgyny* may reflect the fact that musical involvement requires from all performers qualities that are, according to conventional labeling, both masculine (e.g., self-sufficiency) and feminine (e.g., emotional sensitivity).

The preceding personality profile may reflect a bias in the research toward classical musicians. In fact, a more accurate picture of musical temperament must also consider the specific demands of different musical activities (e.g., composing, performing, teaching) and musical genres and cultures (e.g., orchestral, popular styles, folk music). For example, many of the traits of musicians listed previously can be less obvious in a music teacher (see chapter 10) but even stronger in a composer, seen as a "musician *par excellence*" by Kemp (1996, pp. 215; see figure 9.4 and chapter 7, this volume). A number of studies have examined the personality characteristics of pop and rock performers as compared with musicians of other styles. Such popular performers do not show

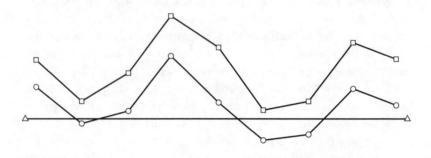

Aloof	Dominant	Expedient	Sensitive	Imaginative	Naive	Radical	Self-sufficient	Undisciplined
A−	E+	G−	I+	M+	N−	Q1+	Q2+	Q3−

Outgoing	Submissive	Conscientious	Tough-minded	Practical	Astute	Conservative	Group-dependent	Controlled
A+	E−	G+	I−	M−	N+	Q1−	Q2−	Q3+

□———□ Composers
○———○ Performers
△———△ Student norms

Figure 9.4. Personality differences between male composers and performers. From *The Musical Temperament: Psychology and Personality of Musicians,* by A. E. Kemp, 1996, p. 200. Copyright © 1996 by Oxford University Press. Reprinted by permission.

as much introversion as their classical counterparts, and they tend to be more enthusiastic and comfortable in loud environments (Gillespie & Myors, 2000).

The fact that research has revealed temperament variations among musicians suggests that there is no single "performer personality." Moreover, aspiring musicians should not feel "doomed" if their personalities do not line up with the trait tendencies described here. There are, of course, many successful musicians whose personalities are notable exceptions to the general trends. Additionally, there is ample evidence that musicians' personalities evolve throughout the life span in response to experiences. In fact, the idea that ones's personality is made up of stable and unchangeable traits has been well debated (Kemp, 1996, pp. 14–15). It should rather be viewed as a disposition to think or act a certain way in particular situations.

Stress and Other Medical Problems

One of the reasons that researchers have investigated the personality characteristics of musicians is the relationship of certain traits to stress and the ability to cope with it. Although the general public may view music as an intrinsically rewarding profession, research has shown that musicians experience high levels of occupational stress. Many regularly deal with financial strain and, as a result, time pressures as they struggle to balance the demands of work and other personal commitments. While "on the job," musicians can experience interpersonal conflicts with colleagues, which arise from intense and criticism-filled working conditions surrounding group performances. Of course, performance anxiety also afflicts many musicians, meaning that some may not even have music making as an enjoyable retreat from the stressors of life (see chapter 8).

It appears that coping with stress is something of a skill that successful musicians develop. Failure to adapt to the pressures can have some very serious ramifications, including depression and other emotional disorders. Depression may be a special risk for individuals who are highly perfectionistic and self-critical, two qualities that, ironically, some musicians consider keys to success in the field. Drug and alcohol abuse is a well-documented accompanier of anxiety and depression, and it is a problem among some musicians. Treatment often involves educating musicians about potential mental health risks and helping them form realistic expectations for themselves and their careers (see Chesky, Kondraske, Henoch, Hipple, & Rubin, 2002; Raeburn, 2000; Sataloff, Brandfonbrener, & Lederman, 1998).

Stress is also a significant contributor to the physical injuries that musicians can encounter. Performers who carry out repetitive motions with their hands and arms in playing their instruments are at risk for overuse injuries (see the section on amount of practice in chapter 4, this volume). Excessive tension further increases the likelihood of damage. The most common symptom experienced by musicians is musculoskeletal pain, including tendinitis. Another occupational hazard is hearing loss, especially among musicians working in electronically amplified performance environments (Chesky et al., 2002). Hearing loss, like performance-related injuries, can be difficult to deal with because it constitutes a direct threat to the livelihood of performing musicians. Thus some may avoid seeking treatment, fearing that a doctor's prescription would prohibit performance on their instrument. However, other options may exist, and musicians are much better served in the long run to receive proper medical care (Brandfonbrener & Kjelland, 2002; Sataloff et al., 1998). Musicians who deal with stress and other medical problems are strongly encouraged to utilize the resources previously referenced (and under "Further Reading" at the end of the chapter).

Performance expertise in a strictly musical sense (i.e., skill at producing musical sounds on an instrument) is not enough to ensure success as a performer.

Musicians are more likely to succeed if they possess a variety of extramusical performance skills, such as those described throughout this chapter. The idea that these competencies are required for a career in music may challenge some musicians who struggle to find the time to practice their instruments, let alone figure out how to develop additional skills. Others, however, fully realize the great versatility that is demanded of a performing musician.

Study Questions

1. In light of the research on the influence of extramusical performance factors, how might a musician practice and prepare for a solo recital in order to most impress the audience?
2. What are the characteristics of a collaborative group that functions well and provides rewarding musical experiences for its members?
3. What personality traits facilitate a performance career? Are musicians who do not possess these traits necessarily at a disadvantage?

Further Reading

Davidson, J. W., & Correia, J. S. (2002). Body movement. In R. Parncutt & G. E. McPherson (Eds.), *The Science and Psychology of Music Performance: Creative Strategies for Teaching and Learning* (pp. 237–250). Practice strategies for musicians to improve their use of bodily gesture in performance.

Davidson, J. W., & Good, J. M. M. (2002). Social and musical co-ordination between members of a string quartet: An exploratory study. *Psychology of Music, 30,* 186–201. Social dynamics and performance coordination of a student string quartet; presents also a good example of case study methodology.

Sataloff, R. T., Brandfonbrener, A. G., & Lederman, R. J. (1998). *Performing Arts Medicine* (2nd ed.). Perhaps the most comprehensive volume on health concerns of performing artists, covering issues such as hearing loss, musculoskeletal injuries, and psychiatric problems.

10

The Teacher

M ost people who become proficient musicians do so only with the assistance of teachers. Although many teachers work with students within the formal setting of a school or music studio, other people also serve in teaching roles for aspiring musicians. For example, parents supervise their children's home practicing, musical peers provide challenges and motivation, and professional musicians act as role models. Parents, peers, and performers all may possess one or two qualities that foster music learning in those they come in contact with, but music teachers by trade must have many of these qualities to be effective.

As seen in the previous chapter, many skills that are acquired by performing musicians have little to do with music making. But often these skills distinguish the most successful performers from the lesser ones. In the same way, great music teachers possess specialized skills, which are largely distinct from those of the performer. Prospective teachers usually receive professional training in education and psychology as a basis for their teaching skills. Research contradicts the notion that a musician who struggles in a performing career or who burns out on performance can successfully "fall back" on teaching (i.e., "Those who can, do; those who can't, teach").

Over the course of their careers, most musicians find themselves occupying the role of teacher—successful or not—at some time or another. Even those who are never employed on a full-time basis as instructors still encounter many situations in which they are asked to explain musical concepts and techniques or demonstrate their musicianship for the benefit of others. There are many factors that influence how effective people's instructional efforts will be, including the time they allocate to teaching, their verbal and nonverbal behaviors, the type of music activities they engage their students in, and measures they take to specifically improve their teaching (Duke, 2000).

The research reviewed in this chapter supports the following conclusions about the functions, behaviors, and personal attributes of music teachers:

1. The type of relationship a teacher establishes with students affects the learning process. A relationship marked by mutual respect and exchange of ideas may better aid students in realizing the highest levels of music preparation and performance.

2. Developing musicians rely on teachers for quality musical models and feedback on students' own performances. Over the course of their studies, students ideally "internalize the teacher," learning to generate goals for themselves and to self-monitor performances.

3. The behaviors and strategies of expert teachers differ from those of less skilled teachers. Experts' verbal instruction speaks clearly to concrete properties of music while also incorporating imagery and metaphors. More important, expert teachers efficiently deliver instruction, limiting their verbalizations to accommodate greater student participation.

4. Students' music achievement is greatest when teachers fully complete instructional cycles, which consist sequentially of (1) the teacher presenting a performance task to students, (2) students responding by implementing or applying the instruction, and (3) the teacher providing specific feedback to students' response.

5. People are not just born great teachers. The personal qualities that support effective teaching result from background experiences and training, rather than from personality characteristics.

The Functions of the Teacher

The Teacher-Student Relationship

Most people can probably think of at least one teacher who was a great influence during their musical development. It may be a schoolteacher, perhaps an elementary music specialist who made classes enjoyable, or a high school choir director who shared a love for group vocal music. Other musicians may feel indebted to a teacher who gave them one-on-one instruction or private lessons. Whether tutoring a single student or working with an entire class, an effective teacher becomes important in the lives of aspiring musicians by establishing a relationship with them.

Obviously, a student's relationship with a one-on-one tutor can be closer than that with a class music teacher or ensemble director. In educational research, one-on-one tutoring has been shown to be generally more effective than conventional group instruction. The acceptance of private lessons is also seen in music education. A private teacher has more specialized expertise than a group instructor (e.g., a trumpet teacher as opposed to a band director) and can tend to the specific needs of individual students. Private lessons may also be the primary setting in which young musicians learn expressivity (Woody, 2000, 2003). When considering one-on-one and group-learning settings, however, the desired qualities of teachers and instructional strategies are probably more similar than different.

Music teachers have different concepts of what teaching is, as seen in the way they interact with students. There are two broad models for the teacher-student relationship: the *master-apprentice* model and the *mentor-friend* model. In a master-apprentice relationship, the role of teachers is to tell of their experiences and demonstrate their craft (Reid, 1997). It is implicit that students want to emulate their teacher's musical and professional life. This relationship is common, especially in one-on-one settings, and is marked by one-way communication from teacher to student, often resulting in the direct copying of a teacher model (Young, Burwell, & Pickup, 2003).

In contrast, the mentor-friend model reflects greater exchange between teacher and student. Teachers work to facilitate student experimentation and provide musical ideas for the student to consider. Teaching means guiding the augmentation of students' own musical experiences (Reid, 1997). This may allow teachers to be more responsive to the individual needs of the students. Elements of the mentor-friend model allow for greater contribution on the part of students and, as a result, stronger feelings of autonomy. This in turn increases the possibility of intrinsic motivation for music learning (see chapter 3). As we will see later in this chapter, teacher behavior and strategies employed during lessons vary, largely as a result of the relationship a teacher has with students.

Many factors can influence the form that a particular teacher-student relationship may take. For example, the differentials in age and musical skill level between teacher and student affect to what extent the mentor-friend model can be used effectively—as do teaching traditions. Of course, an actual relationship between a teacher and student may fall somewhere in between these two models or reflect elements of each.

Research on exceptional musicians emphasizes the important role a teacher has in the student's development of music performance skills. Relationships with early teachers (when the musicians were just beginning their studies) are usually described in terms of warmth and nurturing (Davidson et al., 1998). Subsequent teachers are credited for their ability to personally challenge students. One thing is consistent: Teachers must have the respect of their students, whether they are well liked for the encouragement they offer or admired professionally for their performance ability.

Charting the Course Ahead

Among the primary responsibilities of a teacher are the tasks of determining what a student should learn and devising the way of accomplishing it. In education,

Cross-Cultural Perspective: The Teacher in Traditional Japanese Music Instruction

Although formal music education in Western society is often dominated by a teacher's verbal instruction, that is not the case in other settings around the world (see Merriam, 1964, chapter 8). Traditional Japanese music training is a perfect example. A traditional lesson, which might be centered on learning to play the *koto* (large plucked string instrument) or *shakuhachi* (bamboo flute), involves very little speaking by teacher or student.

The philosophical foundations behind traditional Japanese culture characterize music as being inexplicable in words. As a result, "verbal explanations are rare in traditional Japanese music instruction. Instead, demonstration and the physical interaction of teacher and student in the clarification of finger and arm positions are common learning strategies" (Campbell, 1991, p. 120). Japanese culture also places great importance on young people showing respect for their elders, and this is clearly reflected in the demonstration-imitation processes of music lessons. A student regards his or her teacher as a master musician whose every performance action is worthy to be emulated. In this system, students' success as developing musicians depends largely on how thoroughly they can observe and imitate their teachers.

This premium placed on observation and emulation also dictates the absence of printed notation of music in lessons. Melodic and rhythmic content is transmitted from teacher to student aurally, either through exact demonstration on an instrument or through vocalized mnemonic syllables. "Because notation detracts from the observation of correct performance position, reading and writing are not permitted during instruction. In the music lesson the student's eye absorbs the subtleties of performance etiquette and execution while his or her ear attends to the sound" (Campbell, 1991, p. 120).

a *curriculum* indicates what content is to be taught and in what order. Components of a formal music curriculum can include rationales for studying music, broad educational goals, more detailed learning objectives (related to specific musical concepts), instructional materials, teaching strategies, learner activities, means of assessing achievement outcomes, and a prescribed sequence for implementing these things. Some curricular direction is provided to those who embrace established music teaching methodologies (e.g., Orff, Kodály, Suzuki) or use a series of graded published music materials. Whether or not they use a written, formal curriculum, all teachers make decisions as to what their students will study and how to go about it. Taken together, the individual decisions they make define the long-term music learning experiences of their students.

In the classical music tradition, much teaching occurs within the context of students learning repertoire assigned by a teacher. Accordingly, many teachers believe that the selection of music is one of the most important decisions they make. For students whose music education is exclusively occupied with the rehearsal of music for performance, the sequence of repertoire in fact forms a curriculum. Some have challenged the effectiveness of this approach, especially when it involves a student working with only a few pieces of music at a time. Extended practicing for a polished performance develops a limited set of musical skills and strategies that differs from that required for performing less familiar music (see chapter 6, table 6.1). To what extent are students able to take what is taught and learned with one particular piece and apply it to the context of a new piece assigned later? Research suggests that little transfer of learning will occur from piece to piece unless teachers explicitly teach generalizable concepts drawn from the repertoire and involve students in decision making while preparing performance (Price & Byo, 2002). Many exemplary teachers consider the rehearsal and performance of music literature not an end but a means to teaching comprehensive musicianship. This might include instruction pertaining to music theory and analysis of compositional structure, as well as providing students opportunities to build their aural memory and improvisation skills (Aiello & Williamon, 2002). The research suggests that building of a broader, more versatile body of musical knowledge seems to have its performance benefits, allowing musicians to more efficiently learn music they practice.

When working with students on specific pieces of music, teachers tend to spend the bulk of time addressing technical aspects of performance. This includes teaching an accurate realization of notated pitches and rhythm, as well as the bodily mechanisms to execute the score. Only after a certain level of technical proficiency has been reached do many teachers turn their attention to the expressive qualities of their students' performance (see chapter 4 for a contrasting approach by an expert). A technique-heavy teaching approach may be especially prominent in a master-apprentice relationship between a teacher and student, and such a teaching style involves more spoken instruction (Young et al., 2003).

The research of Reid (2001) suggests that music students' experiences with learning music progress through a hierarchy. The progression is used to describe young musicians' developing understanding of the nature of music, but it is also analogous to the process many instructors lead their students through when teaching music performance. In the Level 1, Instrument stage, attention is devoted to the physical skills and technical aspects of performance. In the Level 2, Elements stage, the learning additionally focuses on musical elements such as dynamics, phrasing, and articulation. The Level 3, Musical Meaning stage introduces consideration of the meaning found within the music. Students rely heavily on a teacher's advice regarding proper stylistic interpretation in order to express the appropriate "feeling" of a work. In Level 4, Communicating, teachers guide student efforts to convey the implicit meaning of a work to an audience. Finally, in the Level 5, Express Meaning stage, students are encouraged to add self-expression or personal meaning to their performances. Reid's research suggests that reaching this pinnacle is facilitated by elements of the mentor-friend model of a teacher-student relationship. But the levels of understanding laid out by Reid are cumulative, meaning that higher levels depend on competency at lower levels. In order to add expressivity to music, one must have the technical bodily mastery to execute the necessary nuances in performance qualities (see chapter 5).

Building the Cognitive Skills of Music

In addition to teaching technical aspects of performance, instructors serve two other broad functions in equipping their students with the skills needed for quality music performance. First, they often provide a source of musical models for students, including aural models of what well-performed music sounds like. Second, teachers offer specific feedback on student performances. As we will see, these functions of the teacher allow young musicians to build the mental representations needed for performance.

Aural modeling is a commonly used approach among music performance teachers (Dickey, 1991; Lindström, Juslin, Bresin, & Williamon, 2003). An instructor will perform a musical excerpt and ask listening students to then imitate it as exactly as possible in their own singing or playing. This process represents a skill set that expert performers have been shown to do with considerable accuracy and consistency (Woody, 1999). In a review of research on teaching strategies used in music instruction, Tait (1992) pointed out that "children are natural imitators" and concluded that modeling is an effective means for improving performance skills (p. 528). Of course, aural modeling by a teacher is also prominent in the lessons of adult music students (Woody, 2000). Through the modeling of their teachers, students come to discern the desirable sound qualities of performance on their instruments and learn which kinds of variations in sound (e.g., timing, dynamics, and intonation) make for appropriate expression. Teachers may also refer students to sound recordings, which can serve as effective aural models.

Providing feedback to students is another very important task of teachers. From general psychology we have learned that knowledge of results is necessary for improving a skill. Advanced musicians are able to self-critique their performances, but developing music students rely on teachers to supply evaluative feedback. Research shows that more effective teaching is associated with a greater amount of feedback within the verbal instruction delivered to students

(Hendel, 1995). The most constructive feedback is that which expresses the discrepancies between a student's rendition of a piece of music and an optimal version. Expert teachers give more detailed feedback (about specific properties of performance) than general appraisals, such as "That sounded good!" (Goolsby, 1997). Researchers in music education have explored whether the feedback of effective teachers is more often positively or negatively expressed, that is, constituting approval or disapproval (Madsen & Duke, 1985). We might intuitively think that positive comments are more motivating to students and, as a result, are more associated with effective teaching. However, the research paints a slightly different picture. Although positive feedback is likely more helpful with younger learners and in one-on-one instruction (Duke, 1999), music students seem able to put up with and benefit from a great deal of expressed criticism in lessons (Duke & Henninger, 2002).

Over the course of their training, successful music students ultimately learn to evaluate their own performances. This emphasizes just how critical teachers are in young musicians' building the mental representations for music performance that allow them to self-regulate their skill development, especially in practice (see chapter 4). We propose the following representational functions: *goal imaging*, *motor production*, and *self-monitoring* (see Lehmann & Ericsson, 1997b; Woody, 2003, and chapter 1, this volume). Goal imaging, the ability to mentally represent what a piece of music *should* sound like, is developed as students work with the aural models provided by teachers and technical media. Mental representations for motor production enable musicians to execute the movements and physical responses needed to play an instrument and to know how those movements feel. Instruction directed to technical and bodily aspects of performance are crucial here. Self-monitoring, the ability to accurately hear one's own performance (i.e., receive feedback), is also primarily acquired from a music teacher. Young musicians especially rely on teachers for this because so much of their attention is devoted to the production of the music, not to monitoring the resulting sound. Equipped with these skills, musicians can compare the sound image (of their own performance) with the goal image, identify discrepancies therein, and then correct them by adapting the representations for motor production. Research suggests that expert teachers, especially one-on-one teachers, guide students in this diagnostic process in their lessons (Woody, 2003).

Effective Behaviors and Strategies in Teaching

Exactly what defines great teaching? It is probably easier to identify examples of great teachers than it is to say precisely what about their teaching makes them great. One way researchers have sought to analyze effective music teaching is by studying those who have been recognized as expert teachers and comparing their activities, behaviors, and strategies with those of inexperienced teachers.

Self Study: Analyzing Your Own Teaching Practices

In this experiment, you will be examining yourself as a music teacher. Carrying this out will be convenient if you currently serve in a music teaching capacity of some kind. If not, you will need to arrange to give someone a one-time music lesson. Before doing anything else, look over the following lists and respond to each as directed.

Lesson Activities: What percentage of a lesson's total time do you believe should be devoted to the following activities? (Estimate a percentage for each):

Student(s) performing music   _____%
Teacher performing (modeling) music   _____%
Teacher talking/explaining   _____%
Student(s) talking/explaining   _____%

Teacher Verbalization: How important do you believe it is that the following types of teacher comments are present in a lesson? (Circle a rating for each, using the scale 1 = *not important* to 5 = *very important*)

Directions for attaining musical
  accuracy (pitch/rhythm)   1 2 3 4 5
Directions for using proper
  technique (use of body)   1 2 3 4 5
Directions for making the music
  more expressive   1 2 3 4 5
Negative feedback about
  student performance   1 2 3 4 5
Positive feedback about
  student performance   1 2 3 4 5
Questioning student(s) about
  music performed   1 2 3 4 5

Set your responses to the preceding lists aside until after you have taught a lesson. Next, you will need to make an audio or video recording of yourself teaching; make sure to get student permission to record the lesson after you explain why you will be doing it. For the purposes of this experiment, try to record about 15 minutes of your teaching.

After the lesson, you will need to play back the recording at least twice to analyze your teaching. The first time, using a clock or the timekeeper on your playback equipment, keep track of how much time was spent on the four kinds of lesson activities:

Student(s) performing music   _____ minutes
Teacher performing (modeling) music   _____ minutes
Teacher talking/explaining   _____ minutes
Student(s) talking/explaining   _____ minutes

On the second playback of your lesson recording, keep a tally of how many times you made the following types of verbalizations:

Directions for attaining musical accuracy (pitches/rhythms)_____
Directions for using proper technique (use of body)_____
Directions for making the music more expressive_____
Negative feedback about student performance_____
Positive feedback about student performance_____
Questioning student(s) about music performed_____

Now compare your prelesson responses (indicating what you thought *should* take place) with what you actually did. Did your instructional practices line up with your teaching values as far as the prevalence of lesson activities and teacher verbalizations? Did your teaching behaviors surprise you in any way? How might you adapt your teaching to make it more effective?

One thing is certain: *Teaching is not telling.* A teacher's role is not to merely broadcast information that students may or may not receive. The quality of teaching is defined by the learning that takes place, in other words, by its output. In this section, we describe some of the qualities that make a teacher's delivery of instruction effective, but we also emphasize active student involvement in educational activities.

General Teacher Competencies

Even before delivering any instruction to students, teachers can do much to increase the likelihood of success. Preparation for teaching involves having a plan for the lesson or the rehearsal. Research attests to the value of planning a sequence of activities and articulating lesson objectives prior to instruction (Tait, 1992). Advanced planning must be balanced, however, with responsiveness to how music students perform during a lesson so that a teacher is primed to take advantage of unexpected events. Goolsby (1996) compared the rehearsals of expert and novice ensemble teachers and found that the experts more equally divided class time among all pieces to be rehearsed. Less experienced teachers seem to be too easily derailed from plans, spending more time on the first piece rehearsed and less on subsequent pieces. Ultimately what is needed is a balance between instructional planning and mid-lesson improvisation—a teaching methodology that is flexible enough to respond to student needs as they arise.

Inexperienced teachers of large music classes often face challenges in maintaining student attention. This can lead to students ignoring instruction and, worse yet, to behavior problems among them. Expert teachers are able to keep their students and themselves on-task with instructional activities (see figure 10.1). Frequent eye contact with students has been shown to increase the attentiveness of a class (Fredrickson, 1992). Other research has identified a quality called "teacher intensity," marked by wide contrasts in an instructor's use of voice loudness and inflection, physical gesture, and facial expression (Byo, 1990). Effective teachers are also recognized for the pacing of their instruction, that is, the perceived rate at which the activities are progressing. Improperly slow pacing has been linked to too much talking and generally slow speech on the part of the teacher (Price & Byo, 2002). The pace of a music lesson is related to the interchange between teacher instruction and student engagement. Students are most attentive during activities that require active participation—especially

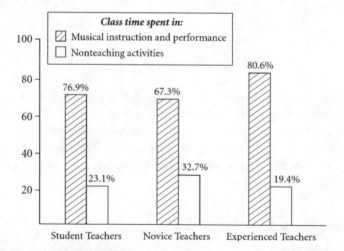

Figure 10.1. Mean percentages of rehearsal time spent on teaching activities and nonteaching activities. The rehearsals of experienced teachers contained the most music instruction. Student teachers' outperforming novice teachers is attributed to their working under the supervision of the experienced teachers. From "Time Use in Instrumental Rehearsals: A Comparison of Experienced, Novice, and Student Teachers," by T. W. Goolsby, 1996, *Journal of Research in Music Education, 44,* 292. Copyright © 1996 by The National Association for Music Education. Reprinted by permission.

music making—and least attentive during teacher lectures and transitions between activities (Duke, Prickett, & Jellison, 1998).

Perhaps in efforts to provide more time for student participation, many effective teachers have learned to optimize the talking they do (see the following subsection). First, their verbal instruction is characterized by clarity, offering efficient explanations of concepts devoid of any vague terms and delivered without unnecessary interjections or "asides." Experienced teachers also question students more often than do novice teachers. Asking questions allows teachers to check for understanding and elicits greater attention from students. Perhaps the most important distinguishing characteristic of expert teachers' verbal instruction is that there is less of it. Excessive talking is almost an epidemic among novice or ineffective music teachers. Research on music teachers' time use in studio lessons and ensemble rehearsals suggests that at least one-third of instructional time is occupied by teachers' lecturing, with some studies reporting over 50% (Duke, 1999; Tait, 1992). Expert teachers, as compared with novices, spend less overall time talking to students, and their individual periods of verbalizing are shorter (Goolsby, 1996, 1999).

Verbal and Nonverbal Music Instruction

Verbal instruction that is specifically related to music varies among music teachers, for example, in content. As addressed previously, teachers tend to lead students through a progression when working on a piece of music, starting with technically oriented aspects of performance and proceeding to more expressive considerations. They also reveal different musical priorities in their verbal instruction to students. Less proficient teachers, who are known to spend more time talking in lessons, are inclined to address technique predominantly, whereas expert teachers focus more efficiently on tone quality, intonation, style, and expression (Cavitt, 2003; Goolsby, 1997, 1999; Young et al., 2003).

The verbal music instruction that teachers give can also be divided into two categories, depending on whether it is made up of (1) imagery and metaphors or (2) direction pertaining to concrete musical sound properties. In reviewing teaching strategies in music, Tait (1992) advanced the place of imagery, metaphors, and extramusical analogies. A teacher might encourage a student to perform a musical phrase to reflect a soaring eagle, a weighty anxious mood, or the feeling of losing a loved one. Research attests to music teachers' widespread use of extramusical images and metaphors, especially those that reflect motion and moods (Barten, 1998; Lindström et al., 2003; Woody, 2000). Teachers may offer extramusical images and metaphors most often when working on expressive performance, intending to intimate a desired sound or to incite emotion in students. This approach is also used to bring about certain physical positions or actions required for performing. For example, Barten (1998) has suggested that it is more fruitful to ask young instrumentalists to imagine a hot potato in their mouths than to give anatomically based instructions about an open mouth cavity. It is clear that a pedagogy steeped in extramusical imagery has the potential to frustrate students and cause conflict in the student-teacher relationship (Persson, 1996). Such problems can occur when teachers make heavy use of metaphors and imagery that students do not understand (e.g., due to cultural differences) or cannot apply to a musical context.

Perhaps for this reason, other music educators advocate verbal instruction that focuses on concrete musical sound properties. Teachers using this approach may describe the qualities of a model sound or point out weaknesses in a student's performance, directly addressing elements such as note duration, tempo, intonation, dynamics, and articulation, among others. Most teachers would see the value of this kind of instruction when dealing with technical aspects of performance (i.e., playing the correct pitches and rhythms), but they could also find this approach effective when working on expressivity, as research suggests. Woody (1999, 2003) found that music students gave better expressive performances when they formed explicit mental representations regarding sound properties, for example, "It gets louder toward the second measure." Many music students, when provided with an extramusical metaphor or imagery example by a teacher, may consciously "translate" it into such explicit plans for their performances.

Of course, sometimes teachers bypass verbal instruction altogether and rely on modeling and imitation. Some of the important aspects of modeling were discussed previously in this chapter. Teacher aural models are common in music classes and ensemble rehearsals, perhaps even more so in individual lessons. This strategy has also been suggested as a necessary complement to a metaphor/imagery teaching vocabulary. Davidson (1989) endorsed a combination of modeling and metaphor to allow students to "attain a multidimensional grasp of the music. . . . The metaphor creates an affective state within which the performer can attempt to match the model" (p. 95). Sloboda (1996) has proposed a theory of "extramusical templates" to explain how students store in memory information heard in an aural model. When a teacher performs a model (with no additional verbal information), an attentive student would be required to process and remember a vast amount of aural performance information. This is made more manageable by abstracting the expressive information into fewer extra-musical analogies, perhaps bodily gesture, vocal intonation, or other expressions of emotion. More research in this area would be desirable.

Completing Instructional Cycles

Whether utilizing verbal or nonverbal means, presenting instruction to students is only one part of effective music teaching. As alluded to earlier, it is critical that students have an opportunity to apply the presented information to their own music making and that teachers provide feedback on their performing. Research in music education suggests a model of "sequential patterns of instruction" consisting of (1) the teacher presenting a performance task to students, immediately followed by (2) students responding (i.e., implementing the initial instruction), and then (3) the teacher giving specific feedback (Price, 1992). It is not until feedback is provided that the instructional pattern or cycle is complete.

Observational studies of music lessons and ensemble rehearsals have shown that effective teaching is marked by an ability to complete the sequence. Goolsby (1997) studied the rehearsal conducted by 30 middle school and high school band directors, who were categorized as expert, novice, and student teachers. The results showed little difference in the occurrence of sequential patterns of instruction between the novice and student teachers, but the experienced directors completed cycles notably more often, almost twice as often as the novices. The experts in this study exhibited shorter periods of lecture and devoted more time to student activity. Table 10.1 shows other important differences in instructional behaviors according to teaching experience. Research analyzing videotaped rehearsals of eminent conductors Bruno Walter and Robert Shaw has suggested that their work from the podium matches the sequential patterns of the instruction model (Yarbrough, 2002).

Each step of the sequential pattern model holds potential pitfalls for teachers. The first step calls for a *task* to be presented. The best initial instruction is that which clearly specifies what students are to do. Thus much teacher verbalization would be disqualified from being considered music instruction if it is merely talk *about* music, without issuing a musical task to students. But perhaps the greatest problem among teachers occurs at the second step, namely, not allowing students adequate opportunity to respond to instruction. As alluded to earlier, time devoted to student performance is surprisingly limited in some music education settings, yet active participation of students is a primary determinant of attentiveness and achievement. This circumstance suggests that effective music learning centers

Table 10.1 Mean Frequencies of Selected Rehearsal Behaviors Exhibited by Student Teachers, Novice Teachers, and Expert Teachers

Rehearsal behaviors	Student-teachers	Novice teachers	Expert teachers
Completed cycles of instruction	7.3	6.3	15.2
Explanations	4.1	3.2	12.8
Unspecific positive feedback	8.3	8.9	3.0
Specific positive feedback	1.4	1.4	5.5
Noninstructional comments	21.8	13.7	2.3
Focused questions to students	3.8	3.2	5.7
Vague questions to students	10.0	9.3	0.7

Table 1 From "Verbal Instruction in Instrumental Rehearsals: A Comparison of Three Career Levels and Preservice Teachers," by T. W. Goolsby, 1997, *Journal of Research in Music Education, 45*, p. 30. Copyright 1997 by MENC: The National Association for Music Education. Adapted with permission.

less on a teacher's presentation of information and more on students' involvement with music. Finally, the third step required to complete an instructional cycle, a teacher's specific feedback to student response, is also often overlooked. Teachers may feel that they have done their job by verbally correcting performance mistakes and letting students try again, but they have failed to offer evaluation of the follow-up performance attempt. Alternatively, teachers may provide only vague feedback to students, such as "good job" and "that's better."

Rehearsing and Conducting

Especially in the United States, most music teachers in secondary schools primarily serve as directors of performance ensembles, such as concert bands, orchestras, and choirs. The role of conductor is viewed as requiring a set of specialized skills in addition to the competencies (described earlier) expected of all music teachers. Varying uses of posture, gesture, and facial expression are all associated with judgments of ensemble performance quality, in part because of their role in eliciting expressivity from performers. Research has shown that music students of all ages readily identify high-intensity conductors, whose behaviors on the podium contain marked contrasts to those of low-intensity conductors (Byo, 1990). Nonverbal behaviors are the means by which conductors try to communicate with their musicians while they are performing. There is both the need to instruct them how they should play or sing and to provide them feedback on how they are actually performing. However, with regard to the ability to effect specific changes in student musicians' performances, nonverbal conducting behaviors by themselves are no alternative to verbal instruction.

Marrin and Picard (1998) developed a "conductor's jacket" that monitored the physiological responses of a conductor. The researchers used this device to gather data from a professional orchestral conductor during several rehearsals. This information was compared with the score of the pieces being rehearsed. Their results confirmed several traditionally held notions about conducting techniques. First, the right hand (used to hold a baton) indicates tempo through a beat pattern, and the amount of force used signifies the desired loudness and style (articulation) of performance. The left hand is used to communicate expressive information. Additionally, the physiological data suggested that a conductor may employ a virtual absence of gesture and motion immediately prior to a major musical event in a piece, as a way of signaling a "heads up" to players.

A conductor's head movements, facial expressions, and gaze are also used to communicate with performers in an ensemble. Poggi (2002) analyzed these nonverbal functions in conductors and concluded that these signals are not idiosyncratic but more systematic in nature. Based on her work, she has created a lexicon that connects specific head or facial signals with their meaning to performing musicians (see table 10.2). As part of instructing an ensemble *how* to perform, a conductor may, for example, display a frowning facial expression to

Table 10.2 The Conductor's Lexicon

Type of Meaning	Signal	Apparent (Literal Meaning)	Real (Indirect) Meaning
Suggest how to play			
Who is to play	Look at the choir		You choir
When to play	Raised eyebrows	I am alerted (emotion)	Prepare to start
	Look down	I am concentrating (mental state)	You concentrate, prepare to start
	Fast head nod		Start now
	Look down	I am not alerted	Do not start yet
What sound to produce			
Melody	Face up		High tune
Rhythm	Staccato head movements		Staccato
Speed	Fast head movements		Svelto
	Frown	I am determined (mental state)	Play loudly
Loudness	Raised eyebrows	I am alarmed (emotion)	It is too loud; play more softly
	Left-right head movements	No! (not that loud)	Play more softly
Expression	Inner eyebrows raised	I am sad	Play a sad sound
How to produce the sound	Wide open mouth		Open your mouth wide
	Rounded mouth		Round your mouth
Provide feedback			
Praise	Head nod	Ok	Go on like this
	Closed eyes	I'm relaxed (emotion)	Good, go on like this
	Oblique head	I'm relaxed (emotion)	Good, go on like this
Blame	Closed eyes + frown + open mouth	I'm disgusted (emotion)	Not like this

Table 4 from "The Lexicon of the Conductor's Face," by I. Poggi, 2002. In P. McKevitt, S. O. Nualláin, & C. Mulvihill (Eds.), *Language, Vision and Music: Selected Papers from the Eighth International Workshop on the Cognitive Science of Natural Language Processing, Galway, Ireland, 1999* (pp. 271–284). Copyright 2002 by Benjamins Publishing Company. Reprinted with kind permission.

evoke a louder dynamic level or show an open, rounded mouth for singers to imitate toward a fuller vocal tone quality. Conductors can also provide feedback this way. For instance, by closing their eyes, they seem to say "Good, I'm enjoying this"; or by shaking their heads back and forth, they indicate that the group is playing too loudly.

Effective rehearsal technique includes more general music teaching proficiencies, such as efficient verbal instruction, quality modeling, and specific feedback to complete sequential patterns of instruction. (Many of the studies previously cited in this chapter were conducted in rehearsal settings.) Ample opportunity for student participation (performance) in proportion to the conductor's spoken instruction is especially important. In fact, an ensemble of advanced music students can improve its performance quality just through the repetition of rehearsing music, devoid of any instruction or feedback from a teacher. It seems that expert conductors come to recognize this, as their rehearsals include a strong element of drill and repetition (Cavitt, 2003; Goolsby, 1997). As compared with less experienced ensemble directors, experts stop the playing or singing of their groups more often in rehearsals, but the stops are shorter in duration because they deliver their instruction so efficiently. Novice conductors, on the other hand, frequently stop and start their ensembles without providing any instruction (Goolsby, 1997).

Stopping and starting during a rehearsal usually revolve around the detection and correction of performance errors. A conductor's precision in detecting errors is affected by a number of rehearsal variables, such as the texture and tempo of the music, as well as the attention devoted to conducting versus listening (Byo & Sheldon, 2000). More generally, however, error detection appears to be a skill that is developed through training, practice, and long-term rehearsal experience. Obviously, a musician's aural skills are of critical importance. Expert conductors can use the music notation of a score to generate auditory images of the music with which an ensemble's performance is compared (Byo & Sheldon, 2000; see also chapter 11). Score study is an accepted preparation strategy among conductors. The error detection abilities of experienced ensemble teachers are likely enhanced by a knowledge of student musicians' performance tendencies (weaknesses), which explains how the teachers target errors for correction even prior to rehearsals (Cavitt, 2003). These experts also show persistence in their correction of identified errors, utilizing a variety of approaches in prescribing solutions (e.g., verbal instruction, teacher and student modeling) and multiple repetitions of target passages in the music (Cavitt, 2003).

Personal Attributes of a Teacher

The way a teacher implements the effective teaching strategies depends partly on his or her personality. For example, someone who in general is socially confident and demonstrative may more readily exhibit the teacher intensity behaviors

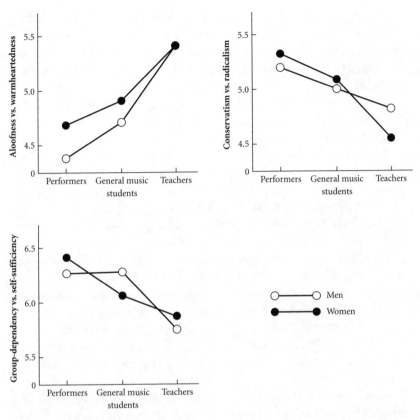

Figure 10.2. Differences in the personality trait measures of outgoingness, conservatism, and self-sufficiency between university students targeting different music specializations (performance, teaching, and no specialization, or general). From *The Musical Temperament: Psychology and Personality of Musicians,* by A. E. Kemp, 1996, Figure 11.2, p. 221. Copyright © 1996 by Oxford University Press. Reprinted by permission.

that have been linked to greater student attentiveness. Some research suggests that certain character traits may play a role in teaching effectiveness. A number of researchers, most notably Kemp (1996), have identified general personality differences between performing musicians and music teachers (see figure 10.2). Whereas performers show a tendency to be introverted, intuitive, emotionally inconsistent, and even aloof (see chapter 9), music teachers are more likely to be extroverted and emotionally stable and to exhibit a feeling-judging temperament (i.e., they can make plans and decisions based on human factors). It is still open to debate how stable those personality dispositions are across situations and longer time spans (Kemp, 1996, p. 14)

Personality trends among teachers are better understood, however, when taking into consideration grade level and areas of specialization within music teaching, such as teaching music in an elementary classroom versus directing an ensemble in a secondary school. Teachers of higher grade levels in strictly performance-oriented instructional settings share some of the prevailing personality characteristics of performers, namely introversion and intuitiveness. This suggests, therefore, that they interact with their students in more theoretical and abstract ways. On the other hand, teachers who work with younger children in general classroom music contexts show greater extroversion and the feeling-judging preference, which might be manifested as a keen awareness of student behaviors in a learning situation.

The findings mentioned as of yet have not taken into consideration teacher effectiveness. In other words, the fact that music teachers tend to display certain character traits does not mean that they aid music learning. When actual teaching effectiveness is considered, the traits that emerge are extroversion and conscientiousness (Kemp, 1996). Certainly an outgoing personality better matches some of the teaching characteristics described in this chapter, such as ample interaction with students and large contrasts in the intensity of verbalization and gesture. Conscientiousness aligns with the need to plan and consider overall learning objectives for students. Drawing on educational research that extends beyond just music teaching, Pembrook and Craig (2002) compiled an extensive list of personality attributes of successful teachers. In addition to the traits already mentioned, this list includes internal qualities, such as self-confidence and enthusiasm, and group management attributes, such as flexibility and proactive leadership.

Also included in the successful-teacher attributes listed by Pembrook and Craig (2002) are a number of traits categorized as "relating to others." An orientation toward others seems to be an important personal quality found in effective teachers. Research has established motivational and achievement differences between pupil-centered and teacher-centered instruction. This could explain why the instruction offered by many "performer-teachers" does not exhibit the characteristics associated with effective teaching. For example, Persson (1996) examined the teaching practices of an acclaimed concert pianist and discovered numerous incidents of teacher-student conflict. The teacher expressed frustration that students were not able to adapt to her methods. Her students, although acknowledging her musical performance expertise, felt that she was not supportive in guiding them to acquire the same skills for themselves. The propensity among some teachers toward certain performer personality traits, namely introversion and self-orientation, seems to interfere with instructional efforts.

The desire to give music-making ability to others is likely the core value of music education. As musicians' belief systems change, perhaps through music education studies in college, they may come to appreciate the satisfaction derived from helping others learn music more than the rewards of their own music making. Becoming a great teacher likely requires diminishing loyalty to one's own musicianship and the adoption of an other-oriented perspective (Kemp, 1996).

It should not be surprising, really, that some music teachers show character traits similar to those of performers. As Kemp has pointed out, most music educators precede their teaching careers with years of isolated practice to develop performance skills, in effect reinforcing character traits of introversion and self-sufficiency. In high school ensembles and college one-on-one lessons, purely musical rewards for teachers are arguably greater than in elementary grades and general classroom situations, which usually include musical novices. This may explain why music teachers in the upper-level settings can retain some of the performer personality traits that would seem to contradict effective teaching characteristics. Moreover, private studio teachers who bypass the specialized training as educators and who can rely only on their experiences as performers may be especially slow to develop the qualities of effective teachers. Their introversion may be manifested as isolation, which can hinder their own development as teachers. By limiting their instructional approaches to those of their own teachers, they can end up perpetuating ineffective teaching methods that are based more on intuition than anything else (Kemp, 1996; see also chapter 1, this volume).

These findings indicate that people are not born great music teachers. The research also verifies that being an effective teacher requires more than just being a skilled performer. Musicians *become* good teachers by choosing teaching as an enterprise and pursuing the skills that teaching demands. It is likely through extensive experience and a deliberate effort to improve that musicians come to take on the personal characteristics described in this section. Music teacher training programs provide young musicians with opportunities to improve specific instructional skills. Research studies have documented the ability of systematic training to increase music education students' use of effective teaching strategies, largely accomplished through (supervised) practice teaching, self-observation, and self-assessment (Duke 2000; Goolsby, 1997).

Study Questions

1. According to research, what teacher characteristics and behaviors are most critical for cultivating the musical development of students? How do expert music teachers come to possess these important qualities and skills?
2. What general conclusions can be drawn from the studies examining the verbal instruction of music teachers? How might you apply these to make your own teaching more effective?
3. Review some of the traditional notions about the role of an ensemble conductor. To what extent are these ideas supported by research on effective rehearsal technique?

Further Reading

Colwell, R., & Richardson, C. (Eds.). (2002). *The New Handbook of Research on Music Teaching and Learning.* Several chapters pertaining to teaching, especially the one by B. Rosenshine, H. Froehlich, and I. Fakhouri (pp. 299–314) on systematic instruction.

Tait, M. (1992). Teaching strategies and styles. In R. Colwell (Ed.), *Handbook of Research on Music Teaching and Learning* (pp. 525–534). A review of music instructional strategies.

Price, H. E., & Byo, J. L. (2002). Rehearsing and conducting. In R. Parncutt & G. E. McPherson (Eds.), *The Science and Psychology of Music Performance: Creative Strategies for Teaching and Learning* (pp. 335–351). A review.

11

The Listener

Hearing is such a normal experience for most of us that we hardly notice it. Imagine the following situation: You are sitting on a bus surrounded by the background noise of the rhythmic rumbling of the bus. Here and there snippets of talk can be heard. A child is spontaneously singing a description of what she sees outside the window until the mother asks her to sing more softly. Elsewhere, two adolescents are exchanging informed opinions on the latest music, throwing in names and terms that ordinary musicologists or music educators do not even understand. In the back, a businessman is talking on the phone to an invisible but certainly highly valued costumer, using a servile tone and frequent jovial laughs. Having planned that the bus ride would be a great time to get some serious work done, you try to focus on the reading material—in vain. Even after mumbling the text to yourself, you still cannot concentrate. Finally, you put in your ear plugs. Seconds later the ambient noises have been reduced to a muffled minimum, and you can start reading.

This scene reveals that our auditory system is continuously receiving information and, unlike the eye, cannot be closed off to the environment. Although a multitude of sounds (even noxious ones) are present at one time and compete for our attention, we allocate our attention selectively and evaluate what we hear. The linguistic difference between hearing (perceiving sound) and listening (paying attention to sound) exists in many languages. Although the details of sound perception lie beyond the scope of this book, we later describe the path of acoustical stimuli from where they emanate to where they are processed in our brains. Although all people of normal hearing can perceive sounds, listening requires active attending to information. Even deaf people can hear extremely loud or low-frequency information through their bodies. When we talk about listening, we mean the conscious attention to some sound source as opposed to the passive intake of background music in stores, ambient noises, or unattended acoustical information. Thus perception, or hearing, precedes the higher order processes associated with active listening.

This chapter addresses the following central points:

1. After briefly describing the pathway of acoustical stimuli, we explain that listening is a highly complicated process by which the acoustical world around us is transformed into some image that we then experience as almost object-like.
2. We show that our musical experience is shaped by a number of cultural and other factors that clearly demonstrate how ephemeral and malleable our internal representation of music is.
3. Listeners experience music emotionally because they can "understand" it—make sense out of its structural features. The performers and composers help us by structuring the musical material.
4. Judging and critiquing music are important skills for some musicians. However, those skills are difficult to develop and are easily disrupted.
5. Along the way we explain some musical phenomena, such as hearing color, having a tune "stuck in the head," and remembering biographically important songs.

Hearing and Listening: Basic Information

It is important for all musicians to have a cursory knowledge of the perceptual processes that give rise to our musical experiences. We do not concern ourselves here with the intricacies of basic sound perception and the physical properties of acoustical events, nor do we deal with the generation of sound by musical instruments and the voice. However, we urge the interested musician to read up on these topics (see Deutsch, 1999, chapters 1–3; Handel, 1993; Butler, 1992, and Yost, 2000, for comprehensive coverage). An intentionally brief and simplified description containing some of the musically relevant information follows.

Although research methods vary considerably, and with them their results, scientists have proven that hearing starts early in human development. As early as the 8th week of gestation, parts of the outer and inner ear emerge, and the cochlea reaches its final size by the 20th week. Neural responses to auditory stimulation have been measured from the 24th week on. Frequency resolution, temporal resolution, and auditory thresholds are initially poor, but they improve over time. Fetal responses to sounds, such as motor movements, have been shown as early as 24 weeks gestational age; first heart- rate changes in response to sound occur about 2 weeks later (see Lecanuet, 1996, for details).

What is there to hear in utero? The prenatal child primarily experiences the maternal background noises associated with respiratory, cardiovascular, and gastrointestinal functions (Lecanuet, 1996). If you have ever listened with your head under water, you know that the sounds are muffled and strongly attenuated in the higher ranges. Somewhat similar is the soundscape experienced by the fetus. The unborn child can still hear outside noises, including voices. However, due to the frequency spectrum of speech, it is mainly able to perceive the prosody (melody) of language rather than individual words (Handel, 1993, p. 65). The mother's voice has the advantage of being transmitted through internal, as well as external, paths (bone conductance and sound waves from the mouth reach the body from the outside). Thus hearing begins in the third trimester of gestation, most likely as a very holistic and crude experience at first but becoming more and more refined and specialized as birth approaches. Once the child is born and its ears are free of water, it perceives sounds as everybody else does.

Hearing actually begins when masses of periodically compressed air molecules (sound waves) reach the eardrum. The air-conducted sound pressure waves hit the eardrum with an extremely small amount of energy. Because of their faintness, the ear has to provide adequate amplification and discrimination to extract information about the spectral components of the sound that informs us about the timbre. Also, the ear has to carry out sophisticated analyses to arrive at the pitch information. The auditory nerve relays information about the ongoing stimulus from the cochlea to the cortex with increasing numbers of nerve fibers. The changing aspects of the stimulus (e.g., onset frequency modulation) are those events that the nervous system responds to by exciting or inhibiting the firing of neurons. At lower levels of the pathway (the nuclei), a functional organization prevails. Similar information is transmitted to different areas of the brain, which extract varying types of information (e.g., pitch and onset) and transmit the results along other independent circuits (Handel, 1993, chapter 12). Obviously, the exchange between information from both ears is important for extracting spatial information; for this, neural information crosses over from one side of brain to the other. At some points in the pathway, the organization of the brain corresponds to dimensions inherent in the stimulus, for example, when high-, middle-, and low-frequency bands are located on adjacent areas on the cortex, just as they are on the cochlea. However, this so-called tonotopic organization is absent in other parts of the pathway. Most of the processing happens in the auditory cortex, where meaning is attached to the incoming neurophysiological activity.

The complexity of the processing is overwhelming and fascinating, and many results from research on other species (e.g., the cat) need to be verified with humans. Because several areas of the brain are involved in processing auditory input, it is largely impossible to say that sounds are processed in the right or left brain hemisphere only. Even in instances when language and music appear together, as in songs, both types of information are processed separately (Besson & Schön, 2003, for a review). Only recently have researchers found out that individual aspects of music, such as timbre, temporal aspects, or contour, are dealt with by specialized modules in the brain. Although there is a tendency to process time structures more in the left temporal lobe of the brain and pitch structures in the right hemisphere, the variability among persons is considerable (see Altenmüller, 2003, for a critical discussion). Further, sound processing relies on modules in different areas, even more so when the listening is associated with memory of past biographical events or with motor activity during performance.

Reconstructing the Outside World Inside

From the preceding it can be inferred that, for several reasons, subjective sound impressions may or may not correspond to those of other persons or to some "objective" acoustical property. Anatomical and physiological factors lead to different sound perception as does one's learning history. First, the physical stimulus is filtered through our perceptual system, and when comparing species we see that the hearing range in animals differs from that of humans. Humans can hear frequencies only between roughly 20 and 20,000 Hertz (20 kHz), whereas bats can hear frequencies way above 100 kHz. Therefore, bat music and conversations do not much matter to humans and probably vice versa. In addition, even within our range of hearing, we are more sensitive in certain frequency bands (especially around 4,000 Hz), regardless of the physical loudness, a fact that is nicely illustrated in equal loudness curves (see figure 11.1). Second, the existence of musical illusions suggests that our ear does not accurately mirror the sounding outside world but that it recreates it for us in a systematic and characteristic way (similar to vision; see chapter 6). Some of the more common musical illusions are the continuous scale and the tritone paradox. The continuous scale is a sequence of tones that evokes the sensation of continuous ascent or descent over many octaves while really remaining in a middle frequency range. The tritone paradox presents simple intervals (diminished fifths) that some people hear as ascending and others perceive as descending (see Deutsch, 1995). Yet all listeners have the clear impression that what they are hearing is unambiguous and true. Given that you can learn to see some optical illusions "the right way," obviously perceptual input requires interpretation. By analogy the same applies to hearing and listening. The truthfulness (veridicality) of auditory input is limited by and dependent on the physiology and psychology of hearing.

The massive amount of incoming information has to be attended to and processed. The most basic processes are those that structure or segment the continuous stream of information. *Segmentation* is the word researchers employ when talking about the structuring of temporal processes. We can also talk about signal detection, in which some musical signal is detected against interfering signals (noise) that could be real background noise. Imagine walking through a

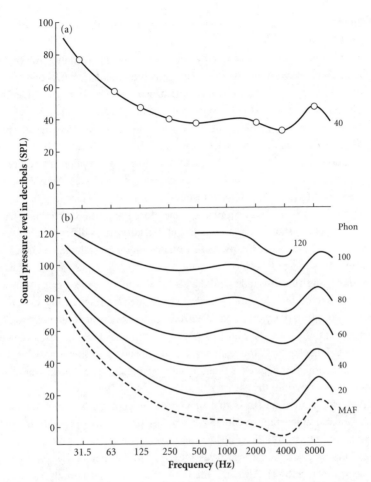

Figure 11.1. Equal loudness curves reveal that our hearing is most sensitive in the range around 3400–5000 Hz (3.4–5.0 KHz), a range important to human communication and music. Higher and lower frequencies require more sound intensity to sound equally loud compared to a given loudness in the most sensitive range. The curve in panel (a) represents intensities of tones that match the loudness of a 1000 Hz tone at 40 dB. The 40 dB curve in panel (a) matches the 40 phon curve in panel (b). Panel (b) shows several of such matches to different loudness levels of the 1000 Hz tone (e.g., 1000 Hz at 60 db). The right axis shows the loudness in phons which is defined as the dB level of the 1000 Hz tone (Stephen Handel, *Listening: An introduction to the perception of auditory events*, MIT Press, 1993, p. 67). Reproduced with permission.

crowded store and all of a sudden attending to the song being played softly on the loudspeakers. You have to filter out all disturbances in order to arrive at the important part of the acoustical scenery, in this case the song with its phrases and tones. The same complicated mechanisms help us filter out language against the acoustical backdrop that surrounds us, for example, when we are talking to a friend in a noisy cafeteria (see Deutsch, 1999, chapter 10, for music; Miller & Eimas, 1995, for speech).

Let us briefly look at two broadly agreed-on concepts of how these things happen. First, perception involves categorization, and second, perception makes use of so-called *Gestalts*. Categorical perception allows us to identify stimulus characteristics as belonging to the same category, although they are somewhat dissimilar. Think of all the visual colors that we recognize as red. Physically speaking, the hue and saturation might vary considerably, yet most people know a red car when they see one. Categorical perception is also prevalent in speech in helping us recognize speech sounds, even when different speakers are uttering them. Spoken instances from the same category (e.g., "r") are perceived as being more similar and therefore harder to discriminate from each other than instances from an adjacent category (e.g., difference between "r" and "l"). These categories partly rely on learning. For example, the Japanese language does not differentiate between "r" and "l," so Japanese people have problems using those sounds deliberately; however, categories can form and change through extensive training, especially through hearing (Lively, Logan, & Pisoni, 1993). Similarly, musicians learn to recognize musical intervals as categorical entities (Burns & Ward, 1978), or even pitches (see the discussion of perfect pitch in chapter 2, this volume). Identifying complex things as belonging to certain learned categories is tantamount to reducing the huge amount of information pouring into the ear.

The second mechanism is that of *Gestalt* perception, whereby we move from rather simple, static events to temporal or spatial groupings. Gestalt perception recognizes "relationships among elements that lead to the perception of objects or events . . . These principles lead to the perception of figures" (Handel, 1993, p. 552). Although the basic theory behind Gestalt perception is borrowed from the visual arts, it can be successfully applied to music (see Handel, 1993, chapter 7, for details). In order to segregate the acoustic stream we receive into discrete channels (e.g., noises emanating from computer, music on TV, someone talking in background, etc.), we have to make sure which sounds belong together, that is, which ones originate from the same sources. Bregman (1990) calls this process "auditory scene analysis." Based on complex but rule-governed analysis of the acoustical features, we can miraculously follow a melody line played by a flute against a background of orchestral instruments in which we also notice the timpani's repeated pattern. Organizational principles, such as similarity, proximity, continuity, common fate, symmetry, and closure, allow elements to be grouped such that they achieve as good a figure as possible. This likely implies predictability and similarity of the grouped elements and is done based on probability computations in the brain. For example, having learned as children to perceptually follow the prosody of our mother's voice even in noisy environments, we may later be able to transfer this perceptual automaton to following a clarinet melody in an orchestral recording. Research in auditory stream segregation has been an important area of investigation and has even produced examples of musical illusions (see Deutsch, 1995). Already J. S. Bach used the principle of proximity intuitively in his solo partitas for violin: With one alternating quickly between high and low notes, he produced the illusion of two simultaneous voices—latent polyphony. This illusion is destroyed by playing the same piece very slowly.

Recent psychoacoustic research on unattended auditory events has shown that attention focuses only on parts of the auditory scene and disregards others. If we knew which ones were unattended, we could eliminate them from the auditory scene without harm to the listener. And this is exactly what modern sound compression in audio equipment does by using a psychoacoustic model. Thus, although we presume that we are attending to all auditory information around us and—in the case of modern audio equipment—receiving all possible information, we are in fact not.

Some people live in a particularly fascinating personal world of multimodality. This phenomenon is called *synesthesia,* which means "joint sensation" (Cytowic, 1993). A few people—Cytowic spoke of 1 in 25,000—experience color hearing, shape tasting, colored days of the week, or other sensory blendings. Synesthetes experience their auditorily triggered visual experiences as projections on a transparent screen several inches away from the face. Moreover, the visual display is involuntary, meaning the person cannot avoid, prevent, or change the type of visual experience that is triggered by some particular sound. Tones might evoke colors, melodies entire moving visual arrays. The medieval composer Hildegard von Bingen was probably a synesthete, and she painted "visions" of sounds, which researchers today believe to have resulted in part from strong migraine headaches. Among musicians, some of the more well-known examples of synesthetes are Alexander Scriabin, Nikolai Rimsky-Korsakov, and Olivier Messiaen. Scriabin associated colors with certain pitches and even wrote a piece titled "Prometheus: The Poem of Fire," with an instrumental part for a keyboard that controlled an array of colored lights. Synesthetes experience these cross-modal phenomena as stable (same stimulation, same response), real, memorable, and emotionally tainted. Unfortunately, they are highly idiosyncratic, so that no two descriptions by synesthetes will match. Synesthetic composers might therefore be inspired by their "visions," but their audiences, synesthetically inclined or not, will unfortunately not be able to share in the composer's experience.

In contrast, cross-modal analogies or correspondences are shared by most people. For instance, high pitches are often experienced as having a lighter shade than lower pitches, and sounds can be classified as dense, pointed, or round, just to mention a few of the many metaphorical associations music can evoke. This type of association can be used productively by composers or teachers to convey musical meaning (see chapter 10). Cytowic (1993) has argued that we are all synesthetic in our brains but that only true congenital synesthetes are privy to those ordinarily hidden processes.

Listening as a Cognitive Experience and Skill

To appreciate the learning processes that are necessary to become active listeners, you could try listening to ethnic music, such as that of the American Indians or African pygmies, and experience the seeming lack of meaning for the uninitiated ear, or try to follow all voices in a five-part fugue. Whereas the first example addresses the effect of acculturation, the latter one implies some degree of formal training that allows hearing the music of one's own culture analytically.

Researchers are still trying to find out how we allocate attention in music. Are we driven by amplitude (loudness), by melody and harmony (cf. Dowling, 1999), by the rhythmic characteristics that drag us along (e.g., Jones & Yee, 1993, for a review), or by what we are trying to do with the music? It is most likely the latter, because when we want to relax, we will attend to certain aspects of the music other than those we do when we want to dance (see chapter 12). As we will see later, attention is not only attracted by the music's properties but can also be consciously allocated.

Listening Analytically

Some persons in our society have trained particular listening skills to a level necessary to function professionally as performers, composers, conductors, music critics, or sound engineers. As a result, they acquire the ability to employ two different ways of listening to music, a holistic ("everyday") and an analytic one. When they listen analytically, that is, direct their attention to specific aspects of the music, even ambiguous musical stimuli become more veridical (Brennan & Stevens, 2002). The octave illusion, for example, sounds to most listeners like a high and a low tone alternating between ears (high right, low left, high right, low left . . .), and the ear receiving the high notes remains constant even if the loudspeakers (headphones) are reversed. However, pipe organists and trained musicians are more likely to avoid being fooled by the octave illusion than less trained persons. Unlike musicians, nonmusicians may even miss a clash of keys between a song and its accompaniment when not specifically directed to pay attention to it (Wolpert, 2000). More examples exist to show differences between analytical and everyday listening.

However, musicians and nonmusicians both have unclear assumptions about what aural capabilities they have. For example, music theorists would be surprised to learn that even trained musicians were unable to hear when a large-scale music piece (sonata) terminated on an unusual key, namely the dominant instead of the tonic (Cook, 1987) or that perceptual evidence for the existence of key mood associations such as "C major sounds 'splendid,' 'clear,' or 'wakeful' " is unconvincing (Powell & Dibben, 2005). In contrast, untrained listeners may be pleased to know that experiments have shown that they segment an ongoing piece of music quite similarly to the way that experts would divide it (Deliège & El Ahmadi, 1990) or that average listeners are surprisingly correct when reproducing pitch and tempo (Halpern, 1992). Music listening is obviously an activity that we all command to some degree, because we have prior experiences dealing with musical sounds.

Previous knowledge allows individuals to establish expectancies or, as the music philosopher Meyer has called them, implications, meaning "guesses (feelings) of how present patterns will be continued and perhaps reach closure" (Meyer, 2001, p. 346). For example, musical expectancies are built up by implications of melodies: Just think of musical jokes that violate such expectancies (see music example 11.1). Similar to the processing of language, people can detect whether a musical phrase is realized according to its implications or not, and the resulting neural activity indicates a possible mismatch. Therefore, even persons who do not play instruments can hear wrong notes in a concert, suggesting that they have a notion of what should be played. In fact, those expectations are so strong that they become "obligatory," and people cannot avoid constructing them (Repp, 1998a). We have already mentioned in the context of music making that the brain undergoes changes in response to habitual stimulation (see chapter 4), and we could repeat it here with regard to music listening. The interplay of long-term memory, which is the source of expectations, and structural properties of the ongoing stimulus allows musical cognition to occur at varying levels of musical structure, from the level of individual intervals to the larger structures of entire musical pieces.

Even at low levels of cognitive processing, differences between musicians and nonmusicians have been found in evoked brain potentials (e.g., Koelsch, Schroger, & Tervaniemi, 1999). Thus, compared with nonmusicians, musicians' early and extensive training may alter the brain to allow processing of stimuli even preattentively. This means that skilled musicians hear their environment differently from nonmusicians, because their brains are always on the lookout for auditory material that can be meaningfully segmented and analyzed as music.

Music example 11.1. U.S. National Anthem modulating to tonic at end of first phrase instead of the dominanat, eliciting a whimsical effect (note: ending on the minor tonic with an E-flat before the final C is even funnier).

Cross-Cultural Perspective: African Drummers and Triple Meters

The correct perceptual and cognitive processing of music provides the ground for its accurate reproduction, a fact we sometimes ignore unless it is explicitly brought to our attention, for example, in the context of amusia (tone deafness). Even professional musicians do not always possess the most useful mental representations. Kopiez, Langner, and Steinhagen (1999; see musical examples at http://musicweb.hmt-hannover.de/ghana) undertook two experiments in an intercultural study of rhythms with Ghanaian master drummers and European (German) drummers. In a first experiment, 12 African drummers rated the performance of six European rhythms performed by European drummers. These performances were selected to vary in levels of performance quality (low, medium, and high) and had previously been rated by European musicians. The systematic agreement between both sets of expert raters was highest when only rhythms that were similarly familiar to all raters were included. The agreement was lower when also including the rhythms that were less familiar to the African drummers.

In a second experiment, 11 African drummers were asked to learn the rhythms by playing along with a tape-recorded model. After a few repetitions, the model stopped and the drummers continued by themselves. The recorded performance data revealed that the Ghanaian drummers used a characteristic off-beat structure by accenting commonly unaccented beats. Particular difficulties were experienced in the performance of an unusual four-measure rhythm and a beat sequence of 3+2+2 (Bolero rhythm).

These experiments provide evidence for the existence of perceptual universals in the evaluation of rhythm performances, which imply common standards of regularity regarding timing and dynamics. At the same time, they demonstrate culture-specific differences in rhythm production. Rhythms are assimilated to preexisting categories, allowing the musician to perform only what he or she can accurately represent. In the absence of triple-meter rhythms in a culture, all perceived rhythms are assimilated to the duple-meter structure. Thus in experts previous knowledge can even inhibit learning of new material (negative transfer).

Musicians do show superior musical memory and recognition of thematic material compared with less trained subjects (Pollard-Gott, 1983), presumably because they develop much more precise and useful representations of musical structure than average people do. However, music students may find it consoling to learn that experts' performance is not as impressive when the music is not tonally constructed or when the excerpt is longer than a few seconds (e.g., Cook, 1987; see chapter 6, figure 6.2, this volume). In an experiment by Ayari and McAdams (2003), European and Arabian listeners of varying levels of musical sophistication were confronted with Arabian improvised music and asked to identify musical ideas and segment the music. A detailed analysis revealed that expert European listeners, "faced with unfamiliar musical structures from another culture . . . would seem to have been unable to describe what they were unable to recognize or represent mentally in a structured fashion, in spite of all being professional musicians or musicologists" (p. 191). This suggests that although experts develop more complicated representations, these representations are specific to a particular type of music, and they are connected with the ability to verbally describe (label) musical features (see chapter 5, section on expressive rules).

As should have become clear from other chapters (chapters 1, 4, 5, 6, and 10), auditory representations allow us to learn, remember, and compare music. But musical representations can also haunt us when our brains produce them involuntarily, as is the case with "tunes in the head." In fact, the brain is so dependent on external information that it will generate its own input in the absence of any, as can be shown in cases of patients who suffer from auditory hallucinations (Raghuram, Keshavan, & Channabasavanna, 1980). Although we know that the areas of the brain involved when imaging music (actually "audiating," as music educators sometimes term it) in the absence of physical sounds are similar to those used when listening to actual music (Halpern, 2003), there are still many unanswered questions about the persistence and etiology of such phenomena.

Music Critics and Jurors

A specific skill in music is required from the music critic or juror. Surprisingly, some studies find a lack of reliability between jurors, either when different jurors do not agree about a given performance or when the same performance is rated twice by the same rater, and the two ratings differ (see Williamon, 1999). Aside from possible disagreements on the appropriateness of an interpretation or a musician's handling of a certain technical difficulty, one would hope that jurors have an agreed-upon basis for their evaluations. The lack of agreement can be explained by two basic mechanisms. One has to do with the floating of our attention (Jones & Yee, 1993), and the second has

Self Study: Self-Deception in Repeatedly Listening to Music

Listen to a short orchestral piece of music (e.g., "Symphonic Dances," Op. 64, by Edvard Grieg) of about 4 to 6 minutes. While listening, imagine that you are attending a fantastic concert by a world-famous orchestra. Take a break of several minutes (or longer) doing something completely different. Then listen to the same recording again, thinking that you are listening to some decent amateur or student orchestra.

When listening to the same piece repeatedly, you will invariably have the impression of hearing something different. This is especially true for pieces you do not know very well. Apart from the fact that attention is never drawn to exactly the same places in the music on repeated hearings, the suggestive information about the performers never fails to influence the ratings and commentaries (e.g. Duerksen, 1972). One of us (AL) has performed this experiment successfully many times in class with advanced music students who did not know that the same recording was played twice. The debriefing was usually met with incredulousness (and finally amusement) on the part of the deceived students.

to do with the interference of competing musical or nonmusical information (e.g., Williamon, 1999; also Lehmann & Davidson, 2002, p. 555; see also chapter 9, this volume).

Imagine that you are presented with a flawless recorded performance. When you hear it the first time, you may focus on different aspects (e.g., by following the orchestration or trying to identify the composer) than you do the second time (e.g., by looking at the CD booklet; realizing that the performer is not your classmate but a highly esteemed professional). Contextual effects, such as contrasts, physical attractiveness of the performer, gender or race, background information, or factors within the juror, such as fatigue, can lead to systematic changes in evaluation. Although these explanations are disillusioning, there are ways to counteract inherent unreliability.

Research on adjudicators and teachers suggests that agreeing on criteria ahead of time or training the juror may be helpful. Contrary to common lore, great musicians do not necessarily make good jurors (Fiske, 1979). Furthermore, general assessments (e.g., a rating-scale "overall impression") may provide more agreement among raters, especially when persons are trained to adjudicate, than multiple or more detailed scales (e.g., "embouchure," "phrasing," "interpretation"; Wapnick & Ekholm, 1997). Although ratings of performance and music criticism will never be "truly objective," in part because individuals cannot completely free themselves from nonmusical influences, raters, especially in educational settings, should try to maintain their impartiality.

From Ear to Heart: Listening as an Emotive Process

The enjoyment of music in terms of its affective content and mood-modulating effect is what listeners are mostly seeking. Among other things, they want to be moved, reminded, and physically and aesthetically stimulated by music (see also chapter 12). The way to investigate this type of complex response is to either ask listeners about their experiences or observe their listening or buying habits. More recently, cognitive neuroscientists have measured physiological parameters, such as heart rate, skin conductance, or brain activity, to judge the effect of music. And although such parameters do not always correlate reliably with the intensity, much less the quality, of the experience, these measurements supplement our knowledge about music listening (see Scherer & Zentner, 2001).

Basic Characteristics of Music

Music can express, or, better, listeners can identify certain emotions in music (see chapter 5), partly because there may be some correspondence between extramusical experiences (e.g., gesture, facial expression, and speech) and the musical stimulus. Fast music with a strong high spectral component evokes different emotions than does music with different acoustical cues. Also, cognitive processes are involved that lead to highly culture-specific responses to music, for instance when major tonality is associated with "happy" and minor with "sad." At the most basic level, researchers have extracted a two-dimensional model using the hedonic tone or valence (happy–sad) as one dimension and activity (active–sleepy) as another one (cf. Schubert, 2003). As early as the 1930s, Kate Hevner investigated the range of musical affect by asking persons to describe music using a set of adjectives. Recent work by Schubert (2003) yielded a list of 46 words in 9 clusters covering the two previously mentioned dimensions (see figure 11.2).

A good example of the complex emotional effects of the musical structure and our learned associations and behaviors is music in films. Here, cognition is influenced by the music, which adds an emotional layer and disambiguates the visual narrative. For example, when two people are kissing good-bye on screen, the music might tell us whether the separation is forever or only for a moment or whether there is danger approaching. In a similar fashion, the soundtrack informs us about the genre of the film: whether it is a comedy, a drama, or something else. Interestingly, viewers do not realize this manipulation through the auditory channel and might even attribute their thoughts to the visual input (see Cohen, 2001, for a review). Many more instances exist in which we use music or music is being used to influence us (see chapter 12).

Cluster	Adjectives describing the dimension
A	Bright, cheerful, happy, joyous
B	Humorous, light, lyrical, merry, playful
C	Calm, delicate, graceful, quiet, relaxed, serene, soothing, tender, tranquil
D	Dreamy, sentimental
E	Tragic, yearning
F	Dark, depressing, gloomy, melancholy, mournful, sad, solemn
G	Heavy, majestic, sacred, serious, spiritual, vigorous
H	Dramatic, exciting, exhilarated, passionate, sensational, soaring, triumphant
I	Agitated, angry, restless, tense

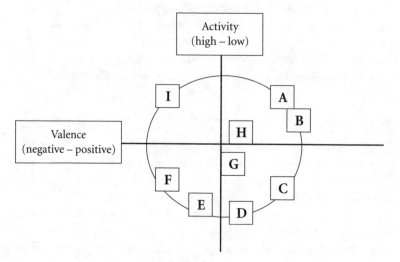

Figure 11.2. Adjective clusters (see table at top) as they emerged in the study by Schubert (2003). One could align them schematically around a circle with activity and valence (pleasantness) as two orthogonal dimensions (see figure below).

Musical Preferences

Interest in musical preferences is most common among marketing and media companies, but music educators have also been interested in what, how much, and why their students listen to particular types of music. In the eighteenth century the Christian missionary Joseph Amiot undertook what amounts to the earliest documented study on music preferences: He played then-fashionable European harpsichord music by Jean-Phillippe Rameau to his Chinese hosts who did not like it and experienced no affective response. Today, European music is widely popular in China, and many professional pianists come from there.

Although early modern research was strictly conducted in the laboratory, more recent studies operate in naturalistic settings (see Miller, 1992; Hargreaves &

North, 1997; Gembris, 2002, for reviews). The most general finding has been that moderate levels of arousal elicit the most liking, whereas too little and too much arousal lead to lower levels of liking. This can be graphically represented by an inverted-U-shaped function (see figure 8.1). Unfamiliar and overly familiar music does not arouse us in a positive way but rather creates overstimulation or boredom. Through repeated exposure to some music, our familiarity with it increases, as does our preference. Radio stations use this phenomenon to plug new and promising songs. Music teachers might use this effect by periodically incorporating certain styles of classical music into their lessons. Note that more complex music requires more exposure in order to reach that optimal middle level of arousal. Becoming familiar with music requires the ability to construct a mental representation of it, which allows us to correctly anticipate its content. Unfortunately, mere exposure to music that was not previously valued does not automatically lead to an increase, but rather a decrease, in preference unless more information on the music is provided to enable a better understanding of it. Overexposure can also have negative effects. Unlike our favorite music, some music might get on our nerves because we hear it too often but cannot avoid exposure to it (e.g., ring tones of a mobile phone). When exposure to our preferred music reaches a point of saturation, we can stop listening to it for a while until it regains freshness. The preceding description is relatively generic and would apply to any musical style.

Reaching the important middle (optimal) level of the arousal curve can be mediated by a number of factors, such as (1) prior arousal, (2) loudness and tempo, (3) further objective structural features, (4) appropriateness of music for the listening situation (see chapter 12), and (5) idiosyncratic factors, that is, the listener's personality and biography. Prior high arousal, such as anger, might lead to someone's wishing to reduce arousal by selecting soothing music. However, when high arousal is to be maintained, that is, when someone wants to stay angry or is at a party, further stimulating music will most likely be chosen. As the previous examples imply, loudness and tempo modulate arousal. When driving a car in heavy traffic or bad weather conditions, for instance, we intuitively avoid such stimulation by turning down the radio, selecting unobtrusive music, or turning the radio off. All of this is to say that processing music requires cognitive resources, and when those are already occupied by other processes, we need to reduce arousal by decreasing the cognitive load. The optimal level of arousal also depends on other musical characteristics that interact with loudness and tempo.

Everybody has at one point or other experienced strong physiological experiences when listening to music. Shivers down the spine, hairs standing on end (so-called "pilo-erection"), tears, "butterflies in the stomach," or laughter are but a few of the reactions that can happen when music deeply moves, "chills," or "thrills" us. Sloboda (1992) tried to link listeners' accounts of such chills to the musical structure and listed about 10 musical devices that may promote the aforementioned reactions (see list below; also the subsection on musical emotion and the brain later in this chapter).

1. Harmony descending cycle of fifth to tonic
2. Melodic appogiaturas
3. Melodic or harmonic sequence
4. Enharmonic change
5. Harmonic or melodic acceleration to cadence
6. Delay of final cadence
7. New or unprepared harmony
8. Sudden dynamic or textural change
9. Repeated syncopation
10. Prominent event earlier than prepared for entrance of a voice

The co-occurrence of these musical devices, especially the degree of (unexpected) change in the musical flow, create pleasantly experienced peaks of emotional intensity. For example, a clear soprano voice with a descending melody line entering against a background of smooth low organ sound will need several seconds to exert its effect on the listener. Researching chills is difficult, because the effects of music are cumulative over time (as music leads up to the critical chill-inducing moment) and involve characteristic time lags of about 1 to 3 seconds. Furthermore, the music has to somehow match the situation, a notion that North and Hargreaves (1997) call "appropriateness." The example they give is Felix Mendelssohn-Bartholdy's "Wedding March," which might have its strongest effect during a wedding and not at other occasions (except maybe when someone thinks about a wedding while listening to the march). More prototypical music, that is, music that most matches the situation, is likely to find the person more predisposed for an emotional response (athletes sometimes wipe away tears after singing their national anthem). Chills do not tend to happen with background music.

The last point to mention is the person. The experience of a certain music as complex, familiar, appropriate, arousing, and so forth is related to the listener's past exposure to it, as well as to age and gender. For example, pieces that are associated in episodic memory with some incident in one's biography will be easily recognized almost immediately and evoke strong emotions. This provides a plausible reason that certain pieces are favored by some and not by other people and that people in different cultures or cultural groups prefer different types of music. Some researchers have posited that the music present during the second decade of human life (and into the early 20s), when emotions are rampant, is central to building identity, managing moods, and helping the transition to adult life (see also chapter 12). This music becomes important for the rest of one's life. As a consequence, even the elderly respond positively when listening to the music of their youth, a phenomenon that can be helpful in music therapy for the elderly. Younger children tend to like swift music and seem more "open-eared" and tolerant of different types of music than adolescents (LeBlanc, 1981). Finally, girls and boys have been found in many studies to differ with regard to their musical preferences, which also help them to build their (in this case gender-specific) identities (cf. Mueller, 2002; Gembris, 2002).

Musical Emotion and the Brain

The nagging question regarding the liking of music is, What does the music do to entice us to listen to it? The simplified answer is that listening to music elicits a reaction similar to the one we have when eating chocolate or making love (Blood & Zatorre, 2001) and is part of the "human biology as expressed in the evolution and development of our cognitive capacities and of our social and environmental interactions" (Cross, 1999, p. 12). The brain circuitry related to our gratification system is stimulated, causing endogenic substances, such as the neurotransmitter dopamine, to be released. Those systems are vital because they constitute an autonomic reward system that reinforces behaviors essential for survival. Researchers and philosophers alike wonder why music evokes such responses even though it seems less vital, if not unnecessary, for the survival of the human race. Music also reduces physiological activity of central nervous structures that signal aversion and fear. Thus bodily reactions to music are complex but generally entail positive effects, which could be the reason music is positively valued everywhere.

Sad- and happy-sounding music resonates in our brains in similar ways, involving both hemispheres and the limbic system, the complex area that wraps around the bridge between the hemispheres and that is responsible for our processing of emotions (Kreutz, Russ, Bongard, & Lanfermann, 2003). The brain might be able to recognize basic emotions even in the absence of higher-order cortical processes (Peretz, 2003). There is mounting evidence that the right hemisphere is more strongly involved in the cognitive mediation of musical emotion than the left one. Recognition and decision processes required for appraisal and preference judgments certainly require activity of the frontal cortex. Much more research will be necessary to unravel the mystery of musical affect.

It is plausible that some persons experience music more strongly than others (see the following subsection). In several studies, musicians reported a heightened awareness of music and its emotion (e.g., Lehmann, 1997). We do not know whether this responsiveness is genetically determined or a result of training and an ensuing better understanding for the potential "pleasure" that can be extracted from a piece of music. Gender-specific effects also exist, as discussed earlier. In general, knowing more about music does not seem to impair emotional response; in fact, expression in unfamiliar music (e.g., non-Western music) is impossible to extract because the structural cues are meaningless to the noninitiated (see chapter 5).

When the Music Stops Playing

Although we would think that deaf people cannot hear at all, they often have residual hearing, depending on when, why, and to what extent they lost their hearing (see Yost, 2000, chapter 16). Of course, residual hearing differs markedly from normal hearing in that it creates frequency distortions or attenuations in different frequency bands. Whether or not music can still be enjoyed probably depends on the individual and his or her interests, but neuroanatomically, music can often still be perceived. Persons with hearing impairments start to depend more on the visual cues that accompany music because these visual stimuli can activate the auditory cortex (Finney, Fine, & Dobkins, 2001). Also, the auditory cortex of deaf people can restructure to sense vibrations (Shibata et al., 2001), and, as a consequence, people with hearing impairments enjoy music and engage actively with it (Calabrese & Olivetti-Belardinelli, 1997). They can even become successful dancers or musicians, like the percussionist Evelyn Glennie, or continue to be musically creative, like Ludwig van Beethoven. Thus, listening also occurs with less-than-perfect hearing.

Just as there are some people who have problems producing or understanding speech (aphasics), there are, unfortunately, people in this world who do not enjoy music despite intact hearing. The prevalence of this phenomenon, called *amusia,* is about 4 in 100 persons, who, despite normal language, memory, and intellectual abilities, have trouble making sense out of music (Peretz, 2003; see chapter 2, this volume, for a discussion in the context of musical talent). Although some amusics are born with normal processing capabilities and incur their disability through sickness or accident, other tone-deaf persons are born that way ("congenital amusia"). In former times, insights about amusics stemmed from injury and stroke patients: Damage to the left hemisphere resulted most often in problems of speech and impairment of movement in the right side of the body, whereas damage to the right hemisphere hindered movement in the left side and affected some music-related tasks. Today, amusia is studied under controlled conditions in the laboratory. Although most patients show a main deficit in the pitch dimension—that is, they cannot identify or sing back tunes—there are also problems with timing ("arrhythmia"). Researchers attribute the deficits to a faulty circuitry for fine-grained pitch (and rhythm) perception. Peretz (2003) has also reported a case study in which a person had perceptual problems and was unable to classify melodies as familiar or unfamiliar; however, the participant could still tell whether the melodies were happy or sad. Although the reported case studies provide a plethora of information, the phenomenon has yet to be definitively explained. This is not surprising, as music processing is modular and distributed across the brain in interconnected networks.

Study Questions

1. Explain how people come to prefer one music over another and why their musical tastes might change over time. Use the '50s "rock-n-roll generation" as an example.
2. Discuss the contribution of musically immanent (structural) and extramusical factors in the listener's understanding of and preference for certain music.
3. What problems do music critics or jurors (especially in "blind" competitions) face when evaluating performances?

Further Reading

Juslin, P. N., & Sloboda, J. A. (2001). *Music and Emotion: Theory and Research*. Covers aspects on listening in chapters 15 through 19.

Deutsch, D. (Ed.). (1999). *The Psychology of Music*. Several chapters cover particular aspects of basic music perception.

Hodges, D. A. (Ed.) (1996). *Handbook of music psychology*. Several chapters on music perception and higher-order processes

Gembris, H. (2002). The development of musical abilities. In R. Colwell & C. Richardson (Eds.), *The New Handbook of Research on Music Teaching and Learning* (pp. 487–508). Musical preferences in the context of life-span development.

12

The User

Work-Focused and Person-Focused Approaches to Music

Consider three situations involving the same piece of music, a Beethoven piano sonata. In the first situation, a music lover has paid a substantial sum of money (and traveled a considerable distance) to sit in a downtown concert hall and hear an internationally renowned concert pianist play the piece. In the second situation, two parents are sitting in a suburban school hall, listening to their daughter play this same piece in her first concert. In the third situation, a taxi driver has put a CD containing this piece into his car audio system, and it plays in the background while he cruises the city center looking for customers. From the perspective of the people hearing the music, how similar are these three musical experiences?

One of the ways of thinking about musical experiences, which has been somewhat overencouraged within the classical tradition, is what we might call a "work-focused" approach. In simple terms, this approach posits that the composition (often identified with the printed or written score) exists in and of itself as an autonomous, pure object, detached from any specific performance of it or any specific context in which it might be heard. Traditional musicology has encouraged this way of thinking by promoting such activities as score analysis, in which the structure and content of the music are analyzed in a way that makes little or no explicit reference to actual performances. This perspective would focus on the similarity that the three situations share, namely, the same piece is being heard on each occasion. The sonata has a certain structure, aesthetic quality and context, and set of mood transitions; taken together, these things are central to determining the nature and meaning of the experience for all listeners, regardless of their situation, motivations, and background.

A different way of thinking about music is what we might call a "person-focused" approach. This approach would claim that there is no such thing as pure music. Every musical object or event is situated in a social context and involves human actors, with their assumptions, backgrounds, and motivations. Musical objects and events thus have rich social meanings and purposes for all of the parties involved—composers, performers, and listeners. No music happens unless it is fulfilling a purpose for someone, or is being *used* for something. This perspective would focus on the specific differences in the three situations arising from the different environments, social constructions, and purposes surrounding the musical act. From such a perspective the three situations may have very little in common. In the first situation, for instance, the listener may be experiencing disappointment that the performance, for all its technical perfection, is much less satisfying than one heard earlier and wondering whether the time and expense have been worth it. In the second situation, although the performance might have all kinds of technical and expressive flaws, the parents are so full of pride in the achievement of their daughter that they are moved to tears. In the third situation, the taxi driver may not even know the name of the piece he is listening to, sensing only that it tends to calm him down as he drives around the stressful city or noticing that certain customers like it.

Both ways of thinking about music are valid and can yield important insights into music and its significance. However, the work-focused approach has been very dominant in the music education world during most of the twentieth century and has influenced the way people think about music in quite profound ways. It has framed conventional aesthetics, philosophy, and musicology (e.g., Dahlhaus, 1991). In particular, the work-focused approach has been associated with a school of thought that asserts that there is a valuable repertoire (or canon, containing the masterworks of such renowned composers as Bach, Mozart, Beethoven, and Brahms, to name but four) that transcends time and culture. Such works are "all-time greats," whose value lies within themselves. If this is true, then no further justification is needed for studying and performing such works. No justification is needed for spending money to support the training and development of elite musicians to provide high-quality performances of these works. The works themselves justify the resources put into them and will always justify such resources—in all places and at all times.

Although we may not hear statements quite as strong as this being uttered every day, it is our experience that many people in the classical music world think like this. As a result, a rather settled philosophy pervades some institutional settings. It is assumed that there will always be symphony orchestras and classical soloists performing a rather limited core of classical repertoire, that there will always be concert halls for them to play in and audiences eager to pay to hear them, and that the job of institutions is to provide the best possible training for musicians hoping to fill traditional symphony and soloist positions.

Self Study: Everyday Music Diary

Think back over everything you did yesterday. Write a brief diary in which you list as many occasions as you can remember in which music was happening (including music you were directly involved in making, but also music in the environment around you); Or keep a diary over the course of a specific day.

If you are working in an environment connected with music (e.g., a music college), think particularly hard about times outside that environment when music took place. For each occasion, write down where you were, what you were doing, who you were with, what the music was (anything you can remember), and what effect, if any, the music had on you.

Now go back over the list and identify those events in which you had some choice over the musical experience. For each of these events, write down why you made the choice you did and to what extent the music helped you fulfill whatever purposes you had in mind.

Finally, compare it with the list produced by someone else. How many different types of musical experience can you identify? How many different purposes were being fulfilled by the music? How much waking time is not accompanied by music? What does this tell you about the role of music in everyday life?

This chapter explores the person-focused approach to music in more detail. The reason is not that we think there is no merit in the work-focused approach. On the contrary, deepening our understanding of specific works is at the heart of effective musicianship, as we have argued in several places. However, taking a person-focused perspective can be a useful way of expanding and enriching the way we think about and approach our musical activities. Also, this approach is increasingly prevalent in contemporary musicology (Cook, 1998), ethnomusicology (Small, 1998), and studies of music education at all levels (Green, 1997; Kingsbury, 1988). It is also increasingly being forced on performing musicians and the institutions that train them as a result of the inexorable decline of classical concert audiences and sales of classical music recordings over the last few decades (e.g., British Phonographic Industries [BPI], 2003).

Although we explore these issues from the perspective of classical music (which is the tradition in which we all were trained and work), the implications of the issues we discuss are ones for all performing musicians, whatever genre they specialize in. Indeed, a breaking down of overrigid barriers between classical and nonclassical music is one of the most encouraging signs of contemporary musical life.

Music Skills Develop to Meet Cultural Needs

Major musical forms emerge because lots of people use them; they have cultural functions. The skills that are encouraged and developed in musicians are totally a function of society's values and requirements on the music profession (see chapter 1). Society creates the constraints for skill development, and a good way to see how cultures create musical skills is to look back over the history of musical performance in specific regions of the world and note the significant changes. There were glass harmonica virtuosi in the eighteenth and ninetheenth centuries, and famous composers (among them Mozart, Berlioz, and Weber) wrote for this now extinct instrument. Today, music students are lucky to have even heard of this instrument that Benjamin Franklin invented. Today, we have virtuosi playing the electric guitar, invented only half a century ago.

Different skills rise and fall as the need for them rises or falls. People with the potential to become skilled glass harmonica players were not more common in the nineteenth century than they are now. Society institutionalizes skill according to changing need and fashion, and musicians change their skill profiles to suit. In this context it becomes clear again that the specific skills of classical performance cannot be "innate." Genes cannot possibly select skills that come and go over periods measured in decades and centuries.

When one is immersed in a particular music tradition (such as the classical tradition), questions about its purpose are not often consciously considered. It is easy for classically trained musicians or musicians trained in any other art music tradition of the world to focus on the details of what they do in their everyday lives and not to look at the bigger picture. This bigger picture indicates that the whole gamut of classical repertoire accounts for less than 5% of the music economy worldwide, that is, 1 in 20 CDs sold (BPI, 2003; see table 12.1).

To offer readers a broadened perspective, we explore two important questions. First, what are the broad types of uses and functions that music has been able to fulfill for people in different times and places? Second, how varied are the situations in which music takes place? More specifically, how typical is the classical music culture of the range of musical cultures that exist? The chapter concludes with some implications of these findings for the contemporary music performer, both in training and in working life. In reviewing these issues, we draw on other disciplines in addition to psychology—specifically, cultural studies, anthropology, and sociology.

Table 12.1 Sales of Albums by Music Type in 2000 and 2002

Genre	2000 (%)	2002 (%)
Pop	32.4	30.3
Rock	25.9	31.0
Dance	13.3	9.5
Rhythm & Blues	8.5	7.4
Middle of Road	4.6	6.1
Classical	4.0	3.5
Hip-hop/Rap	3.9	5.1
Country	1.7	1.5
Folk	1.1	1.4
Jazz	1.0	2.0
Reggae	0.9	0.7
World	0.6	0.4
Childrens'	0.5	0.3
New Age	0.5	0.1
Blues	0.4	0.3
Spoken word	0.2	0.1
Other	0.5	0.3
Total	100	100

Data from "Sales by type of music, 2002," from *British Phonographic Industries: Market Information, 204,* p. 2. Copyright 2003 by The British Phongraphic Industry. Reprinted by permission.

Uses and Functions of Music

Different kinds of musical experience, such as those described in the three "vignettes" that began this chapter, reflect different uses or functions for the people involved. The impetus for trying to categorize and understand these functions within contemporary music studies came originally from anthropology. The branch of anthropology that deals with music is commonly known as ethnomusicology (Myers, 1992), or sometimes comparative musicology (Nettl & Bohlman, 1991). Sociologists have also dealt with the question of function and music (e.g., Adorno, 1976).

For much of the twentieth century, Western ethnomusicologists focused their attention on musical cultures other than their own, often in less industrialized societies. Authors such as Barz and Cooley (1997) and Merriam (1964) have attempted to list systematically the primary functions of music evident from these studies. For instance, Gregory (1997) lists 14 functions of traditional music (including lullabies, games, work music, dance music, ceremonial and festival music, battle music, etc.). What most of these functions have in common is that they are participatory and social in nature, and they bind people together in joint activity. In many situations, music is owned by whoever is present in the situation (be it a mother singing a lullaby to her baby or a group of women working in the fields and singing a work song). Even where some members of a group may be given status as specialized musicians, everyone present can join in the music, leaving virtually no bystanders. This is rather different from the state of affairs in twenty-first-century industrialized societies, where in very many situations there is a clear and rigid distinction between musical participants (the performers, sound engineers, presenters) and the essentially nonparticipatory musical spectators (the listener or the audience). Participatory cultures are, in fact, the norm in the world's history. Even the Western classical tradition was probably more participatory 150 years ago than it is now, partly because the music performed was music of the time.

Social and Cultural Functions of Music

Because so many of the world's musical situations have involved everyone doing things together, in coordination or harmony, the expression of group identity and group solidarity appears to be a fundamental function of music. Magowan (1994), for instance, described how the Aboriginal people of the Northern Territory of Australia use songs to express clan identity. Certain songs may be sung only by someone belonging to a specific clan, and these songs often portray how ancestral laws give a particular clan rights to a particular locality. In Western societies, all sorts of groups use music as an essential "badge of identity." These range from soccer supporter clubs (who sing their "anthem" from the terraces during a match as an expression of identity "against" the opposing club, which simultaneously attempts to dominate the arena with its own, different song; Kopiez & Brink, 1998) to motorbike gangs (such as "biker boys" who use specific types of music to "psych" themselves up for the fast—and extremely dangerous—rides that are the central expression of their cultural identity; Willis, 1978). Music also expresses national identity (Folkestad, 2002). For instance, immediately after the terrorist attacks of September 11, 2001, in the United States, there was a significant increase in broadcast performances of patriotic songs, such as "The Star Spangled Banner," but also of the Enya song "Only Time," which became a manifestation of national mourning. Music can also be used by threatened national groups to assert their identity against assimilation or oppression. A good example of this was the use of Estonian choral music as a focus for political resistance against Soviet rule in Estonia during the cold war.

In relation to identity, one phenomenon of contemporary industrialized society is so pervasive as to merit special mention. This is the way in which adolescents' overtly expressed musical choices and tastes function as statements about youth identity (Mueller, 2002). Statements about the personal choice of music indicate personality, beliefs, and behaviors. Although there are many specialized musical subcultures, research shows that music can be divided into two overarching groups. In one group are genres such as pop, dance, and indie, which the majority of adolescents like. In the other group are genres such as classical, jazz, and heavy metal, which an equally large majority dislike. According to Tarrant, Hargreaves, and North (2001) adolescents believe that people who like pop or dance music are more "in touch with youth issues," easier to get along with, more fashionable, and more fun than people who like classical music or jazz. Similar research findings strongly suggest that an adolescent will seriously prejudge an adult based on the adult's musical tastes. This being the case, we should not be surprised that adolescents with minority musical tastes will sometimes hide these tastes in public—so strong is the wish to be liked and accepted within the peer group (Finnäs, 1989).

Through social uses of music, such as those described here, associations can be created that have their own functional power. Music associated with key people, groups, or events can invoke personal reminiscences of emotional relationships. It often has a memory or nostalgic component (John Booth Davies has aptly called this the "Darling, they're playing our tune" effect). In a study of 91 freewritten responses to a mail survey about personal meanings of music, 50% of respondents spontaneously mentioned that they used music to remind them of valued past events (Sloboda & O'Neill, 2001, see table 12.2). This was by far

Table 12.2 Percentage of Mass Observation Respondents Reporting Various Functions and Activities Chosen for Music

Functions	
Reminder of valued past event	50
Spiritual experience	6
Evokes visual images	2
Tingles/goosepimples/shivers	10
Source of pleasure/enjoyment	6
To put in a good mood	16
Moves to tears/catharsis/release	14
Excites	2
Motivates	2
Source of comfort/healing	4
Calms/soothes/relaxes/relieves stress	8
Mood enhancement	8
To match current mood	6

Taken from table 18.1 in "Emotions in Everyday Listening to Music" by J. A. Sloboda and S. A. O'Neill, 2001. In P. N. Juslin & J. A. Sloboda (Eds.), *Music and Emotion: Theory and Research,* pp. 420. Copyright Oxford University Press, 2001. Adapted by permission.

the most frequent function cited. Although people are quite often alone when they use music in this way, the function is still implicitly social; It points to a relationship or a social situation that goes outside the individual.

Another way in which social meanings find their way into musical situations is through prestige effects. Simply being told something about the reputation of the composer or the performer of a particular piece can influence the degree to which people are prepared to engage with the music and rate it highly. For instance, Weick, Gilfillian, and Keith (1973) showed, in a cleverly controlled study, that members of a jazz orchestra rated the same piece of music more or less highly, devoted more or less effort to learning it, and performed it more or less well according to the way in which the composer of the piece was described to them in a prerehearsal handout (as a "serious" or "nonserious" jazz composer). In another study, teenagers rated the artistic merit of classical, New Age, and jazz compositions that were attributed to either male or female composers (North, Colley, & Hargreaves, 2003). The authors found that the jazz excerpts were particularly gender stereotyped. Males rated the excerpts attributed to females lower on artistic merit than when the same excerpts were attributed to males. Female listeners rated the compositions of female composers higher on artistic and technical grounds than those of males. Every musical culture has a socially constructed hierarchy of values. For instance, within classical music, there is general consensus that J. S. Bach was a better composer than Telemann, a prolific contemporary of Bach's (Farnsworth, 1969).

Membership in any musical culture entails making discriminations and judgments that are generally in accord with the consensus. But the criteria for value are different in different cultures, and they can shift over time within a culture. Cook (1998), for instance, has described how the Beethoven cult (which he describes as "the central pillar in the culture of classical music") has come under increasing attack in recent years. One of the most important sources of "deconstruction" of Beethoven's preeminence is based on the insights brought to musicology through feminist theory (e.g., McClary, 1991). From these perspectives much of Beethoven's music has been characterized as masculine, aggressive, and domineering. As early as 1882, Sir George Grove was talking (with obvious approval) of "the strong, fierce, merciless coercion, with which Beethoven forces you along, and bows and bends you to his will." In contemporary industrialized society, gender equality is increasingly valued (and often enshrined in law), whereas male dominance is associated with unwanted outcomes, such as domestic violence and sexual abuse. From such a cultural standpoint, there are those who find it difficult today to take an unambiguously positive view of the "Beethoven cult"—at least on a theoretical level.

The ability to engage knowledgeably with a body of music (or any other cultural product) and to be able to take part in informed debates about the relative worth of different items is in itself an important sign of social status. Possessing what has been called "cultural capital" (Bourdieu, 1979) allows a person to be accepted as a "connoisseur" within the domain (Frith, 1996). Many people who have no significant performing skills have nonetheless become connoisseurs of particular genres or styles of music. Sometimes connoisseurship, or "fandom," takes very specific forms (for instance, knowing and possessing every composition by a specific composer or every track by a particular singer; Mueller, 2002). Acquiring this kind of detailed and highly articulated knowledge is a skill in its own right, especially for performers. Unless performers become connoisseurs within their chosen styles and genres, they will not be able to exercise independent aesthetic judgment—they will simply be "reheating" other people's cultural judgments. What is more, such performers may be less skilled in the art of musical judgment than many members of their audiences! Given the huge pressures on young performers to compete, oversight of cultural and historical issues is understandable but may, in the long run, be self-defeating.

One area in which certain groups of musicians can distinguish themselves from other musicians concerns "authentic," or historically informed, performance practice and scholarship. Although proponents of Baroque music from the mid-twentieth century onward have made authenticity a central aspect of their aesthetic, the notion of authenticity can be applied to every type of musical performance. Note that in rock or popular music, authenticity has more to do with how honest or credible a performer appears than with the performance tradition. A mature independent musical judgment can only be made where there is experience of a range of different approaches to authenticity.

Individualistic Functions of Music

The functions described here have echoes and resonances in many of the cultures of the world and across history. However, in industrialized societies, where music can be separated from the act of production through recordings and miniaturization of reproduction, new or enhanced functions have emerged. Music can be used far from its originally intended setting, and an individual alone can engage with a very wide range of music. The portable mp3 players or radios allow us to hear music wherever we are and whatever we are doing. It is virtually always possible for an individual to choose what music to listen to just by pressing a button, selecting a song, or scanning the Web. Once we have the basic technology, we don't need to relate to anyone else in our music consumption. We can be solitary, self-contained, and self-regarding.

Several research studies have now begun to paint a picture of how individuals use music as a private resource to manage and enhance everyday life (Behne, 1997; De Nora, 2000; Sloboda & O'Neill, 2001). Two very important general conclusions emerge from this research. First, music in everyday life is generally used as "background." Recorded music will be playing, but the user will usually be doing something else, as well as listening to the music. The activities that music is used to accompany are varied and include domestic chores (cooking, cleaning), study, travel, and social encounters. This means that the concentrated silent attention expected of people in the concert hall is almost entirely absent from everyday contemporary music listening. If they are aware of the music at all, people in these situations focus on music for "snippets"; but they benefit more from the overall mood and soundscape of the music than from any close tracking of the melodies or structure (see chapter 11). The second important conclusion to draw from the research is that listening to music in this way remains valuable to people. It almost invariably improves their moods and their abilities to handle or enjoy the situations they are in. The mood improvement is greatest in those cases in which people can exercise high degrees of choice over what music they hear and when they hear it.

Although music can be heard in almost any life context, the research results so far available suggest that travel is the activity most likely to be accompanied by music listening (Sloboda, O'Neill, & Ivaldi, 2001). In industrialized societies, people spend huge amounts of time in cars, buses, trains, and airplanes. In all of these contexts, recorded music is used not simply to pass the time but very often chosen deliberately to assist a transition in mood or energy that is required during the journey. This is sometimes called "mood management." For instance, someone driving to work may listen to upbeat, energetic music to obtain energy and engagement for the working day. The same person driving home after a hard day's work may choose mellow, soothing music to help iron away the stresses of work and prepare for a relaxing evening at home. Increasingly, cars are apparently becoming the concert halls of the twenty-first century, where people may listen to the music of their choice, at the time of their choosing, and without having to account for their choice or their mode of listening to anyone else (Oblad, 2000).

At certain junctures in life, music may be used not simply to help with everyday moods and emotions but as a resource to assist with life-threatening or life-changing circumstances. For example, music may help to elicit the cathartic tears that one needs to shed in relation to a loss or a hurt. Cathartic emotions are those that release and purge negative feelings. Music may inject hope into what may seem a hopeless situation. Research has suggested that many, if not most, people can recall an incident in which music made a "life-changing" impact on them (Gabrielsson, 2001). What is particularly interesting is that many of these experiences take place when the listener is alone with the music. It is almost as if the music takes on the role of friend or comforter and is preferred, in some cases, to a real person. Expression of emotions in public, particularly emotions of vulnerability and pain, appear to be problematic for many people in industrialized societies. For instance, one respondent in Sloboda's (1999) survey study wrote:

When I'm down I listen to this and go down as far as I can, then I cry, I cry deep from inside. I wallow in self-pity and purge all the gloom from my body. Then I dry my eyes, and wash my face, do my hair, put on fresh makeup, and rejoin the world. (p. 367)

Indeed, the contemporary propensity for privacy and autonomy can mean that music in social settings becomes a source of conflict and discord rather than of group cohesion and shared identity. Research has suggested that the home is often a location for musical conflict, as people with different tastes battle for control of the acoustic environment. The teenager playing loud rock music in his or her bedroom to the annoyance of the rest of the household has become almost a clichéd stereotype for generational domestic disharmony. In another example from Sloboda's (1999) study, one female respondent said, "The car is the only place where I can listen to music loud enough without annoying other people." Desire for autonomy and control can help explain why people differ so much in their reactions to music.

Music (usually prerecorded) now finds its way into a wide array of public places in the industrialized world, including shops, restaurants and bars, hotels, transportation, and workplaces. The vast amount of money spent by commercial companies on providing such music suggests that it is believed to be serving important functions for the companies and organizations who buy it. For instance, music has been claimed to increase work productivity on the factory floor, increase sales in shops, decrease vandalism in shopping malls, decrease anxiety in airline passengers, decrease the amount of anesthetic necessary in hospital operations, and increase performance and pro-social behaviors in school classrooms— to name just a few of music's benefits (see Hallam, 2000; Hargreaves & North, 1997; see also chapter 11).

Recent discussions about the transfer effect of music, sometimes called the Mozart effect, show that people want to use music and are willing to believe in the powers of music. Although the empirical evidence for music's effect on intelligence is thin and possible effects can be alternatively accounted for by arousal, mood, and motivation (e.g., Husain, Thompson, & Schellenberg, 2002), there is no doubt that music has a positive effect on human behavior in many areas (cf. Gruhn & Rauscher, 2002).

Rather than attempting to assess the accuracy of these claims or to understand how these effects might be brought about, it is appropriate to observe that the composer and the performer are normally no party at all to the way their music is being used. In fact, they probably never envisaged their activities as fulfilling the functions that commercial interests have bestowed on them. This is very different from the situation that has persisted until recently in most of the world's musical cultures, in which the performer (who is also often the composer) gets to decide exactly where and when the music is performed and so can exert a great deal of control over how it is experienced and used.

Moreover, it is important to note that recipients of what has sometimes been called "canned music" (as found in shops and other public places) are not simply passive "victims" of the intended effects of such music. Accounts given by informants in these studies suggest, instead, that those who program the music make a conscious decision to use music as a resource, whether it be to facilitate buying decisions directly or to project a certain image that offers a sense of identification for its customers. For instance, reactions to music in a restaurant will depend on such factors as how consistent one judges the music to be with the style or ambience of the room (loud rock music would be experienced as more appropriate in a burger bar than in a Japanese restaurant). Personal needs and characteristics also play a part. One respondent in a study reported that she valued music in restaurants and bars to cover awkward silences in conversation and to make it less easy for people at nearby tables to overhear her. Another respondent, who was somewhat hard of hearing, disliked music in the same context precisely because it made conversation more difficult. After complaining about music in shops, a third, elderly male respondent went on to qualify his remarks by saying that he didn't mind "good" music in shops playing quietly (e.g., Mozart in his local bookshop). It was only "bad" music, that is, pop music being played loudly (not his preference), that he objected to.

The conclusion we are inclined to draw from these findings is that, despite occasional mismatches between what is offered and what is desired, music in public places is as often as not of social benefit and that people find complex and personally specific ways of interacting with their environments to maximize these benefits. What is more concerning about almost all the individualistic functions of music is that the musicians who produce the music often play no role at all in deriving or mediating these functions. They are kept at arm's length from their "end users" and so may have lost the social sensitivity and control that would have characterized musicians in other times and places.

Cultural Contrasts in Music Performance

The previous section highlighted some of the widely diverse functions that music fulfills for listeners. Many of these functions take place away from the traditional "concert" setting, in which performers and listeners are in each other's physical presence (see chapter 9). Nonetheless, people still do go to concerts. Live music still exists in a growing variety of settings and locations. Performers exert a very important and direct influence over outcomes in such settings. Therefore, it remains important to understand the more specific functions that such live performance settings have for audiences and the part performers play in fulfilling those functions.

The classical culture, with its symphony and recital halls, makes certain assumptions about how music takes place that are quite different from those made in other settings, both past and present. Comparing classical concert settings to other musical settings brings into clear focus some of the assumptions underlying classical music culture that may limit a performers' potential to respond fully to different cultural settings.

Here we identify six such contrasts, and, in doing so, we draw extensively on the work of Cook (1998), Frith (1996), and, particularly, Small (1998). Each subsection covers a key feature of classical performance contexts and provides contrasting examples from other cultures (similar to the cross-cultural perspectives offered throughout the book).

The Distinct Roles of Performer and Listener

In a classical concert, performers and audiences enter by different doors; they are generally discouraged from interacting with each other (by physical and psychological barriers). Generally, performers produce all the sounds; listeners attend and appreciate. Performers and listeners are also separated economically. By and large, listeners pay to hear music, and performers get paid.

In many other performing situations the boundaries between performer and listener are much more blurred, even to the point of becoming nonexistent. At a rock concert, the activities and movements of the audience (swaying, waving, hand clapping) may become an integral part of the performance itself. In other settings (e.g., karaoke, folk clubs), anyone may step up from the audience and take the performer spot for a while. In some settings (e.g., gospel worship, traditional or tribal rituals), everyone present fulfills the role of performer.

The Performer

In a classical concert, the items to be performed and the order in which they are performed are predetermined a long time ahead (sometimes years) by the performer (or concert managers). This is often seen as necessary because of the preparation required, not only in rehearsal but also in staging, production of program notes, and other technical issues. In other contexts, listeners can play a major role in determining what is played. For instance, bar pianists expect to play the customers' requested tunes on demand; indeed, the pianists would not stay long in employment if they didn't know all the favorite tunes of the particular clientele. A similar claim could be made for the Yugoslavian epic singer (see Cross Cultural Perspective in chapter 6).

The Traditional Listener

Attendance at a classical concert requires massive self-restraint on the part of an audience member. Conversation is forbidden, and even coughing can attract hostile attention. Movement is discouraged (leaving one's seat is considered appropriate only in an emergency). Even facial expressions tend to be muted. A camera roving over the participants at a normal classical concert would suggest to an uninitiated observer that the audience was either in a trance or deeply sedated. It is the normal expectation at a classical concert audience that such immobility should be maintained without complaint for periods of at least an hour at a time. That such behavior is completely conditioned can be seen in concerts for young listeners, who are not quite familiar with the ritual.

In many more music performance situations, listeners have considerable freedom—to vocalize at will (talk, dance, or sing along), to move freely, or to attend to only parts of the performance. This would be true of almost all popular music performance settings in contemporary industrialized society, from discos to large pop festivals. Most first-time attendees of classical concerts are, therefore, likely to be ill prepared for the stringencies demanded of them in the classical concert hall; this may be one reason that it does not appear an attractive or welcoming environment to many people who otherwise would have the capacity to enjoy classical music. They just feel too uncomfortable and restricted. New interdisciplinary art forms, such as sound installations, increase the interaction between music makers and listeners to overcome such feelings of alienation.

The "Ideal" Setting and Accessories for Classical Performance

Classical music venues all over the world have an essential "sameness" that reflects a historically grown and socially constructed consensus about the ideal settings for the reception of classical music. The concert auditorium is usually separated, both spatially and acoustically, from any disturbances, so there is no possibility of interference with the key activity, which is the music taking place on stage. Seating and room construction maximize comfort and are designed to allow everyone to have the most similar visual and acoustic experience possible. Everything possible is done to focus attention onto what is happening on stage. Lighting is dimmed in the auditorium, and décor is often sparse and soothing, with all lines converging on the podium. It is no coincidence that concert halls tend to resemble a large church or cathedral because there is a strong sense of creating a "sacred" space where listeners and performers may leave behind their everyday selves to contemplate the spiritual values enshrined within the music that is afforded the characteristic of "greatness." Even the external appearance of a symphony hall, with its impressive facade, expresses these values to the outside world. It signifies even to the uninitiated that what goes on within its walls is grand, important, and not "everyday."

Today, much performed music takes place in settings that could not contrast more strongly with the classical concert hall. Perhaps the clearest examples of this are the traveling musicians, or "buskers." These musicians perform wherever there are prospective audiences, no matter what the surroundings or the distractions. If they waited until a group of people was sitting in still silent reverence around them, they would never begin a performance! In many traditional cultural settings, performed music takes place in the setting appropriate to the activity it is accompanying. What matters is that the setting is appropriate for the nonmusical activity that forms the context for the music. This is very consistent with informal uses of music in every culture. Consider probably the most common musical act of our own culture: the communal singing of "Happy Birthday to You." What matters in this case is that all the guests take part in congratulating the birthday celebrant. Nothing else about the setting or the context is of the slightest importance. In this respect, music performance is about "seizing the moment," rather than waiting for the best possible moment. There are other, more formal contexts, such as the sounding of a fanfare at the start of an important event. What matters is the symbolism of the music happening at that specific place and time (see Adorno, 1976, for poignant descriptions).

Along with the importance of the venue goes the importance of the instruments used. Most acoustic instruments found on the concert stage have three important characteristics: (1) They need careful handling; (2) they are expensive—sometimes to the point of being insured for higher sums than the average for which a person's life is insured; (3) they require a long learning time to play well. All these factors help to explain the special, and rather protected, environments in which classical music takes place and is learned (most of this also applies to instruments in rock and jazz music).

It may come as a surprise to some classically trained musicians that there have existed successful musical cultures in which no instruments at all have been used. In some cultures, such as the Vedda of Sri Lanka, the Yami of Botel Tobago, the Fuegians of South America, and the Tasmanian Aborigines, all music is performed by means of so-called corpophones, that is, sounds that can be made through dance, song, and the production of percussive sounds by the slapping and stamping of body parts, either on each other or on the ground (Kartomi, 1991). These cultures made no "investment" in artifacts for music making. It is also very apparent within most popular and folk musical cultures that instruments are often less important than the human voice. The instruments may even be of mere functional quality (e.g., the wind instruments of Italian itinerant bands playing operatic music).

Technical Perfection and Faithfulness to the Composer's Intentions

If we expect anything when we arrive at a symphony hall for a concert, it is that the performers will be well rehearsed. In a classical context that means, at the very minimum, that they play the correct notes with confidence and coordination. Intonation and timing should be precise. We also expect that the interpretation should be well articulated and justified. These expectations reflect the value that is placed on high levels of training and the excellence of the teachers, coaches, and conductors that the classical enterprise requires (see chapters 4 and 9). In these respects, our expectations of classical music performers are very similar to those that are placed on a variety of professionals within contemporary industrialized cultures (such as doctors, lawyers, airline pilots, and food manufacturers). In all these cases there are expected standards, arrived at by consensus and designed to ensure that high standards of knowledge are reliably applied.

In contrast, some musical cultures tend to value "genuineness" and "spontaneity" over technical excellence. In such cultures, being too highly "schooled" may be considered a disadvantage and may be seen as an impediment to "authenticity," which is grounded not in formal schooling but in lived experience (often the experience of pain and adversity). Hence the eagerly perpetuated myth of the completely "self-taught" and "illiterate" rock musician. Some schools of contemporary folk and popular music favor a somewhat rough and even "raw" product as a signal of this authenticity. Performances that are too technically polished are seen as suspect and too allied with consumerist values.

Implications for the Classical Performer

This chapter has indicated the variety of ways in which people engage with and use music. It is widely held that this variety has increased in the contemporary industrialized world in that individuals have ever-increasing choice about which music they interact with and how they interact with it. Commentators have talked about the fragmentation of contemporary culture as a symptom of the "postmodern" age. Many of us now experience a shifting set of competing cultural options in which no one option is preeminent (for an elaboration of this argument, see Sloboda, 2001).

During the middle part of the twentieth century, it was possible for many people to assume that Western classical music was the preeminent cultural reference point that other music could reinforce or react against. From that perspective, it made considerable sense to put classical music and classical training at the center of educational and institutional life. We even accepted that many non-Western musical cultures changed (became Westernized) or vanished. Those of us who occupy positions of seniority and influence in schools, universities, conservatories, and government departments were brought up within this rather stable conception, and this is reflected in the structure and organization of those institutions that support and train musicians. However, we are now faced with similar fundamental changes in our own musical world, and our assumptions and skills may increasingly fail to serve either the people we train or the audiences they will need to attract.

Are contemporary audiences less prepared to buy the "unadulterated" classical model? They may not want to sit motionless in a concert hall all evening. We may have to change the concert experience to make it more attuned to their different ways of engaging with music. This may mean dismantling many of the barriers that classical musicians have set between themselves and their audiences. Will the successful classical performer soon be the one who knows how to talk to the members of an audience, makes them laugh, allows them to ask questions, and is able to explain the value they might find in the experience being offered? We feel that many classical performers could learn a lot from the attitudes and skills of the popular, folk, or jazz musicians operating in bars, on the street, or in the community center. Comedians are constantly scanning and adjusting to the reactions of the audience. They don't hide in the green room during the interval or after the performance; they are out in public, interacting with their audiences, offering them opportunities to participate, and seeking their feedback and opinions.

All musical performers must be acutely aware that they are competing with the many thousands of fine CD recordings and music clips now available electronically. In order to persuade audiences to give up time and money to attend a live performance, performers may need to think harder about how they can make that live performance special and turn it into something far more engaging (see chapter 9) than simply reproducing the basic experience that could be available to any listener in the comfort of his or her own home.

In closing, we, the three authors of this book, are passionate devotees of classical music. This passion is at the heart of our motivations to write this book. We want to see classical music survive and prosper. In order for this to be ensured, we believe that more classically trained musicians need to act on the realization that, in the world's musical history, we can be seen as a rather odd and overspecialized type of musician, capable of enacting only a few of the roles that many musicians have taken for granted in other times and places (e.g., entertainer, singer, healer or therapist, composer, improviser). While demand is stable or increasing for classical musicians, this may be fine, but if demand is changing, then being more aware of what people want from music may be the key to our survival as musicians capable of earning an honest living from our craft. At present, we may be in danger of leaving the business of interacting with listeners to the concert-hall managers, the recording companies, and the music marketers. And that would be a long-term disaster, both for us and for the listeners.

Responding to cultural change does not mean abandoning traditionally valued classical performance. It probably means being smarter and more proactive in our choice of repertoire. Even today there are intriguing and underexplored avenues capable of fascinating niche audiences. It means being creative about where we perform our music, not simply hiding inside traditional concert halls. Above all, it means constantly finding new ways of making meaningful and reciprocal contacts with our audiences. We may have to abandon our ingrained beliefs that the flow of value is predominantly one way—that we bestow value on our audiences through our art. The reality is that the flow is two way and that audiences bestow equal value on us by engaging with what we do and by their attention, commitment, and creative responses to us.

Study Questions

1. Contrast the work-focused and person-focused approaches to music. In what ways do research findings lend weight to the distinctions being made?
2. What research evidence supports the everyday observation that there are many different functions of music?
3. What do we know about the capacities and motivations of contemporary audiences? What implications might this have for the classically trained performer?

Further Reading

Hargreaves, D. J., & North, A. C. (Eds.). (1997). *The Social Psychology of Music.* A good compendium of research into social factors that affect music listeners and performers.
The following are key works that highlight the differences between classical and other musical cultures.
Small, C. (1998). *Musicking: The Meanings of Performing and Listening.*
Green, L. (2002). *How Popular Musicians Learn: A Way Ahead for Music Education.*
Frith, S. (1996). *Performing Rites: On the Value of Popular Music.*

References

Adachi, M., & Trehub, S. E. (1998). Childrens' expression of emotion in song. *Psychology of Music, 26*, 133–153.

Adorno, T. W. (1976). *Introduction to the sociology of music* (E. B. Ashton, Trans.). New York: Seabury Press. (Original work published 1962)

Aiello, R., & Williamon, A. (2002). Memory. In R. Parncutt & G. E. McPherson (Eds.), *The science and psychology of music performance: Creative strategies for teaching and learning* (pp. 167–182). Oxford, UK: Oxford University Press.

Allsup, R. E. (2003). Mutual learning and democratic action in instrumental music education. *Journal of Research in Music Education, 51*, 24–37.

Altenmüller, E., & Gruhn, W. (2002). Brain mechanisms. In R. Parncutt & G. McPherson (Eds.), *The science and psychology of music performance: Creative strategies for teaching and learning* (pp. 63–82). Oxford, UK: Oxford University Press.

Altenmüller, E. O. (2003). How many music centres are in the brain? In I. Peretz & R. J. Zatorre (Eds.), *The cognitive neuroscience of music* (pp. 346–365). Oxford, UK: Oxford University Press.

American Psychological Association. (2002). Ethical principles of psychologists and code of conduct (effective date June 1, 2003). Retrieved August 1, 2006 from http://www.apa.org/ethics/code2002.html

American Psychological Association. (2001). *Publication manual of the American Psychological Association* (5th ed.). Washington, DC: Author.

Ashley, R. (2004). *All his yesterdays: Expressive vocal techniques in Paul McCartney's recordings.* Unpublished manuscript.

Askenfelt, A. (1986). Measurement of bow motion and bow force in violin playing. *Journal of the Acoustical Society of America, 80*, 1007–1015.

Asmus, E. P. (1986). Student beliefs about the causes of success and failure in music: A study of achievement motivation. *Journal of Research in Music Education, 34*, 262–278.

Auer, L. (1980). *Violin playing as I teach it.* New York: Dover. (Original work published 1921)

Austin, J. R. (1991). Competitive and non-competitive goal structures: An analysis of motivation and achievement among elementary band students. *Psychology of Music, 19*, 142–158.

Austin, J. R., & Vispoel, W. P. (1992). Motivation after failure in school music performance classes: The facilitative effects of strategy attributions. *Bulletin of
the Council for Research in Music Education, 111*, 1–23.

Austin, J. R., & Vispoel, W. P. (1998). How American adolescents interpret success
and failure in classroom music: Relationships among attributional beliefs, self-
concept and achievement. *Psychology of Music, 26*, 26–45.

Axelrod, H. R. (Ed.). (1976). *Heifetz*. Neptune City, NJ: Paganiniana.

Ayari, M., & McAdams, S. (2003). Aural analysis of Arabic improvised instrumental music (Taqsîm). *Music Perception, 21*, 159–216.

Baddeley, A. D. (1986). *Working memory*. Oxford, UK: Oxford Clarendon Press.

Bahle, J. (1982). *Der musikalische Schaffensprozeß: Psychologie der schöpferischen
Erlebnis- und Antriebsformen*.[Generative processes in music: Psychology of
creative experience and motivation]. Konstanz, Germany: Paul Christiani. (Original work published 1947)

Bakan, M. (1994). Lessons from a world: Balinese applied music instruction and the
teaching of western "art" music. *College Music Symposium, 33/34*, 1–22.

Bamberger, J. (1991). *The mind behind the musical ear*. Cambridge, MA: Harvard
University Press.

Bandura, A. (1986). *Social foundations of thought and action: A social cognitive
theory*. Englewood Cliffs, NJ: Prentice-Hall.

Bandura, A. (1991). Self-efficacy conception of anxiety. In R. Schwarzer &
R. A. Wicklund (Eds.), *Anxiety and self-focused attention* (pp. 89–110). New
York: Routledge.

Barry, N. (1990). The effects of different practice techniques upon technical accuracy and musicality in student instrumental music performance. *Research Perspectives in Music Education, 44*(1), 4–8.

Barry, N., & Hallam, S. (2001). Practice. In R. Parncutt & G. E. McPherson (Eds.),
*The science and psychology of music performance: Creative strategies for
teaching and learning* (pp. 151–166). Oxford, UK: Oxford University Press.

Barry, N. H., & McArthur, V. H. (1994). Teaching practice strategies in the music
studio: A survey of applied music teachers. *Psychology of Music, 22*, 44–55.

Barten, S. S. (1998). Speaking of music: The use of motor-affective metaphors in
music instruction. *Journal of Aesthetic Education, 32*(2), 89–97.

Barz, G. F., & Cooley, T. J. (Eds.). (1997). *Shadows in the field: New perspectives for
fieldwork in ethnomusicology*. Oxford, UK: Oxford University Press.

Bastien, D. T., & Hostager, T. J. (1988). Jazz as a process of organizational innovation. *Communication Research, 15*, 582–602.

Bean, K. L. (1938). An experimental approach to the reading of music. *Psychological Monographs, 50*, 1–80.

Behne, K. E. (1997). The development of "Musikerleben" in adolescence: How and
why young people listen to music. In I. Deliège & J. A. Sloboda (Eds.), *Perception and cognition of music* (pp. 143–160). Hove, UK: Psychology Press.

Beilock, S. L., Bertenthal, B. I., McCoy, A. M., & Carr, T. H. (2004). Haste does not
always make waste: Expertise, direction of attention, and speed versus accuracy in performing sensorimotor skills. *Psychonomic Bulletin and Review, 11*,
373–379.

Berg, M. H. (2000). Thinking for yourself: The social construction of chamber music experience. In R. R. Rideout & S. J. Paul (Eds.), *On the sociology of music
education: II. Papers from the Music Education Symposium at the University of
Oklahoma* (pp. 91–112). Amherst, MA: University of Massachusetts.

Berliner, P. (1994). *Thinking in jazz*. Chicago, Chicago University Press.

Berz, W. L. (1995). Working memory in music: A theoretical model. *Music Perception, 12*, 353–364.

Besson, M., & Schön, D. (2003). Comparison between language and music. In I. Peretz & R. J. Zatorre (Eds.), *The cognitive neuroscience of music* (pp. 269–293). Oxford, UK: Oxford University Press.

Blacking, J. (1973). *How musical is man?* London: Faber & Faber.

Blake, D. T., Byl, N. N., Cheung, S., Bedenbaugh, P., Nagarajan, S., Lamb, M., et al. (2003). Sensory representation abnormalities that parallel focal hand dystonia in a primate model. *Somatosensory and Motor Research, 19*(4), 347–357.

Blood, A. J., & Zatorre, R. J. (2001). Intensely pleasurable responses to music correlate with activity in brain regions implicated in reward and emotion. *Proceedings of the National Academy of Sciences of the USA, 98*(20), 11818–11823.

Bloom, B. S. (1985). Generalizations about talent development. In B. S. Bloom (Ed.), *Developing talent in young people* (pp. 507–549). New York: Ballantine.

Blum, D. (1998). *Quintet: Five journeys toward musical fulfillment.* Ithaca, NY: Cornell University Press.

Bohlman, P. V. (2002). *World music: A very short introduction.* Oxford, UK: Oxford University Press.

Bourdieu, P. (1979). *Distinction: A social critique of the judgement of taste.* London: Routledge.

Boyd, J. (1992). *Musicians in tune: Seventy-five contemporary musicians discuss the creative process.* New York: Simon & Schuster.

Brandfonbrener, A., & Lederman, R. (2002). Performing arts medicine. In R. Colwell & C. Richardson (Eds.), *The new handbook of research on music teaching and learning* (pp. 1009–1022). New York: Oxford University Press.

Brandfonbrener, A. G., & Kjelland, J. M. (2002). Music medicine. In R. Parncutt & G. E. McPherson (Eds.), *The science and psychology of music performance: Creative strategies for teaching and learning* (pp. 83–96). New York: Oxford University Press.

Bregman, A. (1990). *Auditory scene analysis: The perceptual organization of sound.* Cambridge, MA: MIT Press.

Breig, W. (1997). Composition as arrangement and adaptation. In J. Butt (Ed.), *The Cambridge companion to Bach* (pp. 154–170). Cambridge, UK: Cambridge University Press.

Brennan, D., & Stevens, C. (2002). Specialist musical training and the octave illusion: Analytical listening and veridical perception by pipe organists. *Acta Psychologica, 109*, 301–314.

British Phonographic Industries. (2003, April). Sales by type of music, 2002. *BPI Market Information, 204*, 1–4.

Broadbent, P. (1996). *Charlie Christian.* Newcastle, UK: Ashley Mark.

Burland, K., & Davidson, J. W. (2002). Training the talented. *Music Education Research, 4*(1), 121–140.

Burns, E. M., & Ward, W. D. (1978). Categorical perception: Phenomenon or epiphenomenon: Evidence from experiments in the perception of melodic musical intervals. *Journal of the Acoustical Society of America, 63*, 456–468.

Busoni, F. (1983). *Von der Macht der Töne: Ausgewählte Schriften* [The power of sound: Selected writings]. Leipzig: Reclam.

Butler, D. (1992). *The musician's guide to perception and cognition.* New York: Schirmer Books.

Byo, J. L. (1990). Recognition of intensity contrasts in the gestures of beginning conductors. *Journal of Research in Music Education, 38*, 157–163.

Byo, J. L., & Sheldon, D. A. (2000). The effect of singing while listening on under-graduate music majors' ability to detect pitch and rhythm errors. *Journal of Band Research, 36*(1), 26–46.

Calabrese, I., & Olivetti-Belardinelli, M. (1997). Musical abilities in deaf children: Assessment, development and training. In A. Gabrielsson (Ed.), *Third Trien-nial ESCOM Conference: Proceedings* (pp. 87–90). Uppsala, Sweden: Univer-sity of Uppsala.

Campbell, P. S. (1991). *Lessons from the world: A cross-cultural guide to music teaching and learning.* New York: Schirmer.

Cavitt, M. E. (2003). A descriptive analysis of error correction in instrumental mu-sic rehearsals. *Journal of Research in Music Education, 51*, 218–230.

Ceci, S. J. (1990). *On intelligence—more or less: Bio-ecological treatise on intellec-tual development.* Englewood Cliffs, NJ: Prentice-Hall.

Chaffin, R., Imreh, G., & Crawford, M. (2002). *Practicing perfection: Memory and piano performance.* Mahwah, NJ: Erlbaum.

Chaffin, R., & Lemieux, A. F. (2004). General perspectives on achieving musical excellence. In A. Williamon (Ed.), *Musical excellence: Strategies and tech-niques to enhance performance* (pp. 19–40). Oxford, UK: Oxford University Press.

Charness, N., Krampe, R. T., & Mayr, U. (1996). The role of practice and coaching in entrepreneurial skill domains. In K. A. Ericsson (Ed.), *The road to excel-lence* (pp. 51–80). Mahwah, NJ: Erlbaum.

Chesky, K., Kondraske, G., Henoch, M., Hipple, J., & Rubin, B. (2002). Musicians' health. In R. Colwell & C. Richardson (Eds.), *The new handbook of research on music teaching and learning* (pp. 1023–1039). New York: Oxford Univer-sity Press.

Clarke, E. F. (2004). Empirical methods in the study of performance. In E. F. Clarke & N. Cook (Eds.), *Empirical musicology* (pp. 77–102). Oxford, UK: Oxford University Press.

Clarke, E. F., & Baker-Short, C. (1987). The imitation of perceived rubato: A pre-liminary study. *Psychology of Music, 15*, 58–75.

Clarke, E. F., & Davidson, J. W. (1998). The body in performance. In W. Thomas (Ed.), *Composition-performance-reception* (pp. 74–92). Aldershot, UK: Ash-gate.

Clayton, A. M. H. (1985). *Coordination between players in musical performance.* Unpublished doctoral dissertation, University of Edinburgh.

Cohen, A. (2001). Music as a source of emotion in film. In P. N. Juslin & J. A. Slo-boda (Eds.), *Music and emotion: Theory and research* (pp. 249–272). Oxford, UK: Oxford University Press.

Colley, A., Banton, L., Down, J., & Pither, A. (1992). An expert-novice comparison in musical composition. *Psychology of Music, 20*, 124–137.

Colwell, R. (Ed.). (1992). *Handbook of research on music teaching and learning.* New York: Schirmer.

Colwell, R., & Richardson, C. (Eds.). (2002). *The new handbook of research on mu-sic teaching and learning.* New York: Oxford University Press.

Connolly, C., & Williamon, A. (2004). Mental skills training. In A. Williamon (Ed.), *Musical excellence* (pp. 221–245). New York: Oxford University Press.

Cook, N. (1987). The perception of large-scale tonal closure. *Music Perception, 5*(2), 197–205.

Cook, N. (1998). *Music: A very short introduction.* Oxford, UK: Oxford University Press.

Coon, H., & Carey, G. (1989). Genetic and environmental determinants of musical ability in twins. *Behavior Genetics, 19*, 183–193.

Cooper, C. L., & Wills, G. I. D. (1989). Popular musicians under pressure. *Psychology of Music, 17*, 22–36.

Cox, W. J., & Kenardy, J. (1993). Performance anxiety, social phobia, and setting effects in instrumental music students. *Journal of Anxiety Disorders, 7*, 49–60.

Craske, M. G., & Craig, K. (1984). Musical performance anxiety: The three-systems model and self-efficacy theory. *Behavioral Research Therapy, 22*, 267–280.

Cross, I. (1999). Is music the most important thing we ever did? Music, development, and evolution. In S. W. Yi (Ed.), *Music, mind and science* (pp. 10–39). Seoul, Korea: Seoul National University Press.

Csikszentmihalyi, M. (1993). *Flow: The psychology of optimal experience.* New York: Harper Collins.

Cytowic, R. E. (1993). *The man who tasted shapes.* New York: Putnam.

Dahlhaus, C. (1991). *The idea of absolute music* (R. Lustig, Trans.). Chicago: Chicago University Press.

Davidson, J. W. (1993). Visual perception of performance manner in the movements of solo musicians. *Psychology of Music, 21*, 103–113.

Davidson, J. W. (1997). The social in music performance. In D. J. Hargreaves & A. C. North (Eds.), *The social psychology of music* (pp. 209–228). Oxford, UK: Oxford University Press.

Davidson, J. W. (Ed.). (2004). *The music practitioner: Research for the music performer, teacher and listener.* Aldershot, UK: Ashgate.

Davidson, J. W., & Coimbra, D. D. C. (2001). Investigating performance evaluation by assessors of singers in a music college setting. *Musicae Scientiae, 5*(1), 33–53.

Davidson, J. W., & Correia, J. S. (2002). Body movement. In R. Parncutt & G. E. McPherson (Eds.), *The science and psychology of music performance: Creative strategies for teaching and learning* (pp. 237–250). New York: Oxford University Press.

Davidson, J. W., & Good, J. M. M. (2002). Social and musical co-ordination between members of a string quartet: An exploratory study. *Psychology of Music, 30*, 186–201.

Davidson, J. W., Howe, M. J. A., Moore, D. G., & Sloboda, J. A. (1996). The role of parental influences in the development of musical ability. *British Journal of Developmental Psychology, 14*, 399–412.

Davidson, J. W., Sloboda, J. A., & Howe, M. J. A. (1996). The role of parents and teachers in the success and failure of instrumental learners. *Bulletin of the Council for Research in Music Education, 127*, 40–44.

Davidson, J. W., Sloboda, J. A., Moore, D. G., & Howe, M. J. A. (1998). Characteristics of music teachers and the progress of young instrumentalists. *Journal of Research in Music Education 46*, 141–160.

Davidson, L. (1989). Observing a yang ch'in lesson: Learning by modeling and metaphor. *Journal of Aesthetic Education, 23*(1), 85–99.

Davidson, L., McKernon, P., & Gardner, H. (1981). The acquisition of song: A developmental approach. In K. Dean (Ed.), *Documentary report of the Ann Arbor Symposium.* (pp. 301–315). Reston, VA: Music Educators National Conference.

Davidson, L., & Scripp, L. (1988) Young children's musical representations: Windows on musical cognition. In J. A. Sloboda (Ed.), *Generative processes in music: The psychology of performance, improvisation, and composition* (pp. 195–230). New York: Oxford University Press.

Davidson, L., & Scripp, L. (1992). Surveying the coordinates of cognitive skills in music. In R. Colwell (Ed.), *Handbook of research on music teaching and learning* (pp. 392–413). New York: Schirmer.

Deliège, I., & El Ahmadi, A. (1990). Mechanisms of cue extraction in music groupings: A study of perception of Sequenza IV for solo viola by Luciano Berio. *Psychology of Music, 18*, 18–44.

Deliège, I., & Sloboda, J. A. (Eds.). (1996). *Musical beginnings: Origins and development of musical competence.* Oxford, UK: Oxford University Press.

De Nora, T. (2000). *Music in everyday life.* New York: Cambridge University Press.

Densmore, F. (1926). *The American Indians and their music.* New York: Woman's Press.

Deutsch, D. (1995). *Musical illusions and paradoxes* [CD]. La Jolla, CA: Philomel Records.

Deutsch, D. (1999) (Ed.). *The psychology of music.* New York: Academic Press.

Dickey, M. R. (1991). A review of research on modeling in music teaching and learning. *Bulletin of the Council for Research in Music Education, 113*, 27–40.

Dowling, W. J. (1999). Development of music perception and cognition. In D. Deutsch (Ed.), *Psychology of music* (2nd ed., pp. 603–625). New York: Academic Press.

Driskell, J. E., Copper, C., & Moran, A. (1994). Does mental practice enhance performance? *Journal of Applied Psychology, 79*, 481–492.

Duerksen, G. L. (1972). Some effects of expectation on evaluation of recorded musical performances. *Journal of Research in Music Education, 20*, 268–272.

Duke, R. A. (1999). Teacher and student behavior in Suzuki string lessons: Results from the International Research Symposium on Talent Education. *Journal of Research in Music Education, 47*, 293–307.

Duke, R. A. (2000). Measures of instructional effectiveness in music research. *Bulletin of the Council for Research in Music Education, 143*, 1–48.

Duke, R. A., & Henninger, J. C. (2002). Effects of verbal corrections on student attitude and performance. *Journal of Research in Music Education, 46*, 482–495.

Duke, R. A., Prickett, C. A., & Jellison, J. A. (1998). Empirical description of the pace of musical instruction. *Journal of Research in Music Education, 46*, 265–280.

Eagle, D. S. (1997). *Voices of native America.* Liberty, UT: Eagle's View.

Eccles, J., Wigfield, A., Harold, R. D., & Blumenfeld, P. (1993). Age and gender differences in children's self and task perceptions during elementary school. *Child Development, 64*, 830–847.

Elbert, T., Pantev, C., Weinbruch, C., Rockstroh, B., & Taub, E. (1995). Increased cortical representation of the fingers of the left hand in string players. *Science, 270*, 305–307.

Elder, D. (1982). *Pianists at play: Interviews, master lessons, and technical regimes.* Evanston, IL: Instrumentalist Company.

Epstein, H. (1987). *Music talks: Conversations with musicians.* New York: Penguin Books.

Ericsson, K. A. (2004). Deliberate practice and the acquisition and maintenance of expert performance in medicine and related domains. *Academic Medicine, 79*(10 Suppl), 70–81.

Ericsson, K. A., & Chase, W. G. (1982). Exceptional memory. *American Scientist, 70*, 607–615.

Ericsson, K. A., & Kintsch, W. (1995). Long-term working memory. *Psychological Review, 102*(2), 211–245.

Ericsson, K. A., Krampe, R. T., & Tesch-Römer, C. (1993). The role of deliberate practice in the acquisition of expert performance. *Psychological Review, 100*, 363–406.

Ericsson, K. A., & Lehmann, A. C. (1997) Expert and exceptional performance: evidence of maximal adaptation to task constraints. *Annual Review of Psychology, 47*, 273–305.

Ericsson, K. A., & Lehmann, A. C. (1999). Expertise. In M. A. Runco & S. R. Pritzker (Eds.), *Encyclopedia of creativity* (Vol. 1, pp. 695–707). New York: Academic Press.

Ericsson, K. A., & Smith, J. (1991). Prospects and limits in the empirical study of expertise. In K. A. Ericsson & J. Smith (Eds.), *Toward a general theory of expertise: Prospects and limits* (pp. 1–38). Cambridge, UK: Cambridge University. Press.

Eysenck, H. J. (1995). *Genius: The natural history of creativity.* Cambridge, UK: Cambridge University Press.

Farnsworth, P. R. (1969). *The social psychology of music.* Ames, IA: Iowa State University Press.

Finnäs, L. (1989). A comparison between young people's privately and publicly expressed musical preferences. *Psychology of Music, 17*, 132–145.

Finney, E. M., Fine, I., & Dobkins, K. R. (2001). Visual stimuli activate auditory cortex in the deaf. *Nature Neuroscience, 4*, 1171–1173.

Fishbein, M., Middlestadt, S. E., Ottati, V., Strauss, S., & Ellis, A. (1988). Medical problems among ICSOM musicians: Overview of a national survey. *Medical Problems of Performing Artists, 3*, 1–8.

Fiske, H. (1979). Musical performance evaluation ability: Toward a model of specificity. *Bulletin of the Council for Research in Music Education, 59*, 27–31.

Fitts, P. M., & Posner, M. I. (1967). *Human performance.* Belmont, CA: Brooks & Cole.

Fiz, J. A., Aguilar, J., Carreras, A., Teixido, A., Haro, M., Rodenstein, D., et al. (1993). Maximum respiratory pressures in trumpet players. *Chest, 104*, 1203–1204.

Folkestad, G. (2002). National identity and music. In R. Macdonald, D. J. Hargreaves, & D. Miell (Eds.), *Musical identities* (pp. 151–162). Oxford, UK: Oxford University Press.

Ford, L., & Davidson, J. W. (2003). An investigation of members' roles in wind quintets. *Psychology of Music, 31*, 53–74.

Fowler, W. (1990). Early stimulation and the development of verbal talents. In M. J. A. Howe (Ed.), *Encouraging the development of exceptional skills and talents* (pp. 179–210). Leicester, UK: BPS Books.

Fredrickson, W. E. (1992). Research on eye contact with implications for the conductor: A review of literature. *Update: Applications of Research in Music Education, 11*(1), 25–31.

Friberg, A., & Sundberg, J. (1987). How to terminate a phrase: An analysis by synthesis experiment on a perceptual aspect of music performance. In A. Gabrielsson (Ed.), *Action and perception in rhythm and music* (Publication No. 55, pp. 49–55). Stockholm: Royal Swedish Academy of Music.

Frith, S. (1996). *Performing rites: On the value of popular music.* Oxford, UK: Oxford University Press.

Gabrielsson, A. (2001). Emotions in strong experiences to music. In P. N. Juslin & J. A. Sloboda (Eds.), *Music and emotion: Theory and research* (pp. 435–452). Oxford, UK: Oxford University Press.

Gardner, H. (1973). Children's sensitivity to musical styles. *Merrill-Palmer Quarterly of Behavioral Development, 19*, 67–77.

Gardner, H. (1997). *Extraordinary minds*. New York: Basic Books.

Gembris, H. (2002). The development of musical abilities. In R. Colwell & C. Richardson (Eds.), *The new handbook of research on music teaching and learning* (pp. 487–508). New York: Oxford University Press.

Gerard, C., & Rosenfeld, M. (1995). Pratique musicale et régulations temporelles [Musical expertise and temporal regulation]. *L'Annee Psychologique, 95*, 571–591.

Gieseking, W., & Leimer, K. (1972). *Piano technique*. New York: Dover. (Original work published 1932)

Gillespie, W., & Myors, B. (2000). Personality of rock musicians. *Psychology of Music, 28*, 154–165.

Ginsborg, J. (2004). Strategies for memorising music. In A. Williamon (Ed.), *Enhancing musical performance* (pp. 123–142). Oxford, UK: Oxford University Press.

Goodman, E. (2002). Ensemble performance. In J. Rink (Ed.), *Musical performance: A guide to understanding* (pp. 153–167). Cambridge, UK: Cambridge University Press.

Goolsby, T. W. (1994). Profiles of processing: Eye movements during sightreading. *Music Perception, 12*, 97–123.

Goolsby, T. W. (1996). Time use in instrumental rehearsals: A comparison of experienced, novice, and student teachers. *Journal of Research in Music Education, 44*, 286–303.

Goolsby, T. W. (1997). Verbal instruction in instrumental rehearsals: A comparison of three career levels and preservice teachers. *Journal of Research in Music Education, 45*, 21–40.

Goolsby, T. W. (1999). A comparison of expert and novice music teachers' preparing identical band compositions: An operational replication. *Journal of Research in Music Education, 47*, 174–187.

Gordon, E. E. (1967). *A three-year longitudinal predictive validity study of the musical aptitude profile*. Iowa City: University of Iowa Press.

Gordon, E. E. (1979). *Primary measures of music audiation*. Chicago: GIA.

Gordon, E. E.(1987). *The nature, description, measurement and evaluation of music aptitudes*. Chicago: GIA.

Green, B., & Gallwey, W. T. (1986). *The inner game of music*. New York: Doubleday.

Green, L. (1997). *Music, gender, education*. Cambridge, UK: Cambridge University Press.

Green, L. (2002). *How popular musicians learn: A way ahead for music education*. Aldershot, UK: Ashgate.

Gregory, A. (1997). The roles of music in society: the ethnomusicological perspective. In D. J. Hargreaves & A. C. North (Eds.), *The social psychology of music* (pp. 123–140). Oxford, UK: Oxford University Press.

Grove, G. (1882). *Dictionary of music and musicians* (1st ed.). London: Macmillan.

Gruhn, W., & Rauscher, F. H. (2002). The neurobiology of music cognition and learning. In R. Colwell & C. Richardson (Eds.), *The new handbook of research on music teaching and learning* (pp. 445–460). Oxford, UK: Oxford University Press.

Gruson, L. M. (1988). Rehearsal skill and musical competence: Does practice make perfect? In J. A. Sloboda (Ed.), *Generative processes in music: The psychology of performance, improvisation and composition* (pp. 91–112). New York: Oxford University Press.

Hallam, S. (1995). Professional musicians' approaches to the learning and interpretation of music. *Psychology of Music, 23,* 111–128.

Hallam, S. (1997). Approaches to instrumental music practice of experts and novices. In H. Jørgensen & A. C. Lehmann (Eds.), *Does practice make perfect? Current theory and research on instrumental music practice* (pp. 89–107). Oslo, Norway: Norges musikkhøgskole.

Hallam, S. (1998a). *Instrumental teaching: A practical guide to better teaching and learning.* Oxford, UK: Heinemann Educational.

Hallam, S. (1998b). The predictors of achievement and dropout in instrumental tuition. *Psychology of Music, 26,* 116–132.

Hallam, S. (2000). The power of music. Retrieved January 6, 2004, from http://www.prs.co.uk/DocsRepository/4205/The%20Power%20of%20Music%20Report.pdf.

Halpern, A. (1992). Musical aspects of auditory imagery. In D. Reisberg (Ed.), *Auditory imagery* (pp. 1–28). Hillsdale, NJ: Erlbaum.

Halpern, A. (2003). Cerebral substrates of musical imagery. In I. Peretz & R. Zatorre (Eds.), *The cognitive neuroscience of music* (pp. 217–230). Oxford, UK: Oxford University Press.

Halpern, A. R., & Bower, G. H. (1982). Musical expertise and melodic structure in memory for musical notation. *American Journal of Psychology, 95,* 31–50.

Hamann, D. L. (1982). An assessment of anxiety in instrumental and vocal performers. *Journal of Research in Music Education, 30,* 77–90.

Hamann, D. L., & Sobaje, M. (1983). Anxiety and the college musician: A study of performance conditions and subject variables. *Psychology of Music, 11,* 37–50.

Handel, S. (1993). *Listening: An introduction to the perception of auditory events.* Cambridge, MA: MIT Press.

Hargreaves, D., Cork, C., & Setton, T. (1991). Cognitive strategies in jazz improvisation: An exploratory study. *Canadian Journal of Research in Music Education, 33,* 47–54.

Hargreaves, D. J. (1986). *The developmental psychology of music.* London: Cambridge University Press.

Hargreaves, D. J., & North, A. C. (Eds.). (1997). *The social psychology of music.* Oxford, UK: Oxford University Press.

Hassler, M. (1992). Creative musical behavior and sex hormones: Musical talent and spatial ability in the two sexes. *Psychoneuroendocrinology, 17,* 55–70.

Hayes, J. R. (1989). *The complete problem solver* (2nd ed.). Hillsdale, NJ: Erlbaum.

Helmlinger, A. (2005). *Mémoire et jeu d'ensemble. La mémorisation du répertoire dans les steelbands de Trinidad et Tobago* [Memory and ensemble performance. Memorization of repertoire in the steel bands of Trinidad and Tobago]. Unpublished doctoral dissertation, Université Paris X Nanterre, Paris, France.

Hendel, C. (1995). Behavioral characteristics and instructional patterns of selected music teachers. *Journal of Research in Music Education, 43,* 182–203.

Hepper, P. G. (1991). An examination of fetal learning before and after birth. *Irish Journal of Psychology, 12,* 95–107.

Hickey, M. (2002). Creativity research in music, visual art, theater, and dance. In R. Colwell & C. Richardson (Eds.), *The new handbook of research on music teaching and learning* (pp. 398–415). Oxford, UK: Oxford University Press.

Hodges, D. A. (Ed.) (1996). *Handbook of music psychology* (2nd ed). San Antonio: IMR Press.

Houtsma, A. J., Durlach, N. I., & Horowitz, D. M. (1987). Comparative learning of pitch and loudness identification. *Journal of the Acoustical Society of America, 81*, 129–132.

Howe , M. J. A. (1990). *The origins of exceptional abilities* . Oxford: Blackwell.

Howe, M. J. A., Davidson, J. W., Moore, D. G., & Sloboda, J. A. (1995). Are there early childhood signs of musical ability? *Psychology of Music, 23*, 162–176.

Howe, M. J. A., & Sloboda, J. A. (1991). Young musicians' accounts of significant influences in their early lives: 1. The family and the musical background. *British Journal of Music Education, 8*(1), 39–52.

Huron, D. (1999). *Methodology. The new empiricism: systematic musicology in a postmodern age.* (1999 Ernest Bloch lectures, University of California, Berkeley, #3). Retrieved August 1, 2006 from www.musiccog.ohio-state.edu/Music220 /Bloch.lectures/3.Methodology.html.

Husain, G., Thompson, W. F., & Schellenberg, E. G (2002). Effects of musical tempo and mode on arousal, mood, and spatial abilities. *Music Perception, 20*, 151–171.

Jacobson, R. (1974). *Reverberations: Interviews with the world's leading musicians.* New York: Morrow.

Johnson-Laird, P. N. (2002). How jazz musicians improvise. *Music Perception, 19*, 415–442.

Jones, M. R., & Yee, W. (1993). Attending to auditory events: The role of temporal organization. In S. McAdams & E. Bigand (Eds.), *Thinking in sound* (pp. 69–112). Oxford, UK: Clarendon.

Jørgensen, H. (1997). Time for practising? In H. Jørgensen & A. C. Lehmann (Eds.), *Does practice make perfect?* (pp. 123–140). Oslo, Norway: Norges musikkhøgskole.

Jørgensen, H. (2004). Strategies for individual practice. In A. Williamon (Ed.), *Musical excellence* (pp. 85–104). Oxford, UK: Oxford University Press.

Jusczyk, P. W., & Krumhansl, C. L. (1993). Pitch and rhythmic patterns affecting infants' sensitivity to musical phrase structure. *Journal of Experimental Psychology: Human Perception and Performance, 19*, 627–640.

Juslin, P. N. (1997a). Emotional communication in music performance: A functionalist perspective and some data. *Music Perception, 14*, 383–418.

Juslin, P. N. (1997b). Perceived emotional expression in synthesized performances of a short melody: Capturing the listener's judgement policy. *Musicae Scientiae, 1*, 225–256.

Juslin, P. N., Friberg, A., & Bresin, R. (2002). Toward a computational model of expression in music performance: The GERM model. *Musicae* Scientiae Special Issue 2001–2002, 63–122.

Juslin, P. N., & Laukka, P. (2000). Improving emotional communication in music performance through cognitive feedback. *Musicae Scientiae, 4*, 151–183.

Juslin, P. N., & Laukka, P. (2003). Communication of emotion in vocal expression and music performance: Different channels, same code? *Psychological Bulletin, 129*, 770–814.

Juslin, P. N., & Sloboda, J. A. (Eds.). (2001). *Music and emotion: Theory and research.* New York: Oxford University Press.

Juslin, P. N., Friberg, A., Schoonderwaldt, E., & Karlsson, J. (2004). Feedback learning of musical expressivity. In A. Williamon (Ed.), *Musical excellence* (pp. 247–270). New York: Oxford University Press.

Kalmus, H., & Fry, D. B. (1980). On tune deafness (dysmelodia): Frequency, development, genetics and musical background. *Annals of Human Genetics, 43*, 369–382.

Kartomi, M. (1991) *On concepts and classifications of musical instruments.* Chicago: University of Chicago Press.

Kaspersen, M., & Götestam, K. G. (2002). A survey of performance anxiety among Norwegian music students. *European Journal of Psychiatry, 16*, 69–80.

Keele, S., Pokorny, R., Corcos, D., & Ivry, R. (1985). Do perception and motor production share a common timing mechanism? *Acta Psychologica, 60*, 173–193.

Keller, P. E. (2001). Attentional resource allocation in musical ensemble performance. *Psychology of Music, 29*, 20–38.

Kenny, B. J., & Gellrich, M. (2001). Improvisation. In R. Parncutt & G. E. McPherson (Eds.), *The science and psychology of music performance: Creative strategies for teaching and learning* (pp. 117–134). Oxford, UK: Oxford University Press.

Kemp, A. E. (1996). *The musical temperament: Psychology and personality of musicians.* New York: Oxford University Press.

Kemp, A. E., & Mills, J. (2002). Musical potential. In R. Parncutt & G. E. McPherson (Eds.), *The science and psychology of music performance: Creative strategies for teaching and learning* (pp. 3–16). Oxford, UK: Oxford University Press.

Kendall, R. A., & Carterette, E. C. (1990). The communication of musical expression. *Music Perception, 8*, 129–164.

Kendrick, M. J., Craig, K. D., Lawson, D. M., & Davidson, P. O. (1982). Cognitive and behavioral therapy for musical performance anxiety. *Journal of Consulting and Clinical Psychology, 50*, 353–362.

Kessen, W., Levine, J., & Wendrich, K. (1979). The imitation of pitch in infants. *Infant Behavior and Development, 2*, 93–99.

Kingsbury, H. (1988). *Music, talent, and performance: A conservatory cultural system.* Philadelphia: Temple University Press.

Kinsler, V., & Carpenter, R. H. (1995). Saccadic eye movements while reading music. *Vision Research, 35*, 1447–1458.

Koelsch, S., Schroger, E., & Tervaniemi, M. (1999). Superior pre-attentive auditory processing in musicians. *Neuroreport, 26*, 1309–1313.

Kohn, A. (1993). *Punished by rewards.* New York: Houghton Mifflin.

Komlos, J., & Baur, M. A. (2004). From the tallest to (one of) the fattest: The enigmatic fate of the American population in the 20th century. *Journal of Economics and Human Biology, 2*, 57–74.

Konrad, U. (1992). *Mozarts Schaffensweise* [Mozart's method of composing]. Göttingen, Germany: Vandenhoek & Ruprecht.

Kopiez, R. (2002). Making music and making sense through music. In R. Colwell & C. Richardson (Eds.), *The new handbook of research on music teaching and learning* (pp. 522–541). Oxford, UK: Oxford University Press.

Kopiez, R., & Brink, G. (1998). *Fussball-Fangesange. Eine Fanomelogie* [Soccer fan chants: A fanomenology]. Würzburg, Germany: Königshausen.

Kopiez, R., Langner, J., & Steinhagen, P. (1999). Afrikanische Trommler (Ghana) bewerten und spielen europäische Rhythmen [Cross-cultural study of the evaluation and performance of rhythm]. *Musicae Scientiae, 3*, 139–160.

Krampe, R. T., & Ericsson, K. A. (1996). Maintaining excellence: Deliberate practice and elite performance in young and older pianists. *Journal of Experimental Psychology: General, 125*, 331–359.

Kratus, J. (1989). A time analysis of the compositional processes used by children ages 7 to 11. *Journal of Research in Music Education, 37*, 5–20.

Kratus, J. (1991). Growing with improvisation. *Music Educators Journal, 78*(4), 35–40.

Kratus, J. (1993). A developmental study of children's interpretation of emotion in music. *Psychology of Music, 21*, 3–19.

Kreutz, G., Russ, M., Bongard, S., & Lanfermann, H. (2003). Zerebrale Korrelate des Musikhörens. Eine fMRT-Studie zur Wirkung, fröhlicher', und trauriger' klassischer Musik. [Cerebral correlates of music listening: A fMRI-study regarding the effect of happy and sad classical music]. *Nervenheilkunde, 6*, 51–56.

Lamont, A. (1995). Review of Swanwick, K., *Musical knowledge: Intuition, analysis and music education. European Society for the Cognitive Sciences of Music Newsletter, 7* (April), 9–11.

Langner, J., Kopiez, R., Stoffel, C., & Wilz, M. (2000). Realtime analysis of dynamic shaping. In C. Woods, G. Luck, F. Brochard, F. Seddon, & J. Sloboda, (Eds.) *Proceedings of the Sixth International Conference on Music Perception and Cognition.* Staffordshire, UK: Keele University.

LeBlanc, A. (1981). Effects of style, tempo, and performing medium on children's music preference. *Journal of Research in Music Education, 29*, 143–156.

LeBlanc, A., Jin, Y. C., Obert, M., & Siivola, C. (1997). Effect of audience on music performance anxiety. *Journal of Research in Music Education, 45*, 480–486.

Lecanuet, J. P. (1996). Prenatal auditory development. In I. Deliège & J. A. Sloboda (Eds.), *Musical beginnings: Origins and development of musical competence* (pp. 3–36). Oxford, UK: Oxford University Press.

Lehman, H. C. (1953). *Age and achievement.* Princeton, NJ: Princeton University Press.

Lehmann, A. C. (1996). The acquisition of expertise in music: Efficiency of deliberate practice as a moderating variable in accounting for sub-expert performance. In I. Deliège & J. A. Sloboda (Eds.), *Perception and cognition of music* (pp. 165–191). Hove, UK: Psychology Press.

Lehmann, A. C. (1997). Affective response to everyday life events and music listening. *Psychology of Music, 25*, 84–90.

Lehmann, A. C. (2002). Effort and enjoyment in deliberate practice. In I. M. Hanken, S. G. Nielsen, & M. Nerland (Eds.), *Research in and for music education: Festschrift for Harald Jørgensen* (pp. 153–166). Oslo: Norwegian Academy of Music.

Lehmann, A. C., & Davidson, J. W. (2002). Taking an acquired skills perspective on music performance. In R. Colwell & C. Richardson (Eds.), *The new handbook of research on music teaching and learning* (pp. 542–560). New York: Oxford University Press.

Lehmann, A. C., & Ericsson, K. A. (1996). Performance without preparation: Structure and acquisition of expert sight-reading and accompanying performance. *Psychomusicology, 15*, 1–29.

Lehmann, A. C., & Ericsson, K. A. (1997a). Expert pianists' mental representations: Evidence from successful adaptation to unexpected performance demands. In A. Gabrielsson (Ed.), *Proceedings of the Third Triennial ESCOM Conference* (pp. 165–169). Uppsala, Sweden: Uppsala University.

Lehmann, A. C., & Ericsson, K. A. (1997b). Research on expert performance and deliberate practice: Implications for the education of amateur musicians and music students. *Psychomusicology, 16*, 40–58.

Lehmann, A. C., & Ericsson, K. A. (1998a). The historical development of domains of expertise: Performance standards and innovations in music. In A. Steptoe (Ed.), *Genius and the mind: Studies of creativity and temperament in the historical record* (pp. 64–97). Oxford, UK: Oxford University Press.

Lehmann, A. C., & Ericsson, K. A. (1998b). Preparation of a public piano performance: The relation between practice and performance. *Musicae Scientiae, 2*, 69–94.

Lehmann, A. C., & McArthur, V. (2002). Sight-reading. In R. Parncutt & G. E. McPherson (Eds.), *The science and psychology of music performance: Creative strategies for teaching and learning* (pp. 135–150). Oxford, UK: Oxford University Press.

Lehmann, A. C., & Papousek, S. (2003). Self-reported performance goals predict actual practice behavior among adult piano beginners. In R. Kopiez, A. Lehmann, I. Wolther, & C. Wolf (Eds.), *Proceedings of the Fifth Triennial ESCOM Conference* [CD-ROM] (pp. 389–392). Hannover, Germany: University of Music and Drama.

Lehrer, P. M. (1987). A review of approaches to the management of tension and stage fright in music performance. *Journal of Research in Music Education, 35*, 143–152.

Lehrer, P. M., Goldman, N. S., & Strommen, E. F. (1990). A principal components assessment of performance anxiety among musicians. *Medical Problems of Performing Artists, 5*, 12–18.

Levitin, D. J. (1994). Absolute memory for musical pitch: Evidence from the production of learned melodies. *Perception and Psychophysics, 56*, 414–423.

Lim, V., & Altenmüller, E. (2003). Musicians' cramp: Instrumental and gender differences. *Medical Problems of Performing Artists, 18*, 21–27.

Lindström, E., Juslin, P. N., Bresin, R., & Williamon, A. (2003). "Expressivity comes from within your soul": A questionnaire study of music students' perspectives on expressivity. *Research Studies in Music Education, 20*, 23–47.

Linzenkirchner, P., & Eger-Harsch, G. (1995). *Gute Noten mit kritischen Anmerkungen [Documentation of national music youth competition 1984 to 1993]*. Bonn, Germany: Deutscher Musikrat.

Lively, S. E., Logan, J. S., & Pisoni, D. B. (1993). Training Japanese listeners to identify English /r/ and /l/: II. The role of phonetic environment and talker variability in learning new perceptual categories. *Journal of the Acoustical Society of America, 94*, 1242–1255.

Lord, A. B., Mitchell, S., & Nagy, G. (2000). *The singer of tales* (2nd. ed.). Cambridge, MA: Harvard University Press.

MacDonald, R., Hargreaves, D., & Miell, D. (Eds.). (2002). *Musical identities*. London: Oxford University Press.

Mach, E. (1980). *Great pianists speak for themselves*. New York: Dodd, Mead.

Madsen, C. K., & Duke. R. A. (1985). Perception of approval/disapproval in music. *Bulletin of the Council for Research in Music Education, 85*, 119–130.

Maehr, M. L., Pintrich, P. R., & Linnenbrink, E. A. (2002). Motivation and achievement. In R. Colwell & C. Richardson (Eds.), *The new handbook of research on music teaching and learning* (pp. 348–372). New York: Oxford University Press.

Magowan, F. (1994). "The land is our märr (essence), it stays forever": The yothu-yindi relationship in Australian Aboriginal traditional and popular music. In M. Stokes (Ed.), *Ethnicity, identity, and music: The musical construction of place* (pp. 135–155). Oxford, UK: Berg.

Marrin, T., & Picard, R. (1998, September). The conductor's jacket: A testbed for research on gestural and affective expression. Paper presented at the Twelfth Colloquium for Musical Informatics, Gorizia, Italy.

Marsalis, W. (1995a, November). We all need time in the woodshed. *Our Children, 21*(2), 28–29.

Marsalis, W. (1995b). *Tackling the monster* [Video]. New York: Sony Classical.

Matthay, T. (1926). *On memorizing and playing from memory and on the laws of practice generally*. Oxford: Oxford University Press.

McAdams, S., & Bigand, E. (Eds.). (1993). *Thinking in sound*. Oxford, UK: Clarendon.

McClary, S. (1991). *Feminine endings: Music, gender, and sexuality*. Minneapolis: Minnesota University Press.

McCormick, J., & McPherson, G. (2003). The role of self-efficacy in a musical performance examination: An exploratory structural equation analysis. *Psychology of Music, 31*(1), 37–51.

McPherson, G. E. (1995). The assessment of musical performance: Development and validation of five new measures. *Psychology of Music, 23*, 142–161.

McPherson, G. E. (2000). Commitment and practice: Key ingredients for achievement during the early stages of learning a musical instrument. *Bulletin of the Council for Research in Music Education, 147*, 122–127.

McPherson, G. E., & Davidson, J. W. (2002). Musical practice: Mother and child interactions during the first year of learning an instrument. *Music Education Research, 4*, 141–156.

McPherson, G. E., & Gabrielsson, A. (2002). From sound to sign. In R. Parncutt & G. E. McPherson (Eds.), *The science and psychology of music performance: Creative strategies for teaching and learning* (pp. 99–116). Oxford, UK: Oxford University Press.

McPherson, G. E., & Renwick, J. M. (2001). A longitudinal study of self-regulation in children's musical practice. *Music Education Research, 3*, 169–186.

McPherson, G. E., & Zimmerman, B. J. (2002). Self-regulation of musical learning: A social cognitive perspective. In R. Colwell & C. Richardson (Eds.), *The new handbook of research on music teaching and learning* (pp. 327–347). New York: Oxford University Press.

Mendelssohn-Bartholdy, P., & Mendelssohn-Bartholdy, C. (Eds.) (1882). *Briefe aus den Jahren 1830 bis 1847 von Felix Mendelssohn-Bartholdy [F. M.-B.'s letters from the years 1830 to 1847], II*. Leipzig: Mendelssohn.

Merriam, A. P. (1964). *The anthropology of music*. Chicago: Northwestern University Press.

Messenger, J. (1958). Esthetic talent. *Basic College Quarterly, 4*, 20–24.

Meyer, L. B. (2001). Music and emotion: Distinctions and uncertainties. In P. N. Juslin, & J. A. Sloboda (Eds.), *Music and emotion: Theory and research* (pp. 341–360). Oxford, UK: Oxford University Press.

Miller, J. L., & Eimas, P. D. (Eds.). (1995). *Handbook of perception and cognition: Vol. 11. Speech, language and communication* (2nd ed.). New York: Academic Press.

Miller, L. K. (1989). *Musical savants: Exceptional skill in the mentally retarded*. Hillsdale, NJ: Erlbaum.

Miller, R. F. (1992). Affective response. In R. Colwell (Ed.), *Handbook of research in music teaching and learning* (pp. 414–424). New York: Schirmer.

Mishra, J. (2002). Context-dependent memory: Implications for musical performance. *Update: Applications of Research in Music Education, 20*(2), 27–31.

Monson, I. (1996). *Saying something: Jazz improvisation and interaction*. Chicago: Chicago University Press.

Moore, D. G., Burland, K., & Davidson, J. W. (2003). The social context of musical success: A developmental account. *British Journal of Psychology, 94*, 529–549.

Mor, S., Day, H. I., Flett, G. L., & Hewitt, P. L. (1995). Perfectionism, control, and components of performance anxiety in professional artists. *Cognitive Therapy and Research, 19*, 207–225.

Motte-Haber, H. (1995). Der einkomponierte Hörer [The built-in listener]. In H. Motte-Haber & R. Kopiez (Eds.), *Der Hörer als Interpret* [The listener as interpreter] (pp. 35–42). Frankfurt, Germany: Lang.

Mueller, R. (2002). Perspectives from sociology of music. In R. Colwell & C. Richardson (Eds.), *The new handbook of research in music teaching and learning* (pp. 584–603). New York: Oxford University Press.

Münte, T. F., Altenmüller, E., & Jäncke, L. (2002). The musician's brain as a model of neuroplasticity. *Nature Reviews: Neuroscience, 3*, 473–478.

Münzer, S., Berti, S., & Pechmann, T. (2002). Encoding timbre, speech, and tones: Musicians vs. non-musicians. *Psychologische Beiträge, 44*, 187–202.

Murningham, J. K., & Conlon, D. E. (1991, June). The dynamics of intense work groups: A study of British string quartets. *Administrative Science Quarterly*, 165–186.

Myers, H. (Ed.). (1992). *Ethnomusicology: An introduction*. London: Macmillan.

Nager, W., Kohlmetz, C., Altenmüller, E., Rodriguez-Fornells, A., & Münte, T. (2003). The fate of sounds in conductors" brains: An ERP study. *Cognitive Brain Research, 17*, 83–93.

Nettl, B., & Bohlman, P. V. (1991). *Comparative musicology and anthropology of music: Essays on the history of ethnomusicology* (pp. 293–317). Chicago: University of Chicago Press.

Nettl, B., Capwell, C., Bohlman, P., Wong, I., & Turino, T. (1992). *Excursions in world music*. Englewood Cliffs, NJ: Prentice-Hall.

Neuhaus, H. (1967). *Die Kunst des Klavierspiels*. Cologne, Germany: Gerig.

Nielsen, S. G. (1999). Learning strategies in instrumental music practice. *British Journal of Music Education, 16*, 275–291.

North, A. C., Colley, A. M., & Hargreaves, D. J. (2003). Adolescents' perceptions of the music of male and female composers. *Psychology of Music, 31*, 139–154.

North, A. C., & Hargreaves, D. J. (1997a). Experimental aesthetics and everyday music listening. In D. J. Hargreaves & A. C. North (Eds.), *The social psychology of music* (pp. 84–106). Oxford, UK: Oxford University Press.

North, A. C., & Hargreaves, D. J. (1997b). The effect of physical attractiveness on the responses to pop music performers and their music. *Empirical Studies of the Arts, 15*(1), 75–89.

Nubé, J. (1991). Beta-blockers: Effects on performing musicians. *Medical Problems of Performing Artists, 6*, 61–68.

Nubé, J. (1994). Time-series analyses of the effects of propranolol on pianistic performance. *Medical Problems of Performing Artists, 9*, 77–88.

Oblad, C. (2000). On using music: About the car as a concert hall. In C. Woods, G. Luck, R. Brochard, F. Seddon, & J. A. Sloboda (Eds.), *Proceedings of the Sixth International Conference on Music Perception and Cognition* [CD-ROM]. Keele, Staffordshire, UK: Keele University Psychology Department.

O'Neill, S. A. (1997). The role of practice in children's early musical performance achievement. In H. Jørgensen & A. C. Lehmann (Eds.), *Does practice make perfect? Current theory and research on instrumental music practice* (pp. 53–70). Oslo, Norway: Norges musikkhøgskole.

O'Neill, S. (1999). Flow theory and the development of musical performance skills. *Bulletin of the Council for Research in Music Education, 141*, 129–134.

O'Neill, S. A., & McPherson, G. E. (2002). Motivation. In R. Parncutt & G. E. McPherson (Eds.), *The science and psychology of music performance: Creative strategies for teaching and learning* (pp. 31–46). New York: Oxford University Press.

O'Neill, S. A., & Sloboda, J. A. (1997). The effects of failure on children's ability to perform a musical test. *Psychology of Music, 25*, 18–34.

Palmer, C. (1992). The role of interpretive preferences in music performance. In M. R. Jones & S. Holleran (Eds.), *Cognitive bases of musical communication* (pp. 249–262). Washington, DC: American Psychological Association.

Palmer, C. (1997). Music performance. *Annual Review of Psychology, 48*, 115–138.

Palmer, C., & Meyer, R. K. (2000). Conceptual and motor learning in music performance. *Psychological Science, 11*, 63–68.

Palmer, C., & van de Sande, C. (1995). Range of planning in music performance. *Journal of Experimental Psychology: Human Perception and Performance, 21*, 947–962.

Pantev, C., Engelien, A., Candia, V., & Elbert, T. (2003). Representational cortex in musicians. In I. Peretz & R. Zatorre (Eds.), *The cognitive neuroscience of music* (pp. 383–395). Oxford, UK: Oxford University Press.

Papousek, M. (1996). Intuitive parenting: A hidden source of musical stimulation in infancy. In I. Deliège & J. A. Sloboda (Eds.), *Musical beginnings* (pp. 88–114). Oxford, UK: Oxford University Press.

Parncutt, R., & Levitin, D. (2000). Absolute pitch. In S. Sadie (Ed.), *The new Grove dictionary of music and musicians*. London: Macmillan.

Parncutt, R., & McPherson, G. E. (Eds.). (2001). *The science and psychology of music performance: Creative strategies for teaching and learning*. New York: Oxford University Press.

Pembrook, R., & Craig, C. (2002). Teaching as a profession: Two variations on a theme. In R. Colwell & C. Richardson (Eds.), *The new handbook of research on music teaching and learning* (pp. 786–817). New York: Oxford University Press.

Peretz, I. (2003). Brain specialization for music: New evidence from congenital amusia. In I. Peretz & R. J. Zatorre (Eds.), *The cognitive neuroscience of music* (pp. 192–203). Oxford, UK: Oxford University Press.

Peretz, I., & Hyde, K. (2003). What is specific to music processing? Insights from congenital amusia. *Trends in Cognitive Science, 7*, 362–367.

Peretz, I., & Zatorre, R. (Eds.). (2003). *The cognitive neuroscience of music*. Oxford, UK: Oxford University Press.

Persson, R. (1996). Brilliant performers as teachers: A case study of commonsense teaching in a conservatoire setting. *International Journal of Music Education, 28*, 25–36.

Persson, R. S. (2001). The subjective world of the performer. In P. N. Juslin & J. A. Sloboda (Eds.), *Music and emotion: Theory and research* (pp. 275–289). New York: Oxford University Press.

Piaget, J. (1958). *The child's construction of reality*. London: Routledge.

Poggi, I. (2002). The lexicon of the conductor's face. In P. McKevitt, S. O. Nualláin, & C. Mulvihill (Eds.), *Language, vision and music: Selected papers from the*

Eighth International Workshop on the Cognitive Science of Natural Language Processing, Galway, Ireland, 1999 (pp. 271–284). Amsterdam: Benjamins.

Pollard-Gott, L. (1983). Emergence of thematic concepts in repeated listening to music. *Cognitive Psychology, 15*, 66–94.

Powell, J., & Dibben, N. (2005). Key-mood association: A self-perpetuating myth. *Musicae Scientiae, 9*, 289–312.

Pressing, J. (1984). Cognitive processes in improvisation. In W. R. Crozier & A. J. Chapman (Eds.), *Cognitive processes in the perception of art* (pp. 345–363). Amsterdam: Elsevier.

Pressing, J. (1998). Psychological constraints on improvisational expertise and communication. In B. Nettl & M. Russell (Eds.), *In the course of performance* (pp. 47–68). Chicago: University of Chicago Press.

Price, H. E. (1992). Sequential patterns of music instruction and learning to use them. *Journal of Research in Music Education, 40*, 14–29.

Price, H. E., & Byo, J. L. (2002). Rehearsing and conducting. In R. Parncutt & G. E. McPherson (Eds.), *The science and psychology of music performance: Creative strategies for teaching and learning* (pp. 335–351). New York: Oxford University Press.

Proctor, W., & Dutta, A. (1995). *Skill acquisition and human performance*. Thousand Oaks, CA: Sage.

Raeburn, S. (2000). Psychological issues and treatment strategies in popular musicians: A review: Part 2. *Medical Problems of Performing Artists, 15*(10), 6–17.

Raffman, D. (1993). *Language, music, and mind*. Cambridge, MA: The MIT Press.

Raghuram, R., Keshavan, M. D., & Channabasavanna, S. (1980). Musical hallucinations in a deaf middle-aged patient. *Journal of Clinical Psychiatry, 41*(10), 357.

Ramsey, G. P. (2000). The muze 'n the hood: Musical practice and film in the age of hip hop. *Institute for Studies in American Music Newsletter, 29*(2). Retrieved August 1, 2006 from http://depthome.brooklyn.cuny.edu/isam/ramsey.html .

Rasch, R. A. (1981). Julius Bahle's psychology of musical creation. In N. H. Frijda & A. D. de Groot (Eds.), *Otto Selz: His contribution to psychology* (pp. 164–191). Den Haag, Netherlands: Mouton.

Rasch, R. A. (1988). Timing and synchronization in ensemble performance. In J. A. Sloboda (Ed.), *Generative processes in music: The psychology of performance, improvisation, and composition* (pp. 70–90). New York: Oxford University Press.

Rauscher, F. H., & Hinton, S. C. (2003). Type of music training selectively influences perceptual processing. In R. Kopiez, A. Lehmann, I. Wolther, & C. Wolf (Eds.), *Proceedings of the Fifth Triennial Conference of the European Society for the Cognitive Sciences of Music*. Hannover, Germany: University of Music and Drama.

Rayner, K., & Pollatsek, A. (1989). *The psychology of reading*. Hillsdale, NJ: Erlbaum.

Reid, A. (1997). The meaning of music and the understanding of teaching and learning in the instrumental lesson. In A. Gabrielsson (Ed.), *Proceedings of the Third Triennial ESCOM Conference* (pp. 200–205). Uppsala, Sweden: European Society for the Cognitive Sciences of Music.

Reid, A. (2001). Variation in the ways that instrumental and vocal students experience music learning. *Music Education Research, 3*, 25–40.

Renwick, J. M., & McPherson, G. E. (2002). Interest and choice: Student-selected repertoire and its effect on practising behavior. *British Journal of Music Education, 19*, 173–188.

Repp, B. (1998a). Obligatory "expectations" of expressive timing induced by perception of musical structure. *Psychological Research, 61*, 33–43.

Repp, B. H. (1990). Patterns of expressive timing in performances of a Beethoven minuet by nineteen famous pianists. *Journal of the Acoustical Society of America, 88*, 622–641.

Repp, B. H. (1992). Diversity and commonality in music performance: An analysis of timing microstructure in Schumann's "Träumerei." *Journal of the Acoustical Society of America, 92*, 2546–2568.

Repp, B. H. (1996). The art of inaccuracy: Why pianists' errors are difficult to hear. *Music Perception, 14*, 161–184.

Repp, B. H. (1997). The aesthetic quality of a quantitatively average music performance: Two preliminary experiments. *Music Perception, 14*, 419–444.

Repp, B. H. (1998b). The detectability of local deviations from a typical expressive timing pattern. *Music Perception. 15*, 265–289.

Rogoff, B. (2003). *The cultural nature of human development*. Oxford, UK: Oxford University Press.

Roland, D. (1994). How professional performers manage performance anxiety. *Research Studies in Music Education, 2*, 25–35.

Rosenbrock, A. (2002). The composition process in pop and rock music bands. In M. Britta & M. Melen (Eds.), *Proceedings of the ESCOM 10th Anniversary Conference on Musical Creativity* [CD-ROM]. Liège, Belgium: Université de Liège.

Rosenshine, B., Froehlich, H., & Fakhouri, I. (2002). Systematic instruction. In R. Colwell & C. Richardson (Eds.), *The new handbook of research on music teaching and learning* (pp. 299–314). New York: Oxford University Press.

Runfola, M., & Swanwick, K. (2002). Developmental characteristics of music learners. In R. Colwell & C. Richardson (Eds.), *The new handbook of research on music teaching and learning* (pp. 373–397). New York: Oxford University Press.

Sachs, H. (1982). *Virtuoso*. London: Thames & Hudson.

Sadie, S. (Ed.). (2001). *The new Grove dictionary of music and musicians* (2nd ed., Vols. 1–29). London: Macmillan.

Saffran, J. R. (2003). Absolute pitch in infancy and adulthood: the role of tonal structure. *Developmental Science, 6*, 37–45.

Sataloff, R. T., Brandfonbrener, A. G., & Lederman, R. J. (1998). *Performing arts medicine* (2nd ed.). San Diego, CA: Singular.

Scherer, K. R., & Zentner, M. R. (2001). Emotional effects of music: Production rules. In P. N. Juslin & J. A. Sloboda (Eds.), *Music and emotion: Theory and research* (pp. 361–392). Oxford, UK: Oxford University Press.

Schubert, E. (2003). Update of the Hevner adjective checklist. *Perceptual and Motor Skills, 96*, 1117–1122.

Scupin, R. (1999). *Cultural anthropology* (4th ed.). New York: Prentice-Hall.

Seashore, C. E. (1967). *Psychology of music*. New York: Dover. (Original work published 1938)

Seashore, C. E., Lewis, D., & Saetvit, J. G. (1960). *Seashore measures of musical talents* (Rev. ed.). New York: Psychological Corporation of New York.

Segovia, A. (1976). *Andrés Segovia: An autobiography of the years 1893–1920* (W. F. O'Brien, Trans.). New York: Macmillan.

Sergeant, D. (1969). Experimental investigations of absolute pitch. *Journal of Research in Music Education, 17*, 135–143.

Shaffer, L. H. (1984). Timing in solo and duet piano performances. *Quarterly Journal of Experimental Psychology, 36*, 577–595.

Shibata, D. K., Kwok, E., Zhong, J., Shrier, D., & Numaguchi, Y. (2001). Functional MR imaging of vision in the deaf. *Academic Radiology, 8*(7), 598–604.

Shoup, D. (1995). Survey of performance-related problems among high school and junior high school musicians. *Medical Problems of Performing Artists, 10*, 100–105.

Simon, H. A., & Chase, W. G. (1973). Skill in chess. *American Scientist, 61*, 394–403.

Simonton, D. K. (1984). *Genius, creativity and leadership*. Cambridge, MA: Harvard University Press.

Simonton, D. K. (1997). Products, persons, and periods: Historiometric analyses of compositional creativity. In D. Hargreaves & A. North (Eds.), *The social psychology of music* (pp. 107–122). Oxford, UK: Oxford University Press.

Simonton, D. K. (1999). *Origins of genius: Darwinian perspectives on creativity*. New York: Oxford University Press.

Singer, R. N., Hausenblas, H. A., & Janelle, C. (Eds.). (2001). *Handbook of sports psychology*. New York: Wiley.

Sloboda, J. A. (1978). The psychology of music reading. *Psychology of Music, 6*(2), 3–20.

Sloboda, J. A. (1983). The communication of musical metre in piano performance. *Quarterly Journal of Experimental Psychology, 35*, 377–396.

Sloboda, J. A. (1985a). Expressive skill in two pianists: Style and effectiveness in music performance. *Canadian Journal of Psychology, 39*, 273–293.

Sloboda, J. A. (1985b). *The musical mind: The cognitive psychology of music*. Oxford, UK: Oxford University Press.

Sloboda, J. A. (1990). Music as language. In F. R. Wilson & F. L. Roehmann (Eds.), *Music and child development: The biology of music making* (pp. 28–43). St. Louis, MO: MMB Music.

Sloboda, J. A. (1992). Empirical studies of emotional response to music. In M. Riess-Jones & S. Holleran (Eds.), *Cognitive bases of musical communication* (pp. 33–46). Washington, DC: American Psychological Association.

Sloboda, J. A. (1996). The acquisition of musical performance expertise: Deconstructing the "talent" account of individual differences in musical expressivity. In K. A. Ericsson (Ed.), *The road to excellence* (pp 107–126). Mahwah, NJ: Erlbaum.

Sloboda,. J. A. (1999). Everyday uses of music listening: A preliminary study. In S. W. Yi (Ed.), *Music, mind and science* (pp. 354–369). Seoul, Korea: Seoul National University Press.

Sloboda, J. A. (2001). Emotion, functionality, and the everyday experience of music: Where does music education fit? *Music Education Research, 3*, 243–253.

Sloboda, J. A., Davidson, J. W., Howe, M. J. A., & Moore, D. G. (1996). The role of practice in the development of expert musical performance. *British Journal of Psychology, 87*, 287–309.

Sloboda, J. A., Gayford, C., & Minnassian, C. (2003). Assisting advanced musicians to enhance their expressivity: An intervention study. In R. Kopiez, A. C. Lehmann, I. Wolther, & C. Wolf (Eds.), *Proceedings of the Fifth Triennial ESCOM Conference* (p. 92) [CD-ROM]. Hannover, Germany: University of Music and Drama.

Sloboda, J. A., Hermelin, B., & O'Connor, N. (1985). An exceptional musical memory. *Music Perception. 3*, 155–170.

Sloboda, J. A., & Howe, M. J. A. (1991). Biographical precursors of musical excellence: An interview study. *Psychology of Music, 19*, 3–21.

Sloboda, J. A., & Lehmann, A. C. (2001). Performance correlates of perceived emotionality in different interpretations of a Chopin piano prelude. *Music Perception, 19,* 87–120.

Sloboda, J. A., & O'Neill, S. A. (2001). Emotions in everyday listening to music. In P. N. Juslin & J. A. Sloboda (Eds.), *Music and emotion: Theory and research* (pp. 415–429). Oxford, UK: Oxford University Press.

Sloboda, J. A., O'Neill, S. A., & Ivaldi, A. (2001). Functions of music in everyday life: An exploratory study using the Experience Sampling Methodology. *Musicae Scientiae, 5,* 9–32.

Sloboda, J. A., & Parker, D. H. (1985). Immediate recall of melodies. In P. Howell, I. Cross, & R. West (Eds.), *Musical structure and cognition* (pp. 143–167). London: Academic Press.

Small, C. (1998). *Musicking: The meanings of performing and listening.* Hanover, NH: Wesleyan University Press.

Snitkin, H. S. (1997). *Practicing for young musicians: You are your own teacher.* Niantic, CT: HMS.

Sosniak, L. (1985). Learning to be a concert pianist. In B. S. Bloom (Ed.), *Developing talent in young people* (pp. 19–67). New York: Ballantine.

Spahn, C., Strukely, S., & Lehmann, A. (2004). Health conditions, attitudes toward study, and attitudes toward health at the beginning of university study: Music students in comparison with other student populations. *Medical Problems of Performing Musicians, 19,* 26–33.

Steptoe, A., & Fidler, H. (1987). Stage fright in orchestral musicians: A study of cognitive and behavioral strategies in performance anxiety. *British Journal of Psychology, 78,* 241–249.

Sternbach, D. J. (1995). Musicians: A neglected working population in crisis. In S. L. Sauter & L. R. Murphy (Eds.), *Organizational risk factors for job stress* (pp. 283–302). Washington, DC: American Psychological Association.

Sternberg, R. J. (Ed.). (1999). *Handbook of creativity.* Cambridge, UK: Cambridge University Press.

Sudnow, D. (1993). *Ways of the hand: The organisation of improvised conduct.* London: Routledge.

Swanwick, K. (1991) Further research on the musical developmental sequence. *Psychology of Music, 19,* 22–32.

Swanwick, K., & Tillman, J. (1986). The sequence of musical development. *British Journal of Music Education, 3,* 305–339.

Sweeney, G. A., & Horan, J. J. (1982). Separate and combined effects of cue-controlled relaxation and cognitive restructuring in the treatment of musical performance anxiety. *Journal of Counseling Psychology, 29,* 486–497.

Tait, M. (1992). Teaching strategies and styles. In R. Colwell (Ed.), *Handbook of research on music teaching and learning* (pp. 525–534). New York: Schirmer.

Tarrant, M., Hargreaves, D. J., & North, A. C. (2001). Social categorization, self-esteem, and the estimated musical preferences of male adolescents. *Journal of Social Psychology, 141,* 565–581.

Thompson, S., & Lehmann, A. C. (2004). Strategies for sight-reading and improvising music. In A. Williamon (Ed.), *Musical excellence* (pp. 143–159). Oxford, UK: Oxford University Press.

Trainor, L. J., & Trehub, S. E. (1993). What mediates infants' and adults' superior processing of the major over the augmented triad? *Music Perception, 11,* 185–196.

Trehub, S. (2003). Musical predispositions in infancy: An update. In I. Peretz & R. Zatorre (Eds.), *The cognitive neuroscience of music* (pp. 3–20). Oxford, UK: Oxford University Press.

Trehub, S. E., & Trainor, L. J. (1993). Listening strategies in infancy: The roots of music and language development. In S. McAdams & E. Bigand (Eds.), *Thinking in sound* (pp. 278–327). Oxford, UK: Clarendon.

Upitis, R. (1987). Children's understanding of rhythm. *Psychomusicology, 7,* 41–60.

Valentine, E. (2004). Alexander technique. In A. Williamon (Ed.), *Musical excellence* (pp. 179–195). New York: Oxford University Press.

Van Kemanade, J. F., Van Son, M. J., & Van Heesch, N. C. (1995). Performance anxiety among professional musicians in symphonic orchestras: A self-report study. *Psychological Reports, 77,* 555–562.

Vetter, I. (1998). Musik aus dem Jenseits: Der Fall Rosemary Brown und seine soziokulturellen und psychologischen Bedingungen [The case of Rosemary Brown, its sociocultural and psychological context]. In R. Kopiez, B. Barthelmes, & H. Gembris (Eds.), *Musikwissenschaft zwischen Kunst, Ästhetik und Experiment* (pp. 619–633). Würzburg: Königshausen & Neumann.

Walsh, G., Altenmüller, E., & Jabusch, H. C. (2006). Synchronization of contrary finger movements in pipers, woodwind players, violinists, pianists, accordionists and non-musicians (unpublished manuscript).

Wan, C. Y., & Huon, G. F. (2005). Performance degradation under pressure in music: An examination of attentional processes. *Psychology of Music, 33,* 155–172.

Wanderley, M. M. (2002). Quantitative analysis of non-obvious performer gestures. In I. Wachsmuth & T. Sowa (Eds.), *Gesture and sign language in human-computer interaction: Revised papers* (pp. 241–253). Berlin, Germany: Springer.

Wapnick, J., Darrow, A. A., Kovacs, J., & Dalrymple, L. (1997). Effects of physical attractiveness on evaluation of vocal performance. *Journal of Research in Music Education, 45,* 470–479.

Wapnick, J., & Ekholm, E. (1997). Expert consensus in solo voice performance evaluation. *Journal of Voice, 11,* 429–436.

Wapnick, J., Kovacs Mazza, J., & Darrow, A. A. (1998). Effects of performer attractiveness, stage behavior, and dress on violin performance evaluation. *Journal of Research in Music Education, 46,* 510–521.

Wapnick, J., Kovacs Mazza, J., & Darrow, A. A. (2000). Effects of performer attractiveness, stage behavior, and dress on evaluation of children's piano performance. *Journal of Research in Music Education, 48,* 323–336.

Ward, W. D. (1999). Absolute pitch. In D. Deutsch (Ed.), *Psychology of music* (2nd ed., pp. 265–298). New York: Academic Press.

Waters, A. J., Underwood, G., & Findlay, J. M. (1997). Studying expertise in music reading: Use of a pattern-matching paradigm. *Perception and Psychophysics, 59,* 477–488.

Webster, P. (1992). Research on creative thinking in music: The assessment literature. In R. Colwell (Ed.), *Handbook of research on music teaching and learning* (pp. 266–280). New York: Schirmer.

Weick, K. E., Gilfillian, D. P., & Keith, T. A. (1973). The effect of composer credibility on orchestra performance. *Sociometry, 36,* 435–462.

Weisberg, D. (Ed.). (1992). *Auditory imagery.* Hillsdale, NJ: Erlbaum.

Weisberg, R. W. (1999). Creativity and knowledge. In R. J. Sternberg (Ed.), *Handbook of creativity* (pp. 226–250). Cambridge, UK: Cambridge University Press.

Wesner, R. B., Noyes, R., & Davis, T. L. (1990). The occurrence of performance anxiety among musicians. *Journal of Affective Disorders, 18*, 177–185.

West, R. (2004). Drugs and musical performance. In A. Williamon (Ed.), *Musical excellence: Strategies and techniques to enhance performance* (pp. 271–290). Oxford, UK: Oxford University Press.

Wigfield, A., O'Neill, S. A., & Eccles, J. S. (1999, April). *Children's achievement values in different domains: Developmental and cultural differences.* Paper presented at the biennial meeting of the Society for Research in Child Development, Albuquerque, NM.

Williamon, A. (1999). The value of performing from memory. *Psychology of Music, 27*, 84–95.

Williamon, A. (Ed.). (2004). *Musical excellence: Strategies and techniques to enhance performance.* Oxford, UK: Oxford University Press.

Williamon, A., & Davidson, J. W. (2002). Exploring co-performer communication. *Musicae Scientiae, 6*, 53–72.

Williamon, A., & Valentine, E. (2000). Quantity and quality of musical practice as predictors of performance quality. *British Journal of Psychology, 91*, 353–376.

Willis, P. (1978). *Profane culture.* London: Routledge.

Wilson, G. D. (1997). Performance anxiety. In D. J. Hargreaves & A. C. North (Eds.), *The social psychology of music* (pp. 229–245). New York: Oxford University Press.

Wilson, G. D. (2002). *Psychology for performing artists: Butterflies and bouquets.* London: Whurr.

Wilson, G. D., & Roland, D. (2002). Performance anxiety. In R. Parncutt & G. E. McPherson (Eds.), *The science and psychology of music performance: Creative strategies for teaching and learning* (pp. 47–61). New York: Oxford University Press.

Wing, A. M., & Kristofferson, A. B. (1973). The timing of interresponse intervals. *Perception and Psychophysics, 13*, 455–460.

Winner, E. (1996). *Gifted children: Myths and realities.* New York: Basic Books.

Wolpert, R. (2000). Attention to music in a nondirected music listening task: Musicians vs. nonmusicians. *Music Perception, 18*, 225–230.

Woody, R. H. (1999). The relationship between advanced musicians' explicit planning and their expressive performance of dynamic variations in an aural modelling task. *Journal of Research in Music Education, 47*, 331–342.

Woody, R. H. (2000). Learning expressivity in music performance: An exploratory study. *Research Studies in Music Education, 14*, 14–23.

Woody, R. H. (2002). The relationship between musicians' expectations and their perception of expressive features in an aural model. *Research Studies in Music Education, 18*, 53–61.

Woody, R. H. (2003). Explaining expressive performance: Component cognitive skills in an aural modelling task. *Journal of Research in Music Education, 51*, 51–63.

Yarbrough, C. (2002). Sequencing musical tasks: The teaching artistry of Robert Shaw. *Update: Applications of Research in Music Education, 21*, 6–11.

Yost, W. A. (2000). *Fundamentals of hearing.* San Diego, CA: Academic Press.

Young, V., Burwell, K., & Pickup, D. (2003). Areas of study and teaching strategies in instrumental teaching: A case study research project. *Music Education Research, 5*, 139–155.

Index

ability
  versus competence, 36
  as innate, 41
  testing of, 36, 38, 110
  statistical distribution of, 17
  See also talent
absolute pitch, 38
affect. *See* expression; emotion in
    listening
amusia, 30, 222
anxiety
  description of, 145
  lack of, 156
  reasons for, 153, 155, 160
  symptoms of, 146
  and task demands, 159
  treating, 150, 154, 157, 158, 161
  as a trait, 152
aptitude. *See* ability
automaticity, 79, 103, 117, 134, 137

brain
  and ability, 36
  activation in imaging music, 20
  changes in response to training, 36,
    69, 222
  and emotion in listening, 221
  See also amusia

capacity. *See* ability
chills, 219. *See also* peak experience
chunking, 111, 116, 118, 122. *See also*
    memory

classical culture
  instruments of, 238
  vs. nonclassical culture, 235
  setting of, 237
colors and hearing. *See* synesthesia
common sense, 7
competence, 36. *See also* ability
composition
  attention during, 132
  contrasted with improvisation, 129
  intention of, 238
  learning, 137, 141
  by a paranormal medium, 138
concerts
  audience expectations, 120, 153,
    167, 216
  culture, 155, 169, 171, 224, 235
conducting, 198. *See also* rehearsal
creativity
  and age, 140
  and altered states, 137
  development of, 137
  in everyday life, 127
  theories of, 133, 140
  types of, 127
cross-cultural aspects, 15. *See also*
    non-Western music

development
  of musical abilities, 141
  normal path, 31
  stages of, 31
  of rhythm representations, 110